9/85

6.03 17 3/03

CFD 11/93 ⑪

3/86 ③

✓

Palo Alto City Library

The individual borrower is responsible for all
library material borrowed on his or her card.

Charges as determined by the CITY OF PALO
ALTO will be assessed for each ov

Damaged or non-returned prop
billed to the individual borrower by
PALO ALTO.

NAZIS IN SKOKIE

Notre Dame Studies in
Law and Contemporary Issues

Volume One

The University of Notre Dame Press gratefully acknowledges the generous support of The Honorable James J. Clynes, Jr., of Ithaca, New York, in the publication of titles in this series.

NAZIS IN SKOKIE

FREEDOM, COMMUNITY, AND
THE FIRST AMENDMENT

DONALD ALEXANDER DOWNS

UNIVERSITY OF NOTRE DAME PRESS
NOTRE DAME, INDIANA

Library of Congress Cataloging in Publication Data

Downs, Donald A. (Donald Alexander)
Nazis in Skokie.

Bibliography: p.
Includes index.
1. Freedom of speech—United States. 2. Freedom of
speech—Illinois—Skokie. 3. Jews—Illinois—Skokie.
4. National Socialist Party of America. 5. Skokie (Ill.)
—Demonstration, 1977. I. Title.
KF4772.D69 1985   322.4′4′097731   84-40294
ISBN 0-268-00968-6

Manufactured in the United States of America

FOR SUSAN

Reason and vicissitude . . . At bottom they are but two forms of reason: the one pure reason which "starts from concepts, proceeds by concepts and terminates in concepts" — thus Plato defines dialectics — the other historical reason which arises fulminantly from the nature of things . . .

Cicero was clearly aware of this interplay of reason and experience as he was of the other point implied in Polybius: that vicissitudes or political struggles are not necessarily negative events, indicative of social disease, but on the contrary may help to bring forth a better state . . .

Far from extolling internal peace or regarding public life as a matter of suave urbanity, Cicero held *dissensiones civiles* to be the very condition on which the welfare of the state is based and from which it derives . . .

On the other hand, a society obviously relies for its existence upon common consent in certain ultimate matters. Such unanimity Cicero calls *concordia* and he defines it as "the best bond of permanent union in any commonwealth." How does one tally with the other? Quite easily, if we picture the body of opinions from which the life of a nation draws its sustenance as made up of various layers. Divergencies in surface layers produce beneficent conflicts because the ensuing struggles move upon the firm ground of deeper concord. Questioning certain things but not questioning all, minor divergencies serve but to confirm and consolidate the underlying unanimity of the collective existence.

But if dissent affects the basic layers of common belief on which the solidarity of the social body lastly rests, then the state becomes a house divided, society dis-sociates, splitting up into two societies.

—Ortega y Gasset
Concord and Liberty

Contents

Preface

The empirical data for this work consists of in-depth interviews with over thirty prominent leaders from all major groups in the controversy, as well as data gathered from press reports and books on Skokie and from printed material and correspondence of major political and interest groups in the controversy.

Interviews with six survivor leaders (including the two most prominent ones) provide us with evidence of the most important harms and benefits which occurred at Skokie, and of the most important events and actions. The Skokie story is largely the story of the survivors' resistance, and the way this resistance interacted with and affected other groups and policies.

The number of survivor interviews is limited. Yet the fact that the six survivors interviewed were leaders in the survivor community means that they were well situated to report on the reactions of Skokie's Jewish community as a whole, as well as to describe their own reactions. But as leaders, these six were especially "strong," and, therefore, generally more able to deal with the stress of the past, and present reminders of the past, than the weaker survivors. Accordingly, the conclusions concerning the harms and benefits of the controversy we derive may well be biased in the direction of positive consequences—the harms may well have been greater for many other survivors, and the positive consequences less pronounced (assuming they were even present). Yet, because I will eventually conclude that the harms perpetrated at Skokie outweigh the benefits, this bias in the data base will actually serve to strengthen my arguments, as there were likely greater costs than my data suggests. Furthermore, we will see that even the stronger survivors suffered substantial trauma in reaction to the Chicago Nazis' proposals, so their statements about trauma appear to be representative.

Another important point attests to the validity of generalizing (with due caution) from the interviews of this small sample. A remarkable uniformity characterized the observations and opinions of virtually all interviewees and other commentators concerning the nature of the survivors' reactions as the controversy wore on. Even ACLU leaders came to agree with the most avid Skokie supporters about the nature of the harms the survivors experienced. This consistency of opinion suggests, at least to some degree, that the conclusions reached below are valid. After conducting numerous interviews of survivors of the disastrous, massive mud slide at Buffalo Creek, West Virginia in the early 1970s, Kai Erikson discovered to his surprise that all the individual depictions were extraordinarily alike. The impact of the disaster was so intense and profound that all individuals affected observed its impact in roughly similar fashions. Different people may have had somewhat different personal experiences and responses (e.g., more or less *personal* loss), yet there was striking agreement about the general effects and their categorizations. Similarly, the survivor interviewees (as well as all other observers at Skokie) were quite consistent in their portrayals of the effect of the conflict, despite their individual perspectives. Accordingly, the small size of the survivor sample need not undermine the validity of my conclusions. Nonetheless, I will strive to be cognizant of differences in opinion concerning claims and impact whenever such differences exist.

Non-survivor interviews and data will aid in this regard. I also conducted interviews with Nazi leader Frank Collin of the National Socialist Party of America and his leading legal advocates in the Illinois division of the American Civil Liberties Union, David Hamlin, David Goldberger, Franklyn Haiman, and Michael Gelder. These interviews will aid in our understanding of the development of the controversy. The Collin interview will provide important data concerning the intended impact of the NSPA's speech actions at Skokie; and the ACLU interviews will help to illuminate the nature of present First Amendment doctrine that supported the NSPA's speech rights.

Acknowledgments

I would like to thank those who contributed to making this book. First, there were those who read earlier drafts, mainly at the dissertation stage of progress. Michael Rogin read many versions and made characteristically thoughtful suggestions. Michael also taught me much of what I know about psychology. William Muir also read several versions and taught me how to think about the strategies of conflict and human motivation. Martin Shapiro read a draft and compelled me to consider the possible impact of new doctrines on the First Amendment. Victor Rosenblum, who participated in the Skokie conflict as an advocate and a scholar, offered many helpful comments after reading the finished dissertation upon which this book is based.

I also wish to thank those who assisted me in gathering data in Skokie and the Chicago area. Among those who extended me their time and resources were Eugene DuBow, Abbott Rosen, Rabbi Laurence Montrose, Charles Conrad, Jerome Torshen, Franklyn Haiman, and David Hamlin. Many others contributed in this vein, yet the aforementioned individuals were especially helpful.

However, I must single out an even more select few for special thanks. Fred Richter gave me several interviews and exhaustive data on the Skokie conflict. His contributions gave me an understanding of the contours of the controversy which enabled me to build a book. His encouragement also is appreciated. A special thanks is due to those who were the center of the controversy: my Skokie survivor interviewees. Erna Gans was my major survivor informant and a link to other survivor informants whose names have been changed in the book in order to shield them from prankster reprisals. Without Erna's comments, suggestions, and assistance, this book would have lacked its soul. I express my deep appreciation and debt to her. I am also indebted to my other survivor sources, though I cannot mention their names. Their importance to the book will be conspicuous to the reader.

I also want to thank survivor Sol Goldstein for granting me an important interview.

Three other debts must be acknowledged. Nelson Polsby arranged a grant from the Center for National Policy Studies at the Institute for Governmental Studies, University of California, Berkeley. This grant enabled me to conduct my survivor interviews at Skokie and to obtain other important data. Kerry McNamara discussed the topic with me many times and enriched my thinking on the issue. And my editor at Notre Dame Press, Joseph Wilder, read several later versions of the work and made many important editorial suggestions. Not only was Joe a pleasure to work with, but some of his comments proved to be invaluable. Whatever the final merits of the book, Joe saved it from several dangerous pitfalls.

I reserve my final and most grateful acknowledgment for Robert Kagan, who set an inimitable standard as my dissertation chairman at Berkeley. On a different plane, Bob was as important to the work as my survivor interviewees. He patiently and painstakingly endured my earliest drafts, making strong suggestions that brought order out of chaos. Furthermore, his substantive comments were enormously helpful. I hope the book has enough merit to reflect Bob's efforts.

1

Skokie and the Communal Purposes of Free Speech

I am criticizing, not our concern with procedures, but our preoccupation, in which we may lose sight of the fact that our procedures are not the ultimate goal of our legal system. Our goals are truth and justice, and professional responsibility.—Dallin Oaks, "Ethics, Morality, and Professional Responsibility"

I. Introduction

On April 25, 1977, a group of Holocaust survivors stood up before the Board of Trustees of the Village of Skokie, Illinois. One survivor pleaded that:

It has come to my attention that on May 1 there is going to be a Nazi parade held in front of the village hall. As a Nazi survivor during the Second World War, I'd like to know what you gentlemen are going to do about it . . . there are thousands of Jewish survivors of the Nazi Holocaust living here in the suburbs. We expect to show up in front of village hall and tear these people up if necessary.[1]

The survivor group took action because the National Socialist Party of America (NSPA), a small Chicago-based Nazi group led by a redoubtable provocateur, Frank Collin, had announced its intention to hold a pro-NSPA and white power demonstration on the steps of Skokie's village hall on May 1, 1977. Collin's announcement shot shock waves through the Skokie survivor community. Although the NSPA hardly represented a reincarnation of Hitler, survivors recoiled at the thought of a party entering their community flaunting Nazi-symbols and doctrine. Collin's threat triggered fears of violence and trauma based on the vulnerability of survivors to symbolic reminders of past persecution. Consequently, village officials were implored to deny a permit to Collin and his fellow pseudo-Nazis. As a survivor informed the Board of Trustees on April 25:

> We don't want to wake up May 2 and find out nothing was done. You must understand our feelings. We might do things we don't know yet. We are a special breed of people, people who went through unbelievable things. History doesn't even know the things that happened to us . . . I appeal to you once more. This thing should not happen in our village.[2]

The survivors prevailed. In late April 1977, village officials obtained an injunction in court that banned the NSPA from appearing in Skokie. And in early May, the village fortified its defense by passing three ordinances that required permits for which the NSPA could not qualify.

Yet Collin refused to acquiesce. With the legal assistance of the American Civil Liberties Union, he sued Skokie on the grounds that Skokie's actions violated his First Amendment free speech rights. After protracted legal struggles that lasted until June 1978, the courts finally ruled in Collin's favor, declaring that speech may not be abridged because of its threatening content. Yet Collin eventually cancelled his plan to appear in Skokie because he knew that his group would make vulnerable targets for angry counterdemonstrators. "The thought of snipers alone must have chilled him often," one ACLU spokesman observed.[3]

The fears and counter-threats of violence engendered at Skokie raise serious questions about the limits of free speech. Should the First Amendment protect the kind of speech the NSPA intended for Skokie? Since the courts vindicated the NSPA's speech rights at Skokie, an inquiry into this question obliges one to examine critically the present constitutional doctrine governing the public forum. The heart of this doctrine is the "content neutrality rule" which holds that *political speech* shall not be abridged because of its *content,* even if that content is verbally assaultive and has an emotionally painful impact; it can be abridged only when it interferes in a physical way with other legitimate activities, when it is thrust upon "captive" or unwilling listeners, or when it constitutes a direct incitement to unlawful behavior which is likely to occur.[4] In the absence of these narrow conditions, political speech in a public forum enjoys well-nigh absolute constitutional protection regardless of its content, the intentions of its speakers, and the *impact* of the speech on non-captive targets.[5] Accordingly, the courts ruled in Collin's favor in the Skokie cases even though (as we will see) he intended his speech (and the antecedent notice of his coming) to inflict severe emotional trauma on survivors.

II. Civil Rights and Procedural Justice

"Realism consists in acknowledging the group process and allowing for it. Group activity is an essential and desirable part of the American system, and indeed the First Amendment recognizes this: it protects the right of assembly and the right of association. But it is simply not true that the play of influence, of competing intensities, is *all there is* to politics. The play of ideas, the sifting of good ideas from bad, of truth from falsehood, of justice from injustice—all these are essential parts of our system as well. One cannot deny this without denying the very essence of the First Amendment. One cannot deny this without letting realism descend into cynicism."—J. Skelley Wright, U.S. Court of Appeals

The most forceful expressions and uses of the content neutrality rule arose in civil rights and anti-war litigation, and the aftermath of these struggles. Protest groups vigorously exercised their First Amendment rights to apprise the public of the injustices they suffered,[6] and the content neutrality rule protected them from unjustified abridgement. Not coincidentally, the First Amendment's content neutrality rule parallels the Court's interpretation of the Fourteenth Amendment's equal protection clause that emerged during this period. Key cases have espoused the view that government may not tamper with the content of speech because of the principle of "equal liberty of expression."[7] All speech claimants must be granted a hearing, regardless of the nature of their views, because each has equal status in the eyes of the law. Accordingly, the content neutrality rule has played a key role in the articulation and achievement (however imperfect) of social justice defined as civil rights and equality.

In addition, the content neutrality rule reflects the logic of "procedural justice" or "due process" which conquered administrative law (and criminal procedure) theory and practice in the years preceding Skokie. This theory maintained that social and political justice could be achieved by opening up the administrative process to as many relevant groups as possible; it represented the judicial articulation of the predominant political theory of the last twenty years: justice and rationality defined as group politics and participation in decision-making processes (this emphasis includes a preoccupation with "polyarchy" or pluralism, and access to the political system).[8] In order to facilitate access for new activists, the courts loosened the standards of standing, ripeness, and other doctrines by which agencies and courts had traditionally controlled or limited access.[9]

The due process and interest-group representation revolutions in administrative law which scholars have depicted[10] represent the increasing respon-

siveness of the legal system to newly organized claims and interests in society. Modern administrative law and civil liberty law constitute the heart
of the "responsive law" model of a legal system fostered by the Warren
Court; such a system strives to generate equality by accommodating a wider
set of social interests than did earlier models or types of legal institutions. [11]
This egalitarian ethic constitutes the core "ethos" of the Warren Court. [12]

This movement toward equal justice stresses procedural rather than substantive justice because it is feared that governmental or legal institutional
determination of substantive justice may unduly limit or jeopardize the
claims of diverse, pluralistic groups. Bernard Decker of the U.S. District
Court expressed a similar logic about the First Amendment's marketplace
of ideas notion in *Collin v. Smith,* the Skokie ordinance case:

> They [the fathers of modern free speech theory] believed that false ideas ex-
> isted; and that the process of free debate could be relied upon to identify
> false ideas, but that the government could not. [13]

Procedural justice is suitable to free speech adjudication in the liberal
political community because it secures participation and self-government
for the largest number of citizens. Self-government means that the citizens
help decide the wisdom of policy prescriptions by the process of open social debate. And as Alexander Meiklejohn, a major advocate of self-
government and free speech, states, *participation* is a key ingredient of this
process:

> The First Amendment is not, primarily a device for the winning of new truth,
> though that is very important. It is the device for sharing of whatever truth
> has been won. Its purpose is to give to every voting member of the body poli-
> tic the fullest possible participation in the understanding of those problems
> with which the citizens of a self-governing society must deal. [14]

This treatment of the common denominators of the civil rights movement, contemporary administrative law, and First Amendment jurisprudence establishes both the difficulty and the opportunity posed for our
analysis. On one hand, the content neutrality rule (as a species of procedural
justice) which the courts explicitly relied upon in the Skokie cases has contributed to the quest for social justice. On the other hand, close consideration of the Skokie case raises questions about the *abuse* of procedural justice and free speech, an abuse that may justify minimal abridgement of
free speech. When the content and the inherent purpose of speech become
immaterial from a legal perspective, freedom of speech may be abused in
a manner which contradicts the basic principles of a free society. Speech

by hate groups can be utilized to willfully inflict injury on the targets of hate, turning the freedom of speech into a defense of unjust action.[15] In later chapters we will see that the NSPA used Skokie and the freedom of speech in precisely this way. We will also see that many prominent participants in the Skokie conflict berated the courts because justice seemed to reside on the survivors' side, not Frank Collin's. Collin was not a *victim,* but rather a *victimizer.* One survivor we will get to know later said that

> the purpose for writing that amendment [the First] was not for people to call to build new ghettos and new concentration camps . . . A person should have a right to express an opposite opinion of the government, an opposite opinion of your opinion. But not one to kill these people — there are two different things . . . as citizens, we also have a right to be protected. Not only Nazis have the right.[16]

In essence, survivors asked the courts to heed the claims of substantive justice in the case rather than limiting their legal considerations to the issue of procedural justice, or equal protection in the public forum. Yet the courts abided by the requirements of the content neutrality rule, which prohibited a consideration of substantive justice.

Some serious writers on the First Amendment have espoused a substantive jurisprudence. Walter Berns, for example, has endorsed an approach to the First Amendment which takes virtue and natural justice into consideration. Berns held that the courts should look at the content of speech and grant First Amendment protection to "good" speech which is consistent with virtue and justice.[17] He cited many examples of cases in which destructive and sometimes vicious speech was protected by the courts in the name of the First Amendment. And he demonstrated how the unthinking defense of procedural justice can harm the substance of justice in certain cases, reminding us that substantive justice is, after all, the reason for procedural justice (in a similar vein, commentators have pointed out that the unfettered due process model in administrative law has often resulted in regulatory chaos or irrationality).[18]

Yet Berns' approach jeopardizes freedom and the principle of self-government by endorsing too much abridgement of speech. Speech could be abridged, in his scheme, simply on the grounds that its content was non-virtuous. And Berns provides no guidelines for adjudication other than vague invocations of justice, thereby threatening speech with overly broad enforcement. In addition to permitting the abridgement of speech which directly inflicted a psychological harm on the targets of speech, Berns' position allows abridgement if the speech *could tend* to lead to anti-democratic results even in the very long term. Berns endorsed the abridgement of communist speech, for example.[19] We should label Berns' approach to free speech adjudication *maximalist.*

A more *minimalist* approach would more precisely delineate the distinction betwen protected and unprotected speech. It would thereby protect speech interests and the principle of self-government, which we should value because of their cardinal importance to democratic life. Such a proposal would allow abridgement only in cases of the *direct infliction of a verbal injury* within the public forum. This method could adequately balance consideration of content with consideration of impact. Surprisingly, as we will see, the present law concerning assaultive speech (or fighting words) often does not allow abridgement in even these cases due to the dominance of the content neutrality rule in the kingdom of procedural justice.

The minimalist approach is justified in three senses. First, it grants speech conducive to self-government First Amendment protection. Second, it focuses upon the most harmful or injurious form of bad speech, that which is assaultive or designed to intimidate. Third, it deals with a usage of the public forum which has become prominent in recent years: racial and ethnic vilification by hate groups to intimidate the targets of hate. Recent investigations by concerned groups show that such behavior has become a major practice of Klan, Nazi, and other hate groups.[20] By focusing on cases of such injurious speech, which present a significant public policy problem, the minimalist proposal is more limited and containable than are more maximal approaches, while also providing for the effectuation of nonspeech interests.

In recent years, however, the Supreme Court has used the content neutrality rule in a manner which has granted First Amendment protection to assaultive speech that may be less worthy of protection. Let us now examine the development of this abuse of an otherwise estimable rule. In this examination we will address the issue of the *ends* of the First Amendment.

III. Chaplinsky v. New Hampshire: The Substantive Values of Civility and Truth

Although the content neutrality rule governs most forms of political speech (including Nazi speech and the speech of other hate groups), it has never been held to protect *absolutely all* categories of expression for the simple reason that not all forms of speech can be protected in any rational society. Justice Holmes' famous maxim that falsely crying "Fire!" in a crowded theatre is punishable expresses a trite yet important reality in political life. Some boundaries must be laid for free speech,[21] and it is within these boundaries that the content neutrality rule holds sway. The Supreme Court has employed what is called "definitional balancing" as a means of establishing the broad boundaries of the protected *categories* of speech *within which* the content neutrality rule is applied. Definitional balancing, espoused in different forms by such theorists as Nimmer, Meiklejohn, Bork, and Frantz,[22] entails establishing the basic types of speech which are consistent with the First Amendment's purposes, and then protecting these forms of speech as fully and consistently as is possible. Political speech, including that of Nazis, has been strongly protected in recent decades by these tests.

The case which provided the foundation for the traditional, substantive form of definitional balancing was *Chaplinsky v. New Hampshire,* decided in 1942. In upholding Chaplinsky's conviction for uttering "fighting words" to a policeman ("words likely to cause an average addressee to fight," according to the state court's interpretation of the New Hampshire statute), Justice Murphy of the Supreme Court established the basic content of the definitional test:

> There are certain well-defined and narrowly limited classes of speech, the prevention and punishment of which have never been thought to raise any Constitutional problem. These include the lewd and obscene, the profane, the libelous, and the insulting or "fighting" words — those which by their very utterance inflict injury or tend to incite an immediate breach of the peace. Such utterances are no essential part of any exposition of ideas, and are of such slight social value as a step to truth that any benefit that may be derived from them is clearly outweighed by the social interest in order and morality.[23]

Chaplinsky establishes the "two-tiered" or "two-level" method of definitional balancing. The First Amendment does not protect obscenity, libel, profanity, and fighting words (i.e., assaultive expression). These forms of expression are either harmful or inconsistent with the First Amendment's purposes, which concern the *communal and individual interest* in the attainment of truth (and the "exposition of ideas") and in order and morality. Thus *Chaplinsky* balanced libertarianism with community moral values by employing a specific notion of substantive justice. The question of justice pertains not to the entire content of speech (Berns' approach), but only to the difference between assaultive and non-assaultive content (or civil and uncivil content) in "fighting" contexts and, in the case of libel, true and maliciously false content.[24]

Chaplinsky's basic philosophical position balanced the community's interest in civility and morality with individual right and liberty.[25] It represented a compromise, as it were, between freedom and order. While it allowed community control over uncivil and assaultive forms of expression, it also established the theoretical basis for the protection of all speech of a political nature, including speech critical of the government. *New York Times v. Sullivan,* the watershed 1964 case in which the Supreme Court ruled that "seditious libel" (i.e., speech critical of the government) is protected by the First Amendment, is entirely consistent with *Chaplinsky*. Indeed, *Sullivan* was decided by definitional balancing.[26]

It could be said that well-nigh absolute protection for non-assaultive political speech through definitional balancing is the most important *basic* protection of individual right and liberty because politics and government are the primary sources of the infringement of rights. The most crucial test of a regime's respect for individual rights is that regime's treatment of political speech, especially speech critical of the regime. Its treatment of other forms of expression is important, but secondary.[27] If so, then *Chaplinsky* protects the most cardinal element of liberty while allowing the abridgement of uncivil forms of expression which constitute an abuse of libertarianism.[28]

In addition, *Chaplinsky*'s fighting words test provided a concrete means of enforcing civility. Fighting words are those which "by their very utterance inflict injury or tend to incite an immediate breach of the peace." Their primary purpose is to assault the target of speech. By excluding such speech from constitutional protection, the Court gave local governments the discretion to honor the norms of civility by punishing assaultive speech.

However, in recent years the Supreme Court has eviscerated the doctrine of fighting words by extending the logic of procedural justice and content neutrality. Though the Court has not abandoned definitional balancing, it has stretched the scope of protected categories (especially political speech) by a rigorous application of the content neutrality standard and the principle of libertarianism. In so doing, the Court has emphasized libertarian values at the expense of concern for social value, altering the basic logic of *Chaplinsky* and ultimately, I will argue, dictating the courts' rulings against Skokie in favor of the NSPA. An understanding of this development is necessary to appreciate the reasons for the Skokie legal decisions.

IV. The Evisceration of Chaplinsky

"The Court has gone far toward accepting the doctrine that civil liberty means the removal of all restraints . . . The choice is not between order and liberty. It is between liberty with order and anarchy without either. There is danger that if the Court does not temper its doctrinaire logic with a little practical wisdom, it will convert the constitutional Bill of Rights into a suicide pact." — Justice Robert Jackson (also, Chief Justice at Nuremburg), dissenting in *Terminiello v. Chicago*

The alteration of the fighting words doctrine emerged in cases emblematic of the later civil rights and anti-Vietnam War movements, in which sometimes virulent and critical debate prevailed. In the face of speech right claims made during these struggles, the Supreme Court accommodated the claims not by constructing a new theory of the substantive value of such speech to the community, but rather by adopting a libertarian logic that entailed a profound skepticism of values other than the right to participate and gain access to the public forum. When Skokie came along, this logic blinded the lower courts (at least in legal terms) to the substantive claims raised by Skokie resisters.

As seen, *Chaplinsky* provided for the punishment of fighting words because they "by their very utterance inflict injury or tend to incite an immediate breach of the peace." The infliction of injury test, however, entails the subjective, value-oriented reaction of the target, so it is presumptively at odds with the content neutrality rule concerning political speech. Because of this conflict, the Supreme Court reinforced the protection of speech during the civil rights movement by prohibiting the abridgement of speech due to the reaction of a "hostile audience," or what Harry Kalven christened a "heckler's veto,"[29] and by virtually doing away with the doctrine of fighting words when the speech was of a political nature and expressed in the public forum.

The key cases in this development concerned protest demonstrations in the civil rights and anti-war movements. The doctrine of the heckler's veto was institutionalized in such cases as *Edwards v. South Carolina, Cox v. Louisiana, Gregory v. Chicago,* and *Cohen v. California.*[30] The first three cases involved quite justified demonstrations in the 1960s against racial segregation and discrimination which were met by potentially disorderly crowds; and the *Cohen* case concerned the prosecution of a man who protested the Vietnam War in a Los Angeles courthouse by wearing a jacket with the words "Fuck the Draft" written across its back. Although the Supreme Court stressed the lack of immediate and substantial danger to the peace in these cases (the respective crowds in *Edwards, Cox,* and *Gregory* were not out of control, and the speech acts were not inherently designed to incite or trigger a hostile reaction), the Court indicated that the first duty of the police is to control the crowd and thereby protect the speech rights of the demonstrators. Allowing hostile audiences to merit the abridgement of speech ("heckler's vetoes") would constitute a de facto content abridgement.

Given the motivations and claims of the demonstrators in *Edwards, Gregory,* and *Cox,* such an approach seems eminently justified and consistent with the goals of a just society and the First Amendment as envisioned by *Chaplinsky.* As the Court said in *Gregory,* "hostile hecklers" must not serve as reasons to abridge unpopular speech.

Yet consistency seems less evident when the doctrine of the heckler's veto is applied to fighting words. Such an application cripples the very principle of fighting words, as the heckler's veto doctrine denies in principle the validity of a hostile reaction except in narrowly conceived situations in which speech is thrust upon an unwilling and "captive" listener.[31] Yet the doctrine of fighting words is different from the doctrine of hostile crowd reaction. The latter concerns legitimate, essentially rational speech which is met with anger because of its unpopularity; the reaction is a by-product, as it were, of a primary motive to protest conditions or actions and to present views about these conditions. On the contrary, fighting words, as depicted in *Chaplinsky*, are meant to harm or insult. In such cases, *the resulting hostile reaction or urge to fight are considered normal and the logical result of the speech* — they are intimately connected with the *raison d'etre* of the speech act. In *Chaplinsky*, the state court construed such words to be "words likely to cause an average addressee to fight," and "face-to-face words plainly likely to cause a breach of the peace by the addressee."[32]

Nonetheless, with *Cohen v. California,* decided in 1971, the Court began to alter the fighting words doctrine in order to make it consistent with the norms and goals of the content neutrality rule and its seeming partner, the hostile crowd reaction (heckler's veto) doctrine. The *Cohen* decision reverberates with a suspicion of the substantive values which support the ends of the First Amendment as well as the notion of a justified hostile response to assaultive speech. In addition, *Cohen* expresses a profound suspicion of the public articulation of primary values. As Justice Harlan stated in his decision:

> While the four-letter word displayed by Cohen in relation to the draft is not uncommonly employed in a personally provocative fashion, in this in-

stance it was clearly not "directed to the person of the hearer." No individual present or likely to be present could reasonably have regarded the words on appellant's jacket as a direct personal insult . . . [nor was the speech] thrust upon unwilling or unsuspecting viewers . . . while the particular four-letter word being litigated here is perhaps more distasteful than most others of its genre, it is nevertheless often true that one man's vulgarity is another's lyric. Indeed, we think it is largely because governmental officials cannot make principled distinctions in this area that the Constitution leaves matters of taste and style so largely to the individual.[33]

Cohen (and its progeny) drastically restricted *Chaplinsky*'s doctrine of fighting words and its principle of social value in three respects: 1) it limited the circumstances under which a speech act could be designated fighting words to "captive" situations in which the target has no reasonable means of escape; 2) it ignored *Chaplinsky*'s notion of the *harm* some assaultive speech may inflict 3) it explicitly articulated an extreme moral skepticism or relativity of value which is inconsistent with the basic normative logic of *Chaplinsky*.[34]

The logic of *Cohen* may be valid in most cases. The political community of liberal democracy does indeed consist of an "experiment" in living, inquiring, and valuing. Political life in a polity which practices self-government is characterized by a certain plasticity of experience (or freedom from necessity) which arises from the very practice of political self-determination.[35] Yet the extension of *Cohen*'s logic to more severe cases of verbal assault could harm the basic communitarian norms of civility and protection which are also legitimate values of the polity.[36]

In cases following in *Cohen*'s wake, the Supreme Court did indeed push *Cohen* into more questionable terrain, at least when fighting words are enmeshed in political concerns. In *Gooding v. Wilson,* decided a year after *Cohen* in 1972, the Court declared a Georgia statute dealing with fighting and offensive words void on grounds of vagueness and overbreadth. The Court's logic intimated that virtually any such statute would be considered vague because of the difficulty of assigning consistent meaning to the value-laden reactions of the targets of offensive and assaultive speech. In *Gooding,* the statute (which made it an offense to "without provocation, use to or of another, and in his [presence] opprobrious words or abusive language, tending to cause a breach of peace") was applied to a black woman who shouted the following words to a police officer: "Whitie son of a bitch, I'll kill you; you son of a bitch, I'll choke you to death."[37] In his dissent in *Gooding,* Justice Burger criticized the majority (per Justice Brennan) for dissecting the terms of the statute so as to lose sight of their common meaning in relation to the context of the overall statute, the speech acts they cover, and the impact of the speech on the community.[38] This type of surgical dissection and concomitant suspicion of meaning (or the ability to discern it) is a common libertarian legal technique, and it invariably renders the meaning of statutes vague in honor of libertarianism divorced from a communal context.[39] That is, it violates the "social value" logic of *Chaplinsky*'s concept of speech.

The Supreme Court continued this approach to assaultive speech in political contexts in *Rosenfeld v. New Jersey, Brown v. Oklahoma,* and *Lewis v. New Orleans* I and II.[40] In *Rosenfeld,* the defendant had rudely addressed a public school board meeting attended by women and children, loudly describing teachers and the school board as "mother fucker" several times; whereas in *Brown,* similar language was used by a Black Panther who had been invited to a political meeting to present the Black Panther view on issues. And *Lewis* involved a black woman who cursed obscenely at a police officer after he had stopped her car. The Court remanded each decision in light of *Gooding* and *Cohen*'s position on vagueness and overbreadth. While the factual situations in the cases differed in terms of the likely degree of harm (Brown had been invited by an audience that should have been prepared for his vehemence, and Lewis addressed a policeman, who is presumably used to such language; Rosenfeld's speech is distinguishable in both of these respects), the majority dealt with each speech act in accordance with the approach of *Gooding* and *Cohen.* In essence, the Court ruled that the fighting words doctrine was inapplicable except in narrow captive audience situations, however intentionally offensive the expression might be in a particular case. But the majority of the Court refused to consider factual distinctions, favoring instead an abstract form of jurisprudence. Justice Blackmun's dissent in *Lewis* II epitomizes the view of critics who claimed that the Court's libertarian alteration of *Chaplinsky* had gone too far, and therefore had lost sight of the political-communitarian context of free speech articulated in *Chaplinsky*'s definitional approach.

> [The vagueness and overbreadth doctrines] are being invoked indiscriminately without regard to the nature of the speech in question, the possible effect the statute or ordinance has upon such speech, the importance of the speech in relation to the exposition of ideas, or the purported or asserted community interest in preventing that speech. And it is no longer happenstance that in each case the facts are relegated to footnote status, conveniently distant and in a less disturbing focus. This is the compulsion of a doctrine that reduces our function to parsing words in the context of imaginary events.[41]

This new approach heeds the abstract rights of speakers and the alleged institutional needs of free speech adjudication over the claims of those who are harmed or naturally offended by the abuse of speech.[42] The approach represented the Burger Court's application (in the free speech area) of a technique that the Warren Court utilized in criminal procedure cases: the construction of a rigid, generalized rule, applied across the board to all relevant cases, regardless of the unique facts and situations in each case, "sparked by the [Warren] Court's despair over the prospect of significantly affecting police practices through its more traditional activity."[43] Later I will seek to show that this libertarian and rigid approach treats the victims of assaultive speech as *means* to societal ends, thereby violating what I shall argue is vital to free speech jurisprudence: the Kantian principle of ultimate ends. Hence, whatever the approach's validity in the area of criminal procedure, it raises serious questions in the adjudication of assaultive speech, as the Skokie cases will now illustrate.

V. The Basic Aspects of the Skokie Cases

The Skokie cases raise questions about the limits of the new libertarian jurisprudence governing free speech. Skokie claimants stressed that the law was blind to the clear purpose of the NSPA's proposed demonstration. "He [Collin] had a special reason to come and hurt us," one survivor told me. "You can see a breakdown of the community protection."[44] Yet the courts refused to legally recognize such claims.

The legal aspects of the Skokie litigation will be covered more fully later, so we will merely address their most basic aspects here. Skokie secured a permanent injunction from the Cook County Chancery Court to keep the NSPA out of Skokie; in addition the village enacted three ordinances designed to abridge Nazi-like expression. Consequently Skokie conducted litigation on two fronts, state (injunction) and federal (ordinances).

The major question in the injunction case, *NSPA v. Skokie*,[45] for the Illinois Supreme Court was whether the NSPA's wearing of the swastika in a demonstration could be enjoined because it constituted a verbal assault or fighting words.[46] The court dutifully stressed that attempts to impose prior restraints (abridgement *before* the speech act) bore a severe burden of justification, and then rather quickly concluded that the doctrines of *Cohen v. California* foiled Skokie's fighting words claim. Quoting several pages of *Cohen* in its rather short decision, the Court held that *Skokie* resembled *Cohen* in all salient respects: neither involved a captive audience or undue interference with privacy interests; there is a disputatious value to speech, as "verbal cacophany" is a "sign of strength"; values are subjective, as "one man's vulgarity is another man's lyric." The reliance upon these principles led to the conclusion that the display of the swastika is symbolic political speech, not fighting words.[47]

The federal courts reached a similar conclusion concerning the Skokie ordinances in *Collin v. Smith*.[48] Judge Decker of the U.S. District Court and Judge Pell of the U.S. Court of Appeals ruled against Skokie's invocation of the fighting words doctrine in its defense of its ordinances.

Judge Decker treated both the Skokie ordinance dealing with permits and the group libel ordinance together, as each dealt with "racial slurs." Ordinance No. 995 stated:

> The dissemination of any materials within the Village of Skokie which promotes and incites hatred against persons by reasons of their race, national origin, or religion, and is intended to do so, is hereby prohibited.[49]

"Dissemination" included "publication or display or distribution of posters, signs, handbills, or writing and public display of markings and clothing of symbolic significance."[50] The permit ordinance, No. 994, required the city manager to deny a permit for any assembly which would

> portray criminality, depravity or lack of virtue in, or incite violence, hatred, abuse or hostility toward a person or group of persons by reason of reference to religious, racial, ethnic, national, or regional affiliation.[51]

Skokie argued that racial slurs, like fighting words, were unprotected speech.[52] In ruling against Skokie's contention, Decker emphasized the following: 1) the fighting words doctrine has been narrowed considerably since *Chaplinsky*; 2) there is no principled way to distinguish assaultive racial slurs from non-assaultive (i.e., protected) yet vehement speech about racial issues; 3) Skokie's ordinances, concomitantly, are vague and overbroad; 4) such laws cannot be used for purposes of prior restraint (the permit ordinance). Ruling against Skokie's fighting words claim, Decker stated:

> The Skokie ordinance punishes language which intentionally incites hatred. This standard is as subjective and impossible to clearly define as the standards found impermissible in *Smith* and *Coates*. *Terminiello* and its progeny establish that there is a constitutional right to incite unrest, dissatisfaction, and even anger with social conditions. The distinction between inciting anger with a social condition and hatred of the person or group perceived to be responsible for that condition is impossible to draw with requisite clarity, and depends to a great extent upon the frame of mind of the listener . . . A society which values "uninhibited, robust, and wide-open" debate [a quote from *Sullivan*] cannot permit criminal sanctions to turn upon so fine a distinction . . . the incitement of hatred is often a by-product

of vigorous debate on highly emotional subjects, and the basic message of *Cohen* is that a great deal of useless, offensive, and even potentially harmful language must be tolerated as part of the "verbal cacophony" that accompanies uninhibited debate.[53]

The problem with Decker's conclusion is not his treatment of Skokie's ordinances, which may indeed have been vague, and, in the case of the permit ordinance, an improper prior restraint. The problem is that Decker appears to intimate as a matter of rigid principle (much like the *Gooding* court) that no statute dealing with assaultive racial slurs could be valid. Would precision of language save a statute directed to racial slurs from unconstitutionality given Decker's logic and terms? It seems unlikely. So we are left, in this view, with the likely blanket unconstitutionality of any laws abridging assaultive racial slurs. Yet the claims of Skokie survivors beckon further analysis, as do the claims of common sense.

VI. The Policy Question and Its Investigation

The central policy question of this work concerns the applicability of such cases as *Cohen* and *Sullivan* to Skokie. Do Skokie and other cases signify the limits of the doctrines of "uninhibited, robust, and "wide-open debate" (*Sullivan*) and a "cacophony of discord" (*Cohen*)? Do they suggest where common values begin and the play of skepticism outlives its utility? If so, what form should these limits take? These questions are among *the* moral questions of our time.

These questions may be addressed in relation to two basic models of citizenship and political community: "republican virtue" and "community security." The republican virtue model embodies many of the most salient justifications of freedom of speech. My definition of republican virtue will be limited to the purposes of this analysis. Republican virtue entails intellectual and moral courage, citizen participation in political matters, and the willingness to face the sometimes harsh truths of social and secular existence. One theoretical example of republican virtue is Machiavelli, whose political teachings stress the obligation of mature political citizens to face and grapple with difficult and compelling political issues despite the human, all too human tendency to ignore or hide from such issues.[54] The republican virtue model is also consistent with the notion of the open community as experimentation (Holmes) and inquiry rather than as the embodiment of static, established truth.[55] It is also consistent with Meiklejohn's notion of political freedom as political participation. Two statements by two free speech champions capture the intimate relation between free speech and republican virtue as I have defined it. In *Whitney v. California,* Justice Louis Brandeis defended free speech in language that reverberates with the respect of republican virtue:

> Those who won our independence believed that the final end of the State was to make men free to develop their faculties, and that in its government the deliberative forces should prevail over the arbitrary . . . They believed liberty to be the secret to happiness and courage to be the secret of liberty. They believed that freedom to think as you will and to speak as you think are means indispensable to the discovery and spread of political truth . . . that the greatest menace to freedom is an inert people; that public discussion is a political duty . . . [that] the fitting remedy for evil counsels is good ones . . . Those who won our independence by revolution were not cowards. They did not fear political change. They did not exalt order at the cost of liberty.[56]

In this remark, Brandeis envisions the First Amendment as promoting self-development, deliberation, the struggle for truth, courage, change, and open public debate about important issues.[57] John Stuart Mill took a similar stand in *On Liberty.* Although Mill emphasized the utilitarian role of free speech in effectuating the discovery of truth,[58] his defense of free speech in *On Liberty* included powerful references to classical notions of republican virtue (as well as individual right). Mill envisioned free speech promoting self-reliance, self-development, and engagement in public debate. And he perceptively understood the *psychology* of republican virtue: the way in which free speech compels speakers and audiences (or the targets of speech) to emotionally engage or commit themselves to the truth or to their cause

> Even if the received opinion be not only true, but the whole truth; unless it is suffered to be, and actually is, vigorously and earnestly contested, it will, by most of those who receive it, be held in a manner of prejudice, with little comprehension or feeling of its rational grounds. And not only this, but . . . the meaning of the doctrine itself will be in danger of being lost, or enfeebled, and deprived of its vital effect on the character and conduct: the dogma becoming a mere formal profession, inefficacious for good, but cumbering the ground, and preventing the growth of any real and heartfelt conviction, from reason or personal experience.[59]

The republican virtue model of citizenship and political community highlights the *positive* aspects which may have resulted from the Skokie events. We will see that exposure to the NSPA threat (even though the NSPA did not actually come to Skokie) galvanized a resistance movement that led to a great deal of commitment, public debate, and participation in politics. These actions contributed to an outpouring of public support for the survivors, and the emphatic rejection of the NSPA's policies by participants and the public. In addition, many survivor activists experienced a sense of self-development. According to one insightful survivor, "In order to overcome something, one must have a feeling of mastery over it. The very fact Collin existed allowed this mastery."[60] That is, resisting Collin enabled survivors to psychologically master their feelings of past humiliation and defeat at the hands of Hitler. For these and other reasons, the hopes of Mill and Brandeis may have been vindicated in stunning and surprising ways at Skokie.

At the same time, however, survivors suffered substantial harms. Exposure to the NSPA threat triggered emotional trauma and a sense of the breakdown of community protection. One prominent Skokie official, corporate counsel Harvey Schwartz, told me that

> the survivors came here for sanctuary. A big problem [in the early going] was that they saw this [quarantine policy] as the acquiescence of their local government in permitting this destructive force to enter their community and inflict itself on them. While the ACLU argued for freedom of speech, their reverse argument was "How dare the government sanctify this thing by permitting this to take place on public property?" . . . Our one area of rights is public. Yet Holocaust victims see it differently. They see the government as a *protector* of rights . . . They saw institutions meant to protect them as *not* protecting them.

Schwartz's observation epitomizes the community security model, which entails a more primitive notion of citizenship and community. Whereas the republican virtue model stresses the responsibility and self-reliance of citizens,[61] the community security model emphasizes the duty of the government and the laws to secure order and justice. *Chaplinsky*'s principles of rationality, morality and order, coupled with its doctrine of fighting and assaultive words, express the constitutional recognition of this notion of community. While an open, developing community is important to the effectuation of republican virtue, a community that does not protect its citizens from unjustified psychological assaults (that does not honor the principle of basic security) is not well ordered and cannot claim legitimacy.[62] It is no accident that in the late 1960s, James Q. Wilson discovered in a survey that Boston residents considered the decay of urban civility (e.g., pornography, crime, uncivil public discourse) to be among the most disturbing features of their environment.[63] A healthy community must balance the values of security and republican virtue.

In addition, while growth, experimentation, and open debate are signs of strength and maturity, a viable political community must affirm basic, cardinal values of order. According to Aristotle:

> It is the peculiarity of man, in comparison with the rest of the animal world, that he alone possesses a perception of good and evil, of the just and the unjust, and of other similar qualities; and it is association in a common perception of these things which makes a family and a polis.[64]

The two models of republican virtue and community civility-security will provide the analytical focus for the ensuing investigation. After looking at the eruption and resolution of the Skokie conflict, we will examine the consequences of the controversy in relation to these two models of political community. This analysis will enable us to answer the following questions: To what extent did the NSPA threat engender republican virtue? To what extent did the NSPA threat harm values concerning civility and community protection? Only after answering these and related questions can we evaluate First Amendment jurisprudence governing Skokie and other cases of assaultive speech.

2

The Exploitation of Liberty

I used it [the First Amendment] at Skokie. I planned the reaction of the Jews. They are hysterical.—Nazi Leader Frank Collin

I. The NSPA at Skokie: The Strategy of Extremism in Modern Media Politics

A. The Road to Skokie

Since the early 1970s, miscreant Frank Collin and the National Socialist Party of America had conducted raucous demonstrations in Marquette Park on the South Side of Chicago, where they made their home.[1] They often encountered friction from those who resented their tactics and messages. The NSPA normally had from ten to twenty-five members at these demonstrations, numbers which were slightly below their estimated membership.[2] The Chicago Park District and the Chicago Police Department also became embroiled in these affairs, fearing the eruption of violence. Because the white, ethnic Marquette Park neighborhood was threatened to the east and the south by the sprawl of the South Side black ghetto, NSPA hate demonstrations incited turmoil on both sides of the racial line. According to a long-time resident, Marquette Park was plagued, in 1977, with a war-like mentality:

> The Marquette Park community is all white and wants to remain so, while during the last two years the community bordering Marquette Park on the east has changed from white to black. Marquette Park residents fear the same pattern will occur in their community. A siege mentality permeates the community of ethnic groups—Lithuanians, Poles, Irishmen, and an increasing number of Latins and Arabs.[3]

Marquette Park suffers from many of the problems which have been associated with "white militancy": life on the fringe of the slums, a sense

19

of insecurity, threatened property values, and an educational background not conducive to drawing fine civil libertarian distinctions.[4] Given these conditions, Marquette Park has provided fodder for racial unrest. Although community groups have publicly disavowed racism on behalf of the majority of Marquette Park residents,[5] racialist emotions erupt at NSPA demonstrations, and the NSPA may represent the tacit racism of the majority. Two seemingly average adult Irish residents told me in a bar that

> Collin, you know, is a bit of a kook. He'd go after us Catholics after he finished off the Jews and niggers . . . But there is a common thread that ties us all together, including Collin — the hatred of the nigger.

While young anti-black toughs allegedly commit most of the violence at demonstrations[6] (this phenomenon is typical of racialist activity in many areas of the country, as adult extremist groups incite racialist emotion in younger groups),[7] it is also likely that the NSPA's expression represents the hostility of a large number of area residents. Marquette Park is "urban life at its ugliest," according to David Hamlin of the American Civil Liberties Union.[8]

In 1975 a group of Chicago blacks formed the Martin Luther King, Jr., Coalition to openly resist racism in Marquette Park and to confront Collin's band at Nazi demonstrations.[9] Predictably, violence escalated. The Chicago Park District, which had unsuccessfully attempted to keep the NSPA out of the area's parks earlier in the decade by assigning NSPA demonstrations to parks far away from their home grounds,[10] reacted to the new level of violence by resurrecting an old unused insurance ordinance. The ordinance required $250,000 of liability insurance for demonstrations in Chicago parks. The insurance requirement effectively barred the NSPA from demonstrating, as the NSPA could not afford to procure the coverage (nor was it likely that insurance companies would sell such coverage, even assuming the NSPA could afford it).[11] As he had earlier in the decade, Collin went to the American Civil Liberties Union for legal assistance. They filed a suit, *Collin v. O'Malley*, in the fall of 1976.[12]

Because Collin made a point of obeying the letter (if not the spirit) of the law, on account of his fear of going to jail,[13] he knew that he could not demonstrate on his home grounds during the months of litigation he faced with the Chicago Park District. Being shrewd in the tactics of street politics and intimidation,[14] Collin struck upon an idea which the Midwest director of the Anti-Defamation League labelled "a stroke of genius."[15] He decided to hold demonstrations in North Shore suburban areas, where many Jewish people reside. Never before had the NSPA taken its messages of hate directly to the heart of the Jewish community. Yet faced with the prospect of long-term litigation with the Chicago Park District,[16] Collin had to do something. What better tactic than to dramatically renew the association of a Nazi party with its historical foe, the Jew? Hamlin of the ACLU depicts Collin's reasoning and motivation:

> Since Collin offers his followers no power, no prestige, and no potential for either, the attention they get in the streets is probably their only remuneration . . . to assure himself that his illusion is working, Collin must be sure that somebody, somewhere, is watching. The instincts he has developed to that end triggered a simple, direct analysis of the Park District's requirement: his audience was gone. Collin moved directly to restore it . . . In January 1977, Frank Collin faced the very real possibility that he would be off the streets and out of the parks for at least a year and perhaps much longer. Collin faced two choices. Either he could wait out the litigation in the hope that he would eventually win and be able to return to Marquette Park and his most easily accessible audience, or he could forget Marquette Park and fill the time with other activities, activities aimed at an entirely different audience.[17]

In pursuit of his new strategy, Collin sent applications for demonstration permits to about a dozen North Shore suburbs in September 1976. Interestingly, only one recipient even deigned to respond: the Skokie Park District. The others simply ignored the requests.

Skokie borders Chicago on the north. It is predominantly white collar and middle to upper-middle class, although not as luxurious or wealthy as some communities further north (in the early 1970s it ranked 44th out of 201 Chicago suburbs in per capita income).[18] Yet, it is a well-educated, cosmopolitan, community. Today Skokie has 70,000 residents with different ethnic and racial backgrounds. At one time it had a substantial German population; and in the 1930s it supported a major German Nazi group (Bund),[19] which died out when America went to war with Germany.[20] Ironically, Skokie's Jewish population mushroomed after World War II. Indeed, Skokie's total population jumped from 14,832 to 59,364 in the 1950s suburban boom.[21] Jews were among this swell, and, as of the late 1970s, their estimated population of 30,000 comprised almost half of Skokie's population of 70,000.[22] Of these 30,000, somewhere from 800 to 1,200 are survivors of Hitler's persecution of Jews in Europe (counting family members, the number is estimated to be 5,000).[23] These survivors are well organized and consider themselves distinct. Their presence as a distinct subcommunity makes Skokie unique in the Chicago area, and, perhaps, in the country.

By responding to Collin's request for a permit, the Skokie Park District ironically contributed to making itself a target. Prior to this response, which occurred on October 25, 1976,[24] the NSPA had not singled out Skokie. But in addition to having sent many letters to numerous communities, it had covered the entire North Shore area at night with thousands of leaflets which proclaimed "We Are Coming!" in large print at the top of the page. The leaflets included vile statements about Jews, blaming them for a variety of social ills, and featured a picture of a swastika choking a stereotyped Jew. Since the NSPA targeted these disturbing leaflets at the entire North Shore suburban area, it took the actions of the Skokie Park District to turn Skokie into a singular target.

On October 25, the Skokie Park District (like the Chicago Park District), informed Collin that he would have to provide $350,000 worth of insurance or bond to receive a permit to demonstrate in the park he requested (at this point he had not intended to demonstrate on the steps of village hall). The Skokie Park District has refused to discuss the issue with anyone, yet according to knowledgeable sources the park district probably hurriedly concocted the requirement after consulting with the lawyers of the Chicago Park District, or by simply acting without advice.[25] At any rate, because of the similarity of the requirement to Chicago's, the action ignited Collin's anger and instinct to go for the jugular.

> When he received the reply from the Skokie Park District, Collin instantly recognized his next target: Skokie had provided him with the perfect issue, a golden opportunity, all in a "predominantly Jewish" community . . . The park district reply provided Collin with the key he had sought, and as quickly as he could Collin began to turn it.[26]

Perhaps not all that quickly, for Collin waited a few months to officially inform Skokie that he intended to hold an assembly on the sidewalk by the steps of the village hall on Sunday, May 1. The purpose of the demonstration? *To protest the park district's denial of a permit.*[27] The Skokie Park District is completely independent of the village government; indeed, the village government was not even informed of Collin's dispute with the park district until March 1977.[28] Yet Collin seized the Skokie Park District's denial of a permit as a rationale for holding the demonstration at the village hall. He opportunistically cloaked his desire to cause turmoil in the garb of the classic petition of redress. As Hamlin of the ACLU states, "Every citizen has the absolute right to disagree with the actions of government and every citizen has the right, within legal limits, to make that disagreement public." Yet even Hamlin admits that Collin's plan constituted "wedding an awful scheme to the law."[29]

Once Skokie governmental officials dealt with Collin, they chose not to counter Collin's plans for village hall. At a meeting held with other local leaders (including local rabbis and Chicago representatives of the Anti-Defamation League) they decided to grant Collin's request for a permit on May 1. They based their decision on the traditional "quarantine policy" of the Anti-Defamation League and other major Jewish organizations such as the American Jewish Committee and the Jewish Federation of Chicago.[30] In essence, to quarantine is to ignore and avoid a demonstration in the hope that it will pass away without causing disturbance and without attaining widespread publicity. At this meeting of leaders in April 1977, not one local leader (including the rabbis) dissented from the quarantine policy decision.

Yet the leaders had not anticipated the virulent reaction of the survivor community. As word spread around the community, survivor resistance and threats of counter-demonstration violence mushroomed, forcing the village to abandon the quarantine policy and to seek legal means of keeping the Nazis out. Once again, Collin asked the ACLU to litigate on his behalf, and the famous court battle over Skokie commenced.

B. The NSPA and the Politics of Extremism

> "We had a picket in Berwyn and got into a brawl with the JDL. Later, we went to the same place on the pretext of picketing for free speech. We got a lot of publicity." — NSPA "Lieutenant" Roger Tedor

1. The Extremist Type in the Media Age. Extremism can mean many things, from being uncompromising to espousing sectarian views well outside of the political mainstream. Here we are interested in a narrower meaning that concerns psychology and strategy. For our purposes, an extremist is somebody whose political values, goals, and strategies are a function of his emotional needs rather than a function of his reason. Though values are inextricably linked to our deepest emotions,[31] reasonable people temper their emotional reactions with deliberation. The views and beliefs of extremists, however, are predetermined by their emotional needs, so their views and beliefs are relatively immune to change when disconfirmed in the real world. Hate groups such as Nazis and Klansmen epitomize this form of irrationality, as do some over-zealous militant reformers. Gordon Allport illustrates the distinction between extremism and reasonable militancy or conviction in his classic, *The Nature of Prejudice*:

> Prejudice . . . exists whenever there is irrational hostility toward a group of people whose evil attributes are exaggerated and overgeneralized . . . Vigor of conviction is not the same as prejudice . . . Conviction is by no means

devoid of emotion but it is a disciplined and differentiated emotion, pointed at the removal of a realistic obstacle. By contrast, the emotion behind prejudice is diffused and over-generalized, saturating unrelated objects.[32]

Prejudice "saturates" unrelated objects. Prejudiced people "project" their own inner anxieties onto the world,[33] thereby substituting their own distorted *image* of things for the *reality* of things. This projection is necessary, according to psychologists such as Allport, because extremely prejudiced people feel deeply insecure. Existential insecurity is assuaged by the molding of the world into one's own image. Projection is temporary self-substantiation, yet it must be renewed because it is not a stable solution to insecurity.[34]

It is not surprising, therefore, that some extremists love to aggressively manipulate the news media. Exposure in the media makes them look more important than they actually are; and the media can be used for the strategic purpose of presenting intimidating messages to the public and to the targets of hate. As Hamlin put it, "to assure himself that his illusion is working, Collin must be sure that somebody is watching." Media politics enhances the *image* of power.

Some groups thrive on what Daniel Boorstin calls "pseudo-events." A pseudo-event entails the following characteristics:

1) It is not spontaneous, but comes about because someone has planned, planted, or incited it . . .

2) It is planted primarily (not always exclusively) for the immediate purpose of being reported or reproduced . . . The question "Is it real?" is less important than "Is it newsworthy?"[35]

Pseudo-events open up avenues for the unimportant to gain importance. The presentation of self escalates by projecting the group image to a wider audience. Boorstin laments: "Within the last century, and especially since about 1900, we seem to have discovered the processes by which fame is manufactured . . . a man's name can become a household word overnight. The Graphic Revolution suddenly gave us, among other things, the means of fabricating well-knownness."[36]

Yet if the hate group lacks enough membership and power to be inherently newsworthy, it must *do* something to attract the media's attention. The Ku Klux Klan has always possessed enough *real* power in terms of membership and influence to make its extremism more than a mere pseudo-event, even though it is no stranger to such events.[37] Yet groups like the NSPA possess no substantial power. To gain graphic fame they must incite disorder and prejudice at spectacular demonstrations. Under normal conditions, the media pay attention to celebrities and the economically and politically powerful. So "those who lack power are harder to reach by journalists and are generally not sought out until their activities produce social or moral disorder news."[38] Disorder news is news about dramatic conflicts that threaten the order of society either with violence or the serious transgression of values.[39] The media is especially interested in such news when the violence concerns what Edward J. Epstein calls "conflictive" or "cosmic" pairs: opposing sides that evoke stereotyped and renowned images of open conflict and which possess inherent public interest.[40] Jews vs. Nazis, students vs. authorities, and ghetto vs. police represent such pairs.

This brief discussion of the politics and psychology of extremism concerns only the most "prejudiced" of groups. And it should be acknowledged that the impact of such activity may be quite severe. The intimidation that hate groups so adroitly practice is itself a real phenomenon to its targets; indeed, its impact may be all the greater in certain circumstances *precisely because* of the irrationality which such groups exhibit.[41] At present we are concerned chiefly with the *motivations* of such groups (the dynamics of prejudice and the quest for power and recognition) rather than the *effects* of their actions on targets and audiences. But it should be kept in mind that if the effect is substantial the "pseudo" quality of the action may be irrelevant from a moral perspective.

2. The NSPA: Extremist Politics and Skokie. The NSPA and Frank Collin are classic extremists. They espouse virulent racial prejudice. A typical NSPA newsletter reads:

> What's White Power all about? It was the slogan hurled (together with bricks and bottles!) at the invaders by the white youth and workers. The battlecry which instinctively arose from the enraged masses has therefore returned to them as the most meaningful and effective slogan to unify and inspire them to defeat the enemies of their race and nation.[42]

This penchant for violence could be interpreted as a projection of self-hate. Allport holds that self-hate and inner frustrations often contribute to the violent dynamics of the prejudiced personality.[43] (Some Jews refer to other Jews as "Kikes.")[44] The thesis helps explain Frank Collin. First, substantial evidence (first divulged by Chicago columnist Mike Royko) shows that Collin is not only half-Jewish, but also the son of a survivor of the Nazis' infamous death camp, Dachau.[45] In attacking Jews and survivors, Collin attacks himself and his own heritage. A deeper self-hate is hard to imagine.[46] Second, in his hyperbolic, vituperative, and race-slurring interview with me, the miscreant stated several times that the NSPA intended to disenfranchise homosexuals once the NSPA "came to power." A few months after the interview, Collin was arrested and convicted of sexually molesting and abusing young boys. His own party purged him by turning him in, and he served time in prison.

Destructive impulses are often directed outward towards substitute objects of hate. NSPA members have not been ashamed to admit that the party thrives on the perpetration of violence for the sake of grabbing attention. When a Chicago reporter asked NSPA "Lieutenant" Roger Tedor, during the Skokie conflict, about the success of earlier NSPA demonstrations, Tedor replied:

> We had a picket in Berwyn and got into a brawl with the Jewish Defense League. Later, we went to the same place on the pretext of picketing for free speech, and there was another brawl. We got a lot of publicity . . . I'm absolutely convinced that what I'm doing is absolutely right, and it's impossible to change my mind.[47]

Tedor's remark is revealing. First, it exemplifies the prejudiced mind, for Tedor's views cannot be disconfirmed by reality testing ("it's impossible to change my mind"). Second, it reveals that the NSPA will seek violence by dissimulating the pursuit of another interest. *The real goal is to cause disorder in order to get what Tedor designates as "a lot of publicity"* (disorder news). *Yet the party justifies itself by ostensibly "picketing for free speech."* Such dissimulation is an old trick espoused by Hitler in *Mein Kampf*—another extremist afflicted with the drive to attain media exposure.[48]

The NSPA's actions concerning Skokie reveal similar proclivities to intimidate, to dissimulate, and to attain publicity. In an interview with me over a year after the Skokie conflict ended, Collin explained to me why the party leaped to retaliate against the actions of Skokie's park district. His statement demonstrates his knowledge of the media's addiction to pseudo-events as well as Collin's own commitment to extremism:

> We fought in the courts from 1975 onward . . . we were constantly denied. We faced the alternatives of either dying or coming up with something so dramatic that we could get it up in the world's headlines. In the courts I was a mouse in a maze, so this was an end-run . . . Skokie was traumatic. We lost many members. Many older people left us because the Jews were on television and said they'd kill us. Even hard core people left us. There's a parallel to Hitler. He had many people until the *Putsch*. Then he found himself

with no movement. But when we started making publicity, we gained numbers all over the country . . . [those who left] weren't fanatical enough. Now I've got *fanatics,* real *revolutionaries* . . .⌊The result was the greatest victory for National Socialism since World War II, because when the smoke cleared, we had a strong base.⌉And [due to court decisions] they can't touch us now. Quite honestly, this is a great victory of National Socialism.

Collin intended to create a great media event at Skokie because "something so dramatic" is an antidote to the "alternative of dying." Graphic incarnation substantiates existence. The press followed instructions faithfully, turning Skokie into what every interviewee considered the media event of the year in the Chicago area.[49]

An early event reveals Collin's (and his group's) drive for media attention. After a dramatic near-confrontation in Skokie in late April 1977 in which the police turned the NSPA back just before it entered Skokie (the closest the NSPA was to come to actually entering Skokie, and a key turning point in the controversy, as we will see in the next chapter), Collin and the NSPA hurried back to party headquarters in Marquette Park to view themselves and the events of the day on television. Rather than lamenting the putative denial of their free speech rights, the party celebrated its instant media success secured on the networks. According to a reporter from *Midweek Magazine,* who accompanied them:

> Back in their Marquette Park headquarters, though, the Nazis seemed anything but dejected about their aborted protest. About a dozen members still in full uniform stood outside their blood-red building posing for network camera crews.
>
> When the television crews left, they moved inside and stood in small groups talking while Collin hooked up a portable TV set so they could watch themselves on the evening news. He flipped the channel to WTTW Auction. "Well, what do you want," Collin asked, "Niggers or Jews? . . . We'll get there [Skokie] if it takes all summer."[50]

In addition to being regenerated by the new limelight, the NSPA needed Skokie because they needed a resource with which to bargain with the Chicago Park District and other authorities in their quest to regain their rights in Marquette Park.⌈Groups that lack political and other forms of power often must rely on a resource of last resort: the threat of violence.⌉ The NSPA, however, did not wish to directly threaten violence itself.⌉Collin wanted to appear "law-abiding" to the courts (but not to the survivors) throughout the conflict in order to foster an image of being persecuted and in order to stay out of jail (where he would be exposed to attack by venge-

ful black convicts).[52] The violence would have to be threatened by others,
but in a way which the NSPA could ultimately control. By threatening the
vulnerable survivor community in Skokie with his presence, Collin could,
in effect, hold Skokie "hostage" to *the survivors'* threat of violence *in reaction* to the NSPA's announced plans.[53] The missing link is the intimidation of his new targets, the Jews and the survivors. Collin explained this
aspect of his strategy to me.

> The key to Skokie is that the right to free speech was denied us here, in Mar-
> quette Park. We fought in the courts from 1975 onward. We were constantly
> denied . . . I've got to come up with something within the law, to use the law
> against our enemy, the Jew . . . I used it [the First Amendment] at Skokie.
> I planned the reaction of the Jews. They are hysterical.

In order to carry out this scheme, the NSPA inundated the North Shore
area with tens of thousands of leaflets that announced their plans. This
action took place in September 1976, months before Skokie became the
single target (so the leafletting was not part of the Skokie plan, per se).
Nonetheless, the NSPA *had* decided on a strategy of intimidation for the
North Shore suburbs at this time, and the leaflets constituted the first step
in the strategy's effectuation. Ab Rosen, Midwest director of the Anti-
Defamation League, told me that his office received numerous complaints
and expressions of fear concerning the leaflets. As seen, the leaflets con-
sisted of the words "WE ARE COMING!" emblazoned in large bold-faced
type, along with smaller print which stated the NSPA's reasons for targeting the North Shore area: "where one finds the most Jews, there one will
find the most Jew haters." The leaflet coaxed "fierce anti-Semites" to action. At the top of the leaflet they printed a hideous picture of a swastika
with hands that reached out to choke a picture of a stereotyped Jew.

The NSPA capitalized on another opportunity to graphically intimidate
when columnist Bob Greene of the *Chicago Sun-Times* wrote an impolitic
column on the problem on September 29, 1976. Greene wrote about the
wording of the leaflet and reactions of the Jews. Then he reported the reply of Collin and another Nazi, Mike Kelley, to Greene's own questions
addressed to them about the vulnerability of survivors to the leafletting
and to the NSPA's future plans. Hundreds of thousands of Chicago area
readers of the popular column read the following reply:

> We want to reach the good people — get the fierce anti-Semites who have to
> live among the Jews to come out of the woodwork and stand up for them-
> selves . . . Good. I hope they're terrified (the survivors). I hope they're
> shocked. Because we're coming to get them again. I don't care if someone's
> mother or father or brother died in the gas chambers. The unfortunate thing

is not that there were six million Jews who died. The unfortunate thing is that there were so many Jewish survivors.[54]

Ab Rosen pointed to Greene's column as a catalyst in the galvanization of intimidation and emotional reaction, and as a prime example of the role the press was to play in making Skokie into a provocative media event of extraordinary proportions:

> Skokie was heralded six or so months before when Collin circulated a leaflet saying "WE ARE COMING!" . . . Then Bob Greene wrote a full column repeating the circular. This act escalated the leaflet's circulation to 600,000. I called up Greene and took him to task. The ADL position is that even though the media has a right to publish, there should be editorial judgment and discretion . . . This is a perfect instance of the media making the news [the entire controversy].

Later we will see that Collin's manipulations paid off. In June 1978, the Federal District Court in Chicago ordered the Chicago Park District to give him back his speech right in Marquette Park. Yet on August 27, 1977, the same court and judge (Judge Leighton) had refused to issue such an order, claiming the NSPA had failed to prove that the park district insurance requirement would cost too much or that failure to obtain a permit would cause the NSPA "irreparable injury."[55] The major difference in the cases was the advent of Skokie.

3. Conclusion. The evidence indicates that the NSPA and Frank Collin exhibit the characteristics of extremism and the willingness to practice the politics of extremism. Collin targeted Skokie not simply to protest the abridgement of the free speech right, or even to present his views concerning politics or the decision of the Chicago Park District, but rather to intimidate a vulnerable group in order to generate a strategic resource: the threat of violence. Intimidation and the threat of violence were not the byproducts of an intention to engage in "free speech," but rather were essential ingredients in the NSPA's primary intention to intimidate. The NSPA needed to hold Skokie hostage as a bargaining chip against the Chicago Park District. With the First Amendment as a veil, Collin's action meant "wedding an awful scheme to the law."

II. Skokie's Legal Reaction

The survivors' reaction also forced the Skokie Village Board of Trustees to seek legal measures to stop the NSPA. Skokie's board consists of the mayor and six trustees, split evenly between Republicans and Democrats. They went to court and obtained an injunction against the NSPA on April 28, 1977, in the case *Skokie v. NSPA*. The injunction applied only to Sunday, May 1.[56] As we will see in the next chapter, Collin pounced on the opportunity provided by the limited scope of the injunction and attempted to come to Skokie on Saturday, April 30, instead. Village police thwarted this attempt at the last moment by obtaining an emergency extension of the original injunction. A Circuit Court judge granted the extension (subject to review the following Monday) due to the violence Collin's invasion would have triggered. The following Monday, May 2, Circuit Court Judge Wosik, who granted the original injunction, extended it indefinitely.[57]

In addition to the injunction, which could have been overturned by courts of appeal at any moment, Skokie officials sought back-up support on May 2 by unanimously passing the three ordinances discussed in Chapter One: the permit ordinance (that included a $350,000 insurance bond and prohibitions against the incitement of racial hatred),[58] the military uniforms prohibition,[59] and the ordinance that prohibited the dissemination of racial hate literature.[60] In early May 1977, the ACLU filed *Collin v. Smith* in response in the Federal District Court in Chicago.[61] Though complex legal maneuvering took place in the next few weeks and months, the injunction (*Skokie v. NSPA*) and the ordinance (*Collin v. Smith*) cases were not decided until 1978.

III. The ACLU: Doctrine of Total Tolerance

"Your Honor, if this Court issues a preliminary injunction in this case, enjoining the demonstration of Mr. Collin and the National Socialist Party of America, I fear that the Village of Skokie will be dancing on the grave of the First Amendment." — David Goldberger at the hearing of *Village of Skokie v. NSPA*, April 28, 1977.

A. The ACLU Takes the Case

We have seen that the NSPA is powerless in terms of the traditional resources and attributes of political power. Accordingly, they rely on intimidation and the concomitant threat of violence to gain power over others. These tactics also gain them media coverage which increases the *appearance* of their power and the real exposure of their ideas and plans.

But while these measures can prove useful in some respects, they do not provide access to courts. Skokie's legal efforts frustrated the NSPA's objectives. Yet the NSPA lacks the financial resources to conduct litigation.[62] For this reason it must rely on free legal assistance in order to sue for its rights in court.

For years the American Civil Liberties Union has come to the rescue. The Illinois ACLU litigated against the Chicago Park District on Collin's behalf in the early 1970s. In the 1960s, it litigated for another Chicago Nazi group against the City of Chicago,[63] as well as for the fabled founder of the American Nazi Party, George Lincoln Rockwell.[64] Other state branches of the ACLU have taken cases for other hate groups, such as the Ku Klux Klan, for years prior to Skokie.[65] Of course, the ACLU does not defend or support their clients' political views, per se, but rather the clients' *rights* to express those views. As Illinois ACLU leaders told me, their real client is the First Amendment.

The ACLU defines the First Amendment in terms of the content neutrality rule. Michael Gelder, president of the Evanston-North Suburban chapter of the ACLU in Illinois (which includes Skokie) exemplified this conception of the ACLU's mission in an interview:

> The ACLU defends the First Amendment itself, regardless who is the client. We also defended Martin Luther King in Cicero. We are very purposive and sensitive to the issue. If we don't take a case, then the First Amendment is hurt. There is an identification of ourselves with the First Amendment.

Despite this allegiance, adversaries during the Skokie controversy criticized the ACLU for providing the NSPA with legal support. Village trustees Topol and Conrad told the press in July 1977, that the ACLU was the "real enemy."[66] Shriller critics, such as the Skokie survivors, execrated the ACLU for its stand, and for assigning a Jew, David Goldberger, to defend Collin.

The ACLU's militancy at Skokie was due to both its traditional commitment to principle and to the fact that it jumped into the Skokie case before it was aware of the social reaction which was in store. When Collin came to David Hamlin and David Goldberger, the two Illinois division leaders who handled the Skokie case (Hamlin, a non-lawyer, handled public reactions, Goldberger handled the litigation), they immediately construed the problem from the perspective of Collin's previous battles with Chicago. Neither knew anything about Skokie's actions until Collin apprised them on April 27. The next day they went to court. Consequently, they initially viewed Skokie's action as simply more of the same "oppression" they suffered in Chicago. Hamlin told me:

The ACLU, for my time and place, was the only place I really belonged . . .
I saw fights involving civil liberties issues very much in a political context
. . . I was trained, and very good at what I did, to think in terms of Nixonian:
"its good guys and bad guys." Along comes this subtle, shaded kind of controversy, which on first blush was another First Amendment confrontation,
and David and I indeed reacted to it in precisely that framework for the first
three or four months of the issue.

As Hamlin put it, they saw only the "legal" as opposed to the "social"
aspect of the case at the beginning.[67] This viewpoint is consistent with the
ACLU's firm commitment to the content neutrality principle of free speech.
According to Hamlin, the ACLU's posture:

> was built on a premise that those who preach changes in constitutional law
> are the enemy, possessed of sinister motive and intent . . . We also knew that
> the stakes in the litigation were extremely high, for, if Skokie could prevail
> on any front, the law governing freedom of speech and assembly would be
> dramatically different.[68]

Despite Hamlin's fears, the Illinois board (as well as the national board
later) supported the Skokie and Marquette Park litigation unanimously.
Yet this commitment to principle exacted a harsh price. On the local level,
after the first court hearing on April 28, hostile phone calls from pro-Skokie
callers avalanched Hamlin's office for months. "The anger which ran
through most of the calls was more than sufficient to create an air of siege
in the office," Hamlin commented.[69] Callers sandwiched the threat to tor-
ture Hamlin's family (to show what the Nazis are like) in between the usual
bomb and murder threats.[70] Massive cancellations of membership accompanied these visceral displays of execration. Hamlin concluded that the Illinois division lost 30 percent of its total income in 1977 alone, and had to
lay off five of the office's thirteen employees.[71] And "the vast majority of
the letters of resignation came from members who identified themselves
as Jews."[72]

A similar pattern of loss appeared at the national level. Although ACLU
membership had been declining anyway with the end of the Vietnam War
and Nixon eras, national director Aryeh Neier estimated that the ACLU
lost about 30,000 members (15 percent of total membership) and about
$500,000 per year because of Skokie.[73] Those who withdrew appear to
have fallen into two categories: those who were knowledgeable about general ACLU policy, but were upset at Skokie; and those who never realized
that the ACLU supported the rights of hate groups until the Skokie drama
forced such realization.[74] In addition, the ACLU had been split in the pre-

vious decade between a left wing faction that favored supporting only left-ist "progressive" causes, and the more traditional wing that supported the rights of all groups, regardless of the substance of their views (content neu-trality). Groups in the former faction opposed the Skokie litigation, as they had opposed previous ACLU support of hate groups.[75] Yet while some state divisions disapproved, the Illinois and national boards (the only boards with direct roles at Skokie) unanimously supported Hamlin and Gold-berger's decision to embark on the litigation.[76]

B. The "Socialization" of the Dispute

The ACLU's decision to take the case provided Collin with the legal re-source he needed to regain control of the events. Dramatic court battles are inherently newsworthy. Accordingly, the Skokie issue first hit the head-lines in the *Chicago Tribune* the day after the U.S. Supreme Court inter-vened on the NSPA's behalf in June 1977 and ordered the Illinois courts to expedite the injunction litigation. The banner headline read "OK Nazi March in Skokie."[77]

The ACLU allowed Collin to "socialize" the conflict. As E. E. Schatt-schneider defines it, "socialization" is the process in which groups at a dis-advantage widen the "scope" of a conflict in order to bring new parties into the conflict as allies.[78] Objects of socialization include outside inter-est groups, the press, public opinion, governmental bodies, courts, and the federal executive branch, each of which may provide leverage against local majoritarian institutions.[79] At Selma in 1965, for instance, the Southern Christian Leadership Council (and Martin Luther King, Jr.), usually a lo-cal minority, conducted a demonstration that appealed to public opinion and the press, and thereby put pressure on Congress to pass the Voting Rights Act of 1965; this pressure in turn threw the Justice Department and the courts into the process of overseeing local elections.[80]

Groups who already have a power advantage normally adopt an oppo-site strategy. "Privatization," according to Schattschneider, involves restrict-ing the scope of conflict in order to prevent a change in power relations.[81] At Selma, and in desegregation cases, local majorities sought to keep the struggle localized in order to maintain the status quo. The invocation of such values as "localism" and "states rights" is designed to justify this main-tenance, while the socialization efforts of minorities typically involve the use of universal terms such as "justice," "equality," and "freedom of speech."[82]

The courts, replete with the values and enforcement powers of the Con-stitution, are primary agents of socialization.[83] They provide not only fo-

cus points for the media, but also the instruments of coercion to effectuate political change. Among other things, the law is a political resource
or ally.[84] By providing the means for the NSPA to take Skokie to the courts,
the ACLU allowed the NSPA to socialize its struggle. In comparison, Skokie officials, acting on behalf of the survivors, sought to privatize the dispute by squelching the NSPA's speech rights in the name of localism.
Charles Conrad, a Skokie trustee, told me:

> Government should support the community, use law as a tool. I think this
> is especially true for local government, which should support its commu-
> nity. There is a greater responsibility to the community at the local level.
> This case, if nothing else, clearly represented the will of the community . . .
> this is the value of the federal system: local government can do more for the
> community, knowing the other institutions back us up . . . The duty of a
> legislator is to pass legislation and not worry too much about the law and
> the Constitution. Let the courts review.[85]

Access to the courts bestowed *power* upon the NSPA's claims of "justice," "equality," and "freedom of speech." By invoking these symbols of
socialization, the NSPA claimed a status of right shared by all Americans.
"This is tyranny. We as Americans are being denied our right to demonstrate. What happens tomorrow if somebody finds the peace symbol ob-
jectionable?" Frank Collin shouted to the press after an unfavorable court
decision early in the controversy.[86]

We will see in the next chapter that Skokie officials eventually failed
to privatize the issue, as the appellate courts began to favor the NSPA, and
survivor groups mobilized in reaction to these rulings. Before long, *both
sides* engaged in the politics of socialization, each striving to gain allies
for the eventual counterdemonstration showdown.

C. Socialization and Principle

The ACLU's commitment to the principle of total tolerance (or the content neutrality rule) at Skokie constitutes another factor in the socialization of the dispute. Socialization and principle sometimes are linked in at
least two respects. First, the invocation of principle — especially principles
concerning public rights such as justice, equality, and free speech — often
accompanies the effort at socialization.[87] Claims of an "ethical character"
are more likely to reach audiences than claims without this character.[88]
Second, disputes over principle tend to generate more conflict than disputes over "interests" or other types of goods, thereby making them more
conducive to political mobilization and struggle. In a material sense, prin-

ciples are less *divisible* than interests, which renders their holders less open to compromise or resignation. Strategically, Collin and the ACLU devoted themselves to a singular course of action by committing themselves to the principle of free speech at Skokie. Ab Rosen of the ADL (a long-term ally of the ACLU until Skokie) pointed out that "the ACLU persisted in making Skokie a *cause celebre*. Goldberger would have been better advised to let the whole thing drop." Groups engaged in the strategy of conflict and bargaining will often attach themselves to a principle in order to signal to the opposition that they cannot budge from their present position.[89] And in a psychological sense, principles involve a deeper level of the psyche than do interests, so a challenge to principle engenders a stronger commitment than does a challenge to "interest." Conflicts of principle often involve senses of self-definition and self-worth. Consequently, such conflict may be more radical and merciless than other types of conflict.[90]

The Illinois ACLU's principled dedication to the First Amendment meant, as Hamlin observed, that their posture at Skokie was uncompromising, for it was "built on a premise that those who preach changes in constitutional law are the enemy, possessed of sinister motive and intent." As a result, the ACLU had "never been greater than during the past year [when] we have been under fire for defending the civil liberties of the enemies of civil liberties," national director Neier told the press after the controversy ended.[91]

But the ACLU's uncompromising commitment to principle in the early going affected more than the NSPA's fortunes. It also polarized Skokie's posture, forcing Skokie to socialize the issue on their own side as the controversy wore on. Skokie participants referred to the intransigence of the ACLU as they proclaimed their own dedication to fighting for their cause to the very end. Skokie trustees vilified the ACLU after one important board meeting in July 1977.[92] Ab Rosen depicted the role of the ACLU in polarizing the conflict:

> We have been treating Skokie as a confrontation between Jews and Nazis, which was its genesis. But then the civil libertarians stepped in; and on the other side, a tremendous outpouring of support by the non-Jewish community all over America resulted. "What can we do to help?" To coin a cliche, there was a reservoir of good will to be tapped.

Hamlin himself came to appreciate how ACLU intransigence heightened tensions and helped Skokie to socialize the dispute. Recalling his response to a press query when Skokie passed the three ordinances, Hamlin admits his words served only to entrench ACLU's extremist image.

I paused for a moment before I answered, thinking about the events of the past few days as well as about the newest piece of news of the controversy. It was, from where I sat, a truly remarkable set of events: Wosik's seemingly tainted hearing and unconstitutional injunction, Sullivan's extension of prior restraint, the telephone calls (still coming into the office at a frantic pace), and now three broadly unconstitutional ordinances. The frustration and anger came out. I told the reporter that as far as I was concerned, "the Village of Skokie shredded the First Amendment."

That sentence haunts me still. It came to be so widely quoted that it cemented in spirit, if not in reality, ACLU's public image for the remainder of the controversy.[93]

D. Postscript: Context and the Limits of Principle

The ACLU's commitment to total tolerance and the First Amendment content neutrality rule poses a normative issue in addition to explaining the ACLU's contribution to the conflict. The ACLU viewed the impact of the NSPA speech act to be legally irrelevant. Hamlin distinguished the "social" from the "legal" aspects of the case at many points in his interview and maintained that he had gained a greater appreciation of the social impact as the conflict wore on. Nonetheless, he adhered to the same legal principle despite this recognition.

An important exchange between David Goldberger, Skokie lawyers Gilbert Gordon and Harvey Schwartz, and Judge Wosik in the first injunction hearing on April 28, 1977, epitomizes the normative issue at stake. As Gordon questioned Frank Collin about his views, Goldberger interjected with objections, claiming that the questions were "irrelevant." Gordon asked Collin, "And are you personally in agreement with the materials that are contained in this leaflet?" Goldberger interjected, "I would object, his personal views are not relevant here." When Gordon asked if Collin intended "to distribute anything pertaining to Jews," Goldberger objected: "It's irrelevant." Further questions and objections led Wosik to exasperation:

> *The Court:* Well, now, I'm going to ask you why do you say it's irrelevant if the pleadings allude to something and this is one of the issues? May I please inquire of you as to your general explanation of relevancy?

> *Mr. Goldberger:* Your Honor, I'm prejudging the outcome of this proceeding. However, it's . . . that a man is on trial not for his views, but for what he intends to do in his conduct. This Village of Skokie wishes to place the man's views on trial; they do not like his views. They wish to shut him down, at least insofar as he wishes to hold an assembly in the Village of Skokie.[94]

Similarly, when Schwartz asked survivor leader Sol Goldstein several questions about the impact of the Nazi demonstration and display of the swastika on him, Goldberger proffered several objections claiming, "It's irrelevant, your Honor, this is 1977."[95]

The problem is that Collin's views are indeed quite relevant to the *impact* and the *meaning* of the speech. And if the consequences of speech are important, as the Supreme Court in *Chaplinsky v. New Hampshire* held, then the ACLU's view is suspect. The consideration of consequences constitutes the core of an "ethic of responsibility" that Max Weber elevated to the highest principle of political action.[96] Why cannot impact be a proper criterion for delimiting the scope of a right? In order to so delimit, however, we would have to treat rights as *divisible,* which is something the ACLU is loathe to do, according to interviewee Franklyn Haiman, national secretary of the ACLU.[97] Similarly, we would have to criticize the logic which defines the viability of a right in terms of its application to the most extreme cases. In his spirited partisan article on Skokie written in the wake of the ACLU's Illinois Supreme Court victory in *Skokie v. NSPA* in January 1978, Hamlin asseverated that "Free speech exists in the most extreme case, or it doesn't exist at all."[98] Goldberger proclaimed a similar view in the Judge Wosik hearing quoted above.[99] Yet this position seems too blithely oblivious of consequences.

On the other side of the ledger, the ACLU's preoccupation with the content neutrality rule is not without its own important justification. Skokie contestants were playing for "high stakes." The ACLU thought that modifying present public forum doctrine would threaten the First Amendment more than reformers intended. The ACLU's extensive battling in the trenches of free speech warfare since its inception during World War I has indelibly marked upon its collective mind the constant dangers of illegitimate abridgement which jeopardize the First Amendment.[100] Because these fears are worthy of due respect, they will not be forgotten when we construct our conclusions.

3

Bearing Witness: The Skokie Survivors and the Politics of Intolerance

We are only messengers.—Elie Wiesel, *One Generation After*

They called themselves the testifiers. Now they testify.—Skokie Rabbi Montrose

I. Survivor Interviewees

Before examining the survivors' reasons for resistance and their strategy of resistance, I must introduce the reader to my survivor interviewees. Their names are Stephen, Alex (and his wife), Judith, Sol Goldstein, and Erna Gans. I do not use their real names in order to protect them from pranksters (during the controversy some received malicious late night calls). Consequently, I substitute pseudonyms, except in the cases of Sol Goldstein and Erna Gans, who are too well known in the Chicago area to justify disguise.

My interviewees stood up and accepted leadership in the conflict. So they were among the stronger survivors. Yet many survivors have been profoundly damaged by their experiences in Europe, according to psychiatrists.[1] Even Erna Gans, one of my most competent interviewees, experienced trauma over the NSPA threat to come to Skokie.[2] One can only imagine the impact on weaker survivors. Eileen, a survivor's daughter (and founder of Children of the Holocaust Survivors in Chicago), expressed the matter quite well:

> She's [Erna] an exception. [You can't generalize] on her. She is what it would be nice to say all the survivors could do. And I don't know what gave her the strength, or whatever. Most of the other survivors . . . would not go to

38

school like Erna did, and go and be very public. Very few of the survivors, men or women, are as involved politically [as Erna], who's run for office, etc. That's a rarity. It's like "don't look at me. I don't want to be noticed."[3]

This observation warns us to extrapolate with care. It also reveals something about the survivor phenomenon which appears to have played a mysterious role in the eruption of the Skokie conflict. The survivor experience under Hitler often *privatized* its victims in a psychological sense, forcing them into inner retreats. The experience split the *inner self* from the *outer self* and the *public world.* Consequently, the outer world sometimes becomes an almost insurmountable obstacle to the "divided self."[4] Thus, Erna Gans is an "exception" because of her mastery of "public" life; others, on the other hand, are afraid of the public (they don't want to be "noticed"). Until the Skokie controversy many survivor interviewees distanced themselves from the public realm and the affairs of non-survivor groups. They performed in the "outer" world, yet maintained allegiance to the world of survivorship, a world apart.

The literature on survivors abounds with references to this privatization which may take solipsistic or group-oriented (communal) forms. Writers such as Elie Wiesel coin terms such as "Night," intimating the darkness which characterizes withdrawal.[5] Psychiatrists write about the psychological "regression" which occurred in concentration and death camps and which entailed a movement of self-conception from the light of the mature ego-constituted adult to the darkness of the "primitive" ego.[6] In interviews, one senses that the speaker at times speaks from both egos, or from one in contradistinction to the other. The interviewer witnesses swings of emotion, tone, and voice, depending on the importance of the point and the emotional stress of the particular moment. Of my interviewees, Erna Gans, Sol Goldstein, and Judith appear to have possessed the most integrated personalities, for they controlled their lapses into emotionalism more than my other interviewees. However, it is hard to draw definitive conclusions from such interviews, so our following conclusions are speculative.

Another view of the psychological privatization thesis is offered by Hannah Arendt. In *The Origins of Totalitarianism,* she illustrates the different sense of reality that prevailed in the Nazi camps, a sense which is essentially incommunicable to the everyday, "normal" world:

> This atmosphere of madness and unreality, created by an apparent lack of purpose, is the real iron curtain which hides all forms of concentration camps from the eyes of the world. Seen from outside, they and the things that happen in them can be described only in images drawn from a life after death,

that is, a life removed from earthly purposes. Concentration camps can very aptly be divided into three types corresponding to three basic conceptions of a life after death: Hades, Purgatory, and Hell . . . Hell in the most literal sense was embodied by those types of camp perfected by the Nazis, in which the whole of life was thoroughly and systematically organized with a view to the greatest possible torment.[7]

The unearthly quality of many survivors' experiences makes communication with people who have not suffered such ordeals difficult.[8] The "outside world" often cannot listen or understand, and many survivors feel unable to surmount inner inhibitions that thwart communication. To a significant extent, the Skokie issue entailed the merging of the disparate world views of survivors and non-survivors. The survivors' stance was a "coming out," or a making public of their pasts. Before the time of the Skokie controversy, they were silent in public about their pasts.

Yet not all survivors are alike. Bruno Bettelheim discerns three basic character types, based on how survivors deal psychologically with the past. The first is the "concentration camp survivor syndrome", the most extreme form of mental disorder following persecution, in which such psychiatric disorders as depression, paranoia, neurosis, and psychosis overwhelm the individual (naturally, there are degrees of affliction). The second is characterized by an attitude of "life as before," in which "one chooses to re-integrate oneself essentially the same way one had been before imprisonment." This form of coping is superior to the survivor syndrome, yet can be shaky because it is premised on "denial" of the emotional changes that have taken place.[9] Bettelheim surmises that this category of survivor "may very well be the majority" of survivors. If so, the Nazi issue at Skokie may have put the integration of some survivors "to a serious test." Finally, "re-integration" constitutes the most successful type of psychological adjustment. Members of this group have learned to integrate their camp experiences into their present personalities. This arrangement allows survivors to deal with deeper psychological forces such as guilt and anxiety more propitiously, for such forces prey on the self more mercilessly when the self is not used to grappling with them.[10] Facing reality fosters strength.[11]

My interviewees do not appear to fit the first category, though at times during the Skokie controversy some experienced great anxiety (by their own accounts and those of others). Three of my interviewees appear to fit the "reintegration" category (once again, this is an educated guess, at best). Erna Gans is representative of this remarkable group and the most politicized. She is involved not only in survivor affairs, but also in larger political issues; she has been the president of Korzcak Lodge in Skokie (the predominant survivor organization) and has run for office as a state representative. In the two interviews I had with her she was emotional, and at times "prejudiced" (in the sense of "militant" devotion to cause that we discussed in the last chapter), but always with intelligence and control. During the war she endured the death camps of Poland, including Auschwitz, and lost most of her family. After liberation, she came to Skokie for the same reason others did: it had gained a reputation as a haven for survivors. Erna strove to grow and assimilate herself to the new country. She went to college and eventually completed all graduate course work in sociology except for the dissertation at Loyola University in Chicago. She also became active in politics, and today runs a very successful printing business with her husband (also a survivor — all my survivor interviewees were married to survivors — a common practice)[12] in a suburb west of Skokie. Far from denying the painful past, she actively confronts it on a regular basis by virtue of her politics. The night before our second interview she had been a major speaker at a large memorial service in Chicago for the Warsaw Ghetto uprising.

Political drive can be suspect when it serves as a channel for negative subconscious needs.[13] Yet political involvement can also promote self-development, confidence, and insight into human affairs. Indeed, when Bettelheim observed the reactions of his fellow inmates in a Nazi concentration camp (1938 and 1939, before the Final Solution), he concluded that two types of inmates were most immune to traumatization: those from the upper socio-economic classes and those who possessed substantial "political education." "The politically educated prisoners found support for their self-esteem in the fact that the gestapo had singled them out as important enough to take revenge on." On the contrary, the "politically uneducated" German middle classes were much more easily traumatized because "they had no consistent philosophy which could give them the strength to make a stand against the Nazis. They had obeyed the law handed down by the ruling classes, without ever questioning its wisdom."[14] So, politics can also engender a worthy self-integration, as in Erna's case. We may view Erna's personality as a "political reintegration." As will be seen, it is possible that many survivors may have used the Skokie issue as a means of actuating such a belated reintegration.

The other political "reintegrationist" survivor is Sol Goldstein. While Erna led the local Skokie survivor community, Goldstein acted as a bridge between this community and the assimilated Jewish establishment downtown in Chicago (the Jewish Federation and its umbrella operating group, the Public Affairs Committee), and as a singular mover within the Jewish establishment itself. A wealthy engineer and businessman with impressive political connections and skills (he is esteemed by Israeli leaders, for example), sources portrayed Goldstein in nearly super-human terms. According to one informant, he "single-handedly turned the Federation around."[15] He earned the respect of all parties in the larger Skokie alliance, except, perhaps, of the most militant survivors, who viewed his less militant position as an unjustified accommodation to the Federation. Commentators described him in such terms as "gifted," "powerful," "great," "internationally known," and "burning with an inner fire."

Goldstein had perhaps the least debilitating personal experience under the German Nazis. Yet he hardly went unscathed. In 1943 Nazis murdered fifty Jewish women in Goldstein's home town of Kovno, Lithuania, by throwing them down a well and covering them with gravel. Goldstein's mother was in this group. Soon thereafter they led thousands of Kovno citizens out into the countryside to be shot.[16] Goldstein, then twenty-nine, managed to escape into the forests, where he fought with the Partisans against the Nazis until the war ended. Yet though he witnessed the destruction of his family, Goldstein did not suffer incarceration in concentration or death camps, nor their debilitating effects. He maintained autonomy and respect by actively resisting the Nazis. Yet his loss caused him to resist Collin with great passion.

Eugene DuBow, who chaired the Federation's final counterdemonstration mobilization committee along with Goldstein, echoed other interviewees with these observations:

> Goldstein is one of the most fascinating men I've ever met. He has a Yiddish accent and speech, yet he's very articulate, emotional, and has a great political sense. He almost single-handedly got the Fed to organize a counterdemonstration . . . Goldstein had a foot in both camps, Skokie and Chicago, the survivors and the Fed. He was the only survivor on the Federation Board . . . Goldstein's magnetism is charismatic. You only run into a few in your entire lifetime, and Goldstein was one . . . He's self-made, and he hears a different drummer . . . I'd meet with him every morning at his desk. He'd start opening his mail and cut you off, as if you didn't exist then. I had to decide to either go with it and hang in there, or have my ego destroyed. I finally decided that it was worth it to hang in. He had such command and such resources. He was like the Godfather—except that it was so situational. When it was all over, he lost a lot of his authority.

Goldstein impressed me as well. He possesses a depth and a seriousness which are extraordinarily rare and even disconcerting. He has seen the enormity of evil in ways which most of us never will ("he hears a different drummer"). Unfortunately, the interview with him was not as fruitful as the others. He did not discuss the issue very well and did not allow me into the sanctum of his world. Accordingly, I quote Goldstein below less than other survivors. Yet he did make several important remarks which will prove to be illuminating. Let us now look at the other survivor informants.

Another indicator of the reintegrated survivor is the ability to talk about the past with a posture of detachment, to be either philosophical or analytical. Judith, my other seemingly "reintegrated" interviewee, represents this type. She called herself an "existentialist." We could call her reintegration the "psychological-existential" reintegration. She works as a psychological counselor at the Kaplan Jewish Community Center in Skokie. During our interview, Judith demonstrated a remarkably lively and probing perspective on the issue of survivorhood and its psychological meaning. Although she appeared to be committed to survivor issues, she was much more objective and analytical than my other survivor informants, who turned the Skokie issue into a personal crusade. For example, she remarked:

> There were some positives [at Skokie, for survivors] in terms of all those issues. In spite of the fact that they felt helpless, they found that they were not as helpless as they thought they were . . . the process of doing — you see, I am very existentialist, really, in many ways. I feel — and I don't know if the war taught me, or whatever — that as long as you are doing, it's okay . . . when you do feel helpless, you feel immobilized . . . In order to overcome something, one must have a feeling of mastery over it. The very fact Collin existed allowed this mastery . . . When someone tells you they don't want the Nazis doing it again, they are saying a lot of things . . . you have to understand and dig out what is beneath the words, to the emotions.

Perhaps her existentialist sense assisted Judith and her husband in escaping from the Warsaw ghetto just before the Nazis burned it to the ground (they escaped through a sewer and eventually found work in Germany under the protective guise of false papers).

The rest of the survivors I interviewed are of equally substantial character. Alex and his wife experienced the death camps of Poland. Their scars were more apparent than Judith's, Erna Gans' and Sol Goldstein's. Yet despite these scars, Alex and his wife played leading roles within the major survivor group (survivors spent all night at their house organizing the April 30, 1977 counterdemonstration). The interview went well, but somewhat more painfully. Alex is a businessman, and a man of exquisite dignity. In the interview, he spoke with a deep resonant voice and with great clarity, choosing his words very carefully. Paradoxically, he seemed both tense and self-possessed early in the interview. Yet once I gained his trust, he opened up and became confident. Suzanne was also present, yet played a secondary role. For the most part, she interjected when she wished to elaborate on her husband's remarks. She appeared to be angrier, and perhaps more militant. While Alex emphasized his more pressing commentary by a measured rise of voice designed to instruct, Suzanne resorted to a shriller invective in pleading the survivors' case. Alex and Suzanne appear to be more insular in their social lives than Erna or Judith, as they told me that before the Skokie conflict they had kept pretty much to their own people at Korzcak Lodge. Perhaps this is one reason I felt a greater gulf existed between them and myself than with Erna and Judith.

Stephen was my final major survivor source. After surviving the death camps of Poland (as did his wife) Stephen came to Skokie in the late 1950s and became, after much struggle, a successful businessman. Stephen's voice often shook with emotion during the interview, and he made many more voluntary references to his own history of persecution. He *personalized* various issues more than the others and tended to single out specific targets of ridicule. He seemed less tolerant of ambiguity, and occasionally engaged in "splitting," or bifurcating too rigidly the categories of good and evil.[17] For instance, while Stephen reverently called Rabbi Montrose (the most militant Skokie rabbi in the issue) a "great man," David Goldberger of the ACLU was "scum." Yet like other survivor activists, Stephen possessed dignity and presence, and spoke with impressive authority. His comments often came across as probing speeches, a fact which reminded me that his speech at Rabbi Montrose's synagogue changed Montrose's position (a matter we will examine later in the chapter). In these "speeches" he explained the survivors' positions with powerful eloquence; and he displayed his disagreements with survivors whom he thought had adopted compromising positions. He also criticized the established ADL and Jewish Federation for the same reason.

In addition to these survivor interviewees, I also interviewed two children of survivors, John (Stephen's son), and Eileen, as well as many nonsurvivor Jewish leaders, in order to attain supplementary perspectives. I will refer to their comments when they may illuminate or aptly challenge a viewpoint presented.

II. The Community of Survivorship at Skokie:
Reasons for Resisting the NSPA

A. The Demise of the Quarantine Policy

The survivors were the key resisters at Skokie. Without them, no conflict would have erupted, as the quarantine policy advocated by the predominant Jewish groups such as the Anti-Defamation League would have prevailed. To quarantine means to ignore: let the Nazis come, ignore them, and they will leave in inconspicuous peace. The ADL, like Collin, knew that the NSPA could not secure a "hostage" and a dramatic issue at Skokie without a hostile Jewish reaction.[18] For political (if not philosophical) purposes speech does not exist if it falls upon deaf or absent ears. Every major Jewish interest group had espoused the quarantine policy since the Second World War.[19] At Skokie, no non-survivor Jews (other than Jewish Defense League members in the Skokie-Chicago area) openly opposed the quarantine policy at the start of the conflict.[20] Accordingly, the survivors started out with a sense of isolation which lowered their trust and increased their militancy.

But threats to commit violence by the organized survivor community forced the village and Midwest divisions of major Jewish groups to change their policies and tactics. Skokie city manager Jack Matzer, a non-Jew who strongly espoused the early quarantine policy, expressed the hopes and futility of the quarantine policy:

> Originally a meeting was called by Mayor Smith for leaders of the community, rabbis, etc. At this point no decisions were made, but there was much discussion. There was some concern over letting them march, but no strong opposition was voiced. It wasn't until the rabbis went to their congregations that opposition arose. Initially an open mind prevailed: let them do their thing and get it over with. There was a lot of discussion about permitting it but have everybody else stay home. Yet not long after this the survivor groups got very active. Two critical elements were the media and the survivors. Soon more people saw the consequences of them coming to Skokie . . . The survivors appeared united to us, with one variance: there was a split between two groups, the DuBow and Goldstein group at the Federation, and the local survivors led by Erna Gans . . . My initial feeling was that I couldn't understand why they couldn't come in and leave. I didn't appreciate the psychological effect until later. There was *no question* that for *survivors* it was a *re-living* of the whole Nazi thing, and I changed my attitude.

Skokie officials and other leaders originally advocated quarantine because they did not understand the survivors' tribulation. The two camps approached the issue from two different perspectives (Arendt's bifurcation thesis). Because of their unique experiences, survivors greeted the advocates of quarantine with wrath. Ab Rosen of the ADL, who ventured to Skokie in April 1977 to advocate quarantine in public meetings attended by survivors, depicted the treatment of quarantine advocates:

> The main individuals were all survivors. They are an integrated part of the community. They are powerful voices. They wouldn't relent. "We'll be out

there with baseball bats," they claimed. Those of us who stood up took a terrible beating. These confrontations took place at individual meetings and at the B'nai B'rith to talk about the Skokie problem. At these meetings survivors would stand up and say "you weren't there." This is an unassailable argument. Logically this is assailable, but not emotionally. I took a terrible emotional battering. The survivors prevailed right from the start, as soon as it was known that Skokie was a target. Collin showed a genius in targeting Skokie.

Due to this pressure, leaders forsook the quarantine policy in late April 1977, a few weeks after Collin's request for a permit to demonstrate at village hall became known.

The reasons for the survivors' hostile resistance are rooted in the relation between the survivor community at Skokie and survivors' experiences in Nazi Europe. We must explore this relation next.

B. Structure and Motivations of the Survivor Community: Roots of Resistance

1. Sociological Structure: The Turf of the Outsider. The Skokie survivor community is somewhat diverse, yet also very organized. Of the 800 to 1200 survivors (no official count exists), over half belong to one or more of the major survivor groups, according to interview sources. The largest and most influential is the Korzcak Lodge, with approximately four hundred families. Erna Gans, the top *local* survivor leader during the conflict, was president of Korzcak during the conflict. Other groups, which overlap with Korzcak, include the Laueum, the Schalom Club, the New Citizens Club, the McCovey Club, and a club of survivors' children which Eileen helped found. The clubs perform many functions, from socializing to community work, education, and politics. Most importantly, they facilitate social interaction and reintegration in the survivors' new world. They are mutual support communities for people who consider themselves special in virtue of their unique past experiences. Suzanne described this function in her interview:

> It happens that we are a group left without family, most of us. Well, we have the families that we built now, after the war. Otherwise sisters, brothers, very few — you have to be very lucky to have that. So we are groups that keep together when we make a bar mitzvah or a wedding. It's like a family. We keep close like a family. Like the Korzcak Lodge: we have four hundred members. It's like one family. Whatever we do, we do together.

Suzanne's portrayal of Korzcak resembles that of other commentators on the lifestyles of survivors.[21] Many of them huddle together, forming a new protective web of community (or "communality")[22] that is *a replacement of the past.* Many survivors name their children after loved ones who died under Hitler; although naming children after deceased family members is a Jewish tradition, sources claim the practice is more prevalent among survivors.[23] Alex linked Korzcak and life in Skokie to the past, intimating that the new communality was bonded by a shared loss:

> Among ourselves, when we gather — would it be a bar mitzvah, would it be a wedding, would it be an anniversary, whatever the occasion comes up — we have a great time. But one evening or one day wouldn't go by when we get together that this issue shouldn't come up about the past of the Holocaust. Always somebody starts it. It's just a thing, it cannot be forgotten.

Past and present, however distinct in geographical and national-cultural terms, interact in the mind; they constitute the temporal aspects of the divided self. Alex's portrayal also evokes what sociologist Richard Sennett terms a "negative gemeinschaft" or "destructive community," one that is grounded on a negative separation from the pluralistic world around it.[24]

Non-survivor leaders at Skokie confirmed the view of the survivors as a community apart. Fred Richter, president of the Northwest Suburban Synagogue Council during the conflict and a major ally of the survivors, told me that "survivors are multifaceted. They enter the community and are like you and me. But there is a barrier." Richter mentioned that many survivors are less assimilated to the mainstream of American culture than other Jews. And this difference contributed to the survivors' willingness to resist Collin in disregard of the First Amendment, which is a cultural value for many assimilated Jews. Richter stated:

> The dynamics are different in Skokie with the high survivor organization. The key variables that explain the difference between, say, Skokie and Evanston, are the fact that Evanston was inhospitable to Jews for a long time, that Evanston had a Rabbi and university which attracted the more intellectual Jews, and that Skokie Jews are Eastern European, whereas Evanston's are German, Western European. German Jews always felt superior, as depicted in Andre Manner's *Poor Cousins.* The American Jewish movement is twofold.[25]

As a result of the survivors' alleged relative lack of assimilation they inclined to put the obligation to support their community ahead of their commitment to the First Amendment when they learned of the NSPA's challenge. When put to this test, their links to the larger community of

Skokie (the public world) proved weaker than their bonds to the survivor community. Ab Rosen reported how the survivors viewed the First Amendment once they felt their communal security was at stake:

> After Skokie, leaders of other towns told me that their people would not react like Skokie did. Those Jews were more integrated into American society. At Hyde Park, the Nazis would be laughed at. There is a difference in socioeconomic status, and it's a matter of educational sophistication. Some folks up there [Skokie] don't understand the American system at all. "Fuck the First Amendment," I heard.

Rosen's comment is consistent with the evidence. Yet it should be noted that my survivor informants revealed a good deal of familiarity with and respect for American values and institutions. They just construed the Skokie case to be *different*. We will see that their claims were actually more sophisticated than many critics thought.

More importantly, the restricted, "negative" survivor community also served a positive function for its members. Like all meaningful communities, it provided membership in a community of shared values and experience; this type of community is exceptionally important for survivors because of the fears they harbor from their past tribulations. Their special community bound them together for protection against these fears.

2. Protection of Turf and Resistance to Collin. Survivor interviewees stressed the relation between their resistance to Collin and their conception of their community as protective turf. When I asked Alex why he resisted Collin at Skokie, but had ignored Collin on the Southwest side of Chicago until this provocation, he replied in a representative manner:

> We haven't done too much before, we haven't paid too much attention, because we were not attacked right at our home. The minute somebody comes and tries to attack my home, I have to defend myself. This is why we felt that we cannot let it happen at our home. We knew of Frank Collin before. But right close here, where I tried to raise a family, I couldn't let it happen.

Alex stressed the "attack" on the "home" and the "family"—the basic institutions of communality dedicated to growth. These institutions take on an added meaning when their relation to the past is recognized: Hitler destroyed communality in its fullest sense, so the new communality becomes all the more precious at the same time that a harsh world confirms its precariousness. Contemporary *signs* of Nazism can be keys that unlock the gates of the nightmare.[26] Therefore, the NSPA's carrying of the swastika *into* Skokie takes on the psychological meaning of an assault on communality itself. The psychological meaning of communality blends with the psychology of the individual survivor to create a special trauma triggered by the recurrence of the symbolization of Nazism targeted at the community. Nazis in Marquette Park (of which Alex was aware) do not galvanize resistance, but their targeting of Skokie does. Even though the NSPA intended to remain only on the public steps of village hall, this plan nonetheless is the psychological equivalent of an "attack right at our home." As Erna affirmed:

> He comes and he says 'here I am.' He comes to our homes; he flaunts his ideas in our faces . . . why should we allow Nazis free access to the community, to espouse their views, their political philosophy against the right of Jews to live? He came to Skokie for a certain reason. He knew that there was a concentration of survivors, and he had a special reason to come and hurt us . . . *you can see a breakdown of the community protection.*

Similarly, Stephen spoke of Nazis on his "porch."

These remarks suggest that Frank Collin's symbols of hate and destruction threatened not only individuals, but the Jewish *community as well.* Psychologist David Guttman of Northwestern University depicted the nature of this phenomenon in his pre-trial deposition taken in the Skokie ordinance case. When ACLU lawyer Goldberger asked Guttman if the Skokie survivors would feel the same kind of terror if Collin demonstrated in a public forum in Chicago, just a few miles away from Skokie, Guttman replied:

> No, whatever the legal definitions of territory might be, there is psychologically a sense of turf, a sense of community, such that an act—an act can have different meanings depending on whether it's performed within that community or outside of it.
>
> I'm not happy, for instance, that Collin appears in the Daly Square, yet for me it doesn't have the same significance, whether as a human being or a psychologist or whatever, as his appearance in Skokie. The one constitutes a public demonstration of offensive ideas, the second constitutes an invasion.[27]

Guttman's articulation of the problem of communality and assault as a kind of invasion at Skokie parallels the findings of students of other crises. In his study of the Buffalo Creek disaster, Kai Erikson found that communality declined after the disaster because the victims' "illusion of safety" had been pierced.

Among the symptoms of extreme trauma is a sense of vulnerability, a feeling that one has lost a certain natural immunity to misfortune, a growing conviction, even, that the world is no longer a safe place to be. And this feeling often grows into a prediction that something terrible is bound to happen again.[28]

Concerning Skokie survivors, Judith told me, "When you've been in fire, it scares you every time you see it."[29]

3. The Community of Obligation: Resistance to Repay the Debt. In addition to the desire to protect their reconstituted community, survivors resisted for another reason: to repay a debt they felt they owed their lost loved ones and the larger Jewish community.

Many survivors of Hitler's persecution feel shame at not preventing the genocide.[30] Eileen spoke of her father who suffered through the same experiences Elie Wiesel depicts in *Night,* a book on Auschwitz.

I think that if you ask most survivors now if they would have done things differently, I think they'd say "sure" . . . They've been in America for thirty years and have had kids who keep asking them "why did you go like sheep?" . . . Whereas I was more rational [concerning Skokie], he was like, "I didn't do this in 1939. I didn't shoot Hitler." He saw Hitler many times in Berlin in the 1920s and I'm sure this was going through his mind.[31]

This feeling of shame translates readily into a sense of debt which survivors *owe* the dead. The debt consists of both the price the dead paid and the inability (or failure) of the survivors to have prevented the exaction of this terrible price. Part of the debt is repaid by "bearing witness" to what happened in Europe before the eyes of the world. Stephen told me:

We did owe it to them. Exactly . . . I cannot forget my very dramatic and tragic departure from my mother. And one thing she mentioned was that if you ever survive, *let the world know.*[32]

Rabbi Montrose, the unofficial rabbi of survivors at Skokie, said, "They called themselves the testifiers. Now they testify." And Erna pointed to "an obligation to the past, to those who were killed, to be witness." These remarks indicate that membership in the Skokie survivor community encompassed international and intergenerational Jewish communities.

The act of resistance becomes necessary to fulfill the debt. On the one hand, it may compensate (at least in part) for past inaction. On the other hand, it confirms the survivors' commitment to the payment of the debt.

Erna Gans depicted the nature of this logic in an interesting and representative statement:

> We could not act in the past. It was a different time frame. But now when we are free to act and don't act, that's a different story. We had to point out the danger. In Germany, Hitler was not faced early. But knowing what history taught us and *then* not acting is inconceivable . . . If I *didn't* do that, I'd question my right to be a survivor.

The obligation to the dead engenders a duty to be vigilant in the present. Erna speaks of a "right" to be a survivor. Rights are claims which signify status in some sort of a community. Yet now that *free agency* (a necessary, if not sufficient, element in moral responsibility or accountability)[33] is possible in America, the entitlement or right to membership in the community of survivorship must be earned by the forthright support of that community when it is threatened by its most profound enemy (or someone posing as that enemy). Only then, when the act of subordination[34] and sacrifice is demonstrated, can the survivor prove that his failure to act in the past was due to circumstances beyond his control. Skokie survivors distinguished past from present opportunities to act in a manner that effectuated this logic. According to Erna, the past "was a different time frame." Similarly, Stephen stated:

> We were accused that we went like sheep. And that's so wrong. This is the greatest injustice. At that time we were hunted by everybody, not just by Nazis, but hunted by every human being . . . But now we must be strong and not be silent. We cannot afford to be weak. We have got to fight.

The sense of obligation which swept through the Skokie survivor community suggests that positive consequences occurred which pertained to the way in which survivor leaders infused the Skokie incident with a political and psychological meaning drawn from the past. Whereas the Jewish community in Europe failed to be strong, the reconstituted community of survivors at Skokie *would* be strong and resist. "But now we must be strong and not be silent. We cannot afford to be weak. We have got to fight." This is not the language of the defeated, but rather the language of republican virtue as envisioned by such advocates of free speech as Brandeis, Meiklejohn, and Mill.

4. The Community of Justice: Resistance as Civil Disobedience. In addition to the motivations of protection and obligation the Skokie survivors appear to have been driven by an aroused sense of injustice. They considered the proposed NSPA demonstration to be an unjustified verbal assault on their peace of mind and dignity, and resisted to express this sense of injustice.

By carrying the brutal message of Nazism into the heart of the Jewish community, Collin was, to the survivors, crossing the line which separated speech worthy of First Amendment protection from speech not so worthy. A lengthy statement by Stephen expresses the survivors' position in detail. The ACLU's position was, for Stephen, "beyond belief":

> We just couldn't believe that this could ever happen. And we didn't believe that the village or any government could ever permit them, that there is any law that would let them come and march whether at Skokie or any place, but especially at Skokie with its large survivor population . . .
>
> Once we decided to unite ourselves, the next problem was how to explain to people how wrong it is when they go by the First Amendment and free speech. We explained to people that the purpose for writing that amendment was not for Nazis, not for people to call to build new ghettos and new concentration camps . . . It is just to listen to someone's opinion. A person should have a right to express an opposite opinion of the government, an opposite opinion of your opinion. But not one to call to kill these people—there are two different things. It's impossible to think that the people who wrote the Constitution, that they would say that a murderer has the right to come and express his opinion and to say that we are going to murder a certain segment of people. Now, is it thinkable: Chicago has a famous mass murderer, John Gacy, who murdered thirty-three people. Do you think it thinkable, because of the Constitution, if he would be out of prison by some way, that he should be allowed to come and march in front of all the victims' families who live in one community? You cannot have a murderer coming on, or these people with the same ideas as those who killed my people or my parents, because he is protected by the Constitution. We need protection from the law because as citizens, we also have the right to be protected. Not only the Nazis have the right.

The key elements in Stephen's representative position are the following: 1) the *targeted* advocacy of murder, either explicit or symbolic, is a form of emotionally assaultive speech the First Amendment should not protect; 2) such speech, and its protection, is morally "unthinkable"[35] (not only do Nazis advocate morally "unthinkable" acts which they acted on in Germany —but the inner moral logic of Nazism is predicated upon transforming the morally "unthinkable" into acceptable moral policy); 3) in a community which does not endorse the morally unthinkable, citizens have a right to be protected by the law and the community against the targeted advocacy of such policy; the lack of such support is itself "unthinkable"; 4) finally,

Stephen stresses the peculiar vulnerability of survivors and/or bereaved as targets of the advocacy of death.

Other survivor sources concurred. Alex asserted that "we could *never believe* that something like this should arise again . . . I live in a free country and I don't have to be afraid." And Erna Gans emphasized that:

> *We never thought in our wildest dreams* that it could happen like that again, that they would have a right to confront us . . . to say those obscene words without being punished. This realization brought back a terror . . . here we are again, in the same position . . .

The survivors wanted protection against what they construed to be assaultive speech. In the absence of such protection, they were prepared to fight. Recall that the New Hampshire statute upheld by the Supreme Court in *Chaplinsky v. New Hampshire* spoke of fighting words as "words likely to cause an average addressee to fight."[36] *Chaplinsky* supports the view that assaultive speech *will* often lead to a hostile reaction. Skokie survivor leaders and their allies took this logic one step further and claimed that in the face of an attack on the community, a hostile reaction *should* take place. Such resistance even justifies breaking the law against hostile reactions to speakers in the public forum, as it signifies a higher moral and communal principle. It may be viewed as a form of civil disobedience. Civil disobeyers normally believe in the rule of law but sometimes feel compelled to break a particular law or group of laws in order to honor a higher principle with which the law conflicts.[37] Often this principle is itself a basic norm that supports the legal system, a fact which distinguishes most civil disobeyers from revolutionaries.[38]

Survivors and their allies at Skokie spoke of their commitment to resistance in the language of civil disobedience. They thought that the application of the First Amendment to Collin's plans violated the basic rights of survivors to be secure in the reconstituted community. They considered the ACLU's position to contradict the basic values of democracy. Alex told me that the survivors "preferred the law . . . we tried everything possible to go by the law . . . we are a group of good citizens." Nonetheless, before Skokie took legal measures to keep the Nazis out, "We were prepared to see what we could do to stop him ourselves." And for Stephen, the decision to physically confront Collin in the event he came to Skokie led to attitudinal dissonance between his commitment to resistance and his duty to obey the law. Though he feared being labeled a "rebel," he stood ready to "go against the police and against the government" if necessary to block the NSPA.[39]

Rabbi Montrose construed the resistance in terms that epitomize the classic posture of civil disobedience:

> I'm in favor of courts, and I will obey any law. But sometimes the natural law takes over in cases like this.
>   The courts said Jews have no right to stop these guys. But we have a right to defend ourselves against a major threat when we are invaded on our own grounds. Would Poles or Italians let someone into their neighborhoods to come and preach their murder? They'd kill them if they came in there preaching their extermination.[40]

Montrose and the survivors linked the moral appeals to natural law to the willingness to fight for one's community when it is "invaded." They divined that the protective function of community is indeed a value, that security is somehow tied up with justice. Their view also suggests that anger itself can be a moral expression under certain circumstances. Indeed, anger can galvanize the sense of justice and moral community, signifying citizens' commitments to these values.[41]

The analysis so far has been limited to the survivor community's *reasons* for resistance in relation to the psychological and attitudinal nature of their community. Let us now turn to an analysis of the political *strategies* of the survivor community to gain allies and socialize the struggle, and to the further unfolding of events.

III. The Mobilization of Support: The Survivors' Socialization of the Issue and the Strategy of Resistance

A. The Basic Strategy: Win Allies and Deter the NSPA

Survivor leaders had two basic, direct goals which they viewed as two sides of the same coin: to compel the local government to pass a law to keep the NSPA out, or to physically *force* the NSPA out in the event the law could not do so.

The willingness to use force entailed another strategic element: *the threat of force to deter the NSPA*. We may profitably view the survivors' actions in the emergence of the conflict as a strategy of deterrence, which Thomas Schelling states "is concerned with influencing the choices that another party will make, and doing it by influencing his expectations of how he will behave."[42] Survivors employed the *threat* of violence to prevent or deter the NSPA from coming to Skokie and to serve as a *long-range* deterrent, notifying hate groups across the nation that Jews would defend their community from attack by all necessary means. Informants construed the passage of protective law the same way: it would protect them not only in the short run, but would also publicly demonstrate that officials were on their side.[43]

In order to effectuate this two-fold deterrence strategy, survivor leaders realized that they would have to *socialize* the conflict. Socialization involved generating a legal response from Skokie officials, as well as mobilizing mass social support to buttress the threat of massive (and potentially violent) resistance. As Jerome Torshen, the head of the *Goldstein* suit legal team and a staunch supporter of the survivors from the beginning, told me, "Collin has no death wish. If we could generate enough resistance to him, he would back down." And the very threat of violence in the wake of an NSPA demonstration in Skokie could, in turn, be used to compel village officials to pass protective law. Given their early isolation, survivors viewed Skokie leaders as additional enemies against whom to deploy the strategies of conflict.

The analysis of the survivor mobilization of resistance will be organized around these two *objects* of strategy and the basic *types* of conflict strategy. The two objects were the NSPA and potential allies in the public and in leadership positions. We will look at each object separately. The basic strategies of conflict which we will utilize (of which deterrence is but a part) include two basic modes of action discussed by William Ker Muir. First, *coercion*: "a means of controlling the conduct of others through threats to harm." Muir emphasizes the "extortionate transaction" in which a victimizer extorts a victim by seizing a "hostage" to gain an end; extortion is an extreme form of coercion. Second, *exhortation*: in which

individuals act, not because they are coerced or tempted, but because they think their action is right, because they are persuaded by the "truth" of the matter that they have a duty to fulfill. They will sacrifice gladly, even kill or be killed, for a cause they believe in.[44]

In dealing with village and Jewish leaders, the survivors utilized both strategies; yet they employed only coercion against the NSPA. This disparity was natural, as outside leaders were viewed ambivalently by survivors, whereas the NSPA was simply an enemy of "war."

In order to understand the survivors' execution of their strategies of socialization and deterrence, it is necessary to elaborate further the development of the conflict. As we have seen, Collin initially intended to come to Skokie on May 1, 1977, but Skokie blocked this plan by attaining an injunction in Cook County Court on April 28. The injunction banned the

NSPA from appearing in Skokie *in uniform.*[45] Yet because the injunction applied only to May 1, Collin announced on the evening of Friday, April 29, that he planned to invade Skokie on Saturday, April 30, instead. Word of Collin's announcement spread quickly through the Skokie survivor community, and leaders plotted resistance deep into the night. By eight o'clock Saturday morning, a large group of about 100 survivors and hundreds of allies (ranging from militant local Jewish Defense League members and less militant Jewish leaders to concerned outside groups) had assembled near the steps of village hall, aching to physically resist. Wholesale violence certainly would have erupted.

Village officials, finally convinced by the survivors' threats of violence, roused themselves and managed to find a local Cook County judge at home who issued an emergency *exparte* injunction (issued, that is, after a non-adversarial hearing in which only one party is present).[46] Skokie police then rushed to the local exit from the Edens Expressway and served the injunction to Collin, en route to Skokie. (Collin had already been stopped by other officers who had followed him from his South Side headquarters and had maintained radio contact with Skokie police.) Collin accepted the new injunction and went home. Back at headquarters he held a press conference and then the party eagerly watched the television's graphic depiction of its "success" (see Chapter Two).[47] The following Monday, Skokie officials acted on their new appreciation of the survivors' claims and went to Cook County Court to get the original injunction extended indefinitely.[48] In addition, they passed the three ordinances to buttress their defense.

In the next few weeks the ACLU struggled in the Illinois courts to attain an expeditious review, which is normally required when a First Amendment claim is at stake.[49] Yet the Illinois Appellate Court refused to review the case (or to grant a stay) with the required dispatch; Hamlin of the ACLU called their delay "unconscionable."[50] Consequently, the ACLU petitioned the U.S. Supreme Court to grant a stay. On June 14, 1977, the Supreme Court, in a 5-4 decision, ordered the Illinois courts to expedite the injunction case which the ACLU had appealed from the Cook County Circuit Court.[51]

The order encouraged Collin and the ACLU; so Collin announced to the press and to Skokie that he desired to hold a rally in Skokie on July 4, even though the injunction and the ordinances were still in effect. In response, survivors and their supporters announced a counterdemonstration for the fourth. At this point the national Jewish Defense League (JDL) entered the fray for the first time. In late June 1977, its leader, the irascible Meir Kahane, came to Skokie to help plan the counterdemonstration. He proclaimed to the press that "the streets of Skokie will run with Nazi blood," and that "If I see a Nazi coming, I will break his head."[52] Kahane's prominently publicized threats set the tone for much of the public discourse which was to prevail up to the end of the conflict.

Despite the impending showdown, and despite the Supreme Court order, the recalcitrant Illinois courts still procrastinated. On June 28, the Illinois Appellate Court scheduled its "expedited" hearing on the injunction to begin in July—too late to clear the NSPA's plans for July 4.[53] But the ordinances, which the ACLU was fighting in the federal courts (they sued in federal court precisely because of the delays they had already experienced in the Illinois courts' handling of the injunction), were still in effect. So Collin had to cancel his July 4 plans. Nonetheless, activists staged a symbolic counterdemonstration at the Kaplan Jewish Community Center in Skokie on that date. The media highlighted the event by focusing on the para-military JDL.[54]

The next few months witnessed a waiting period on the legal side. During this time the survivors and their allies attempted to socialize the issue to gain wide-spread support in the event the courts ruled against Skokie. Meanwhile, on July 11, 1977, the Illinois Appellate Court modified the original county court's injunction by allowing the NSPA to come to Skokie in uniform, *but without swastikas* (which the court held constituted "fighting words").[55] Yet because the NSPA considered the swastika ban equivalent to the original uniform ban ("This is my party identification, that is my symbol, and we will not be parted from it," an NSPA spokesman pleaded to the press after the ruling),[56] the appellate court's opinion had little legal significance other than to signal the long-range trend of the courts to favor Collin.

Another legal event had more symbolic and theoretical importance than legal impact. An elite group of lawyers with the moral support of the Jewish Federation's Public Affairs Committee and the ADL filed a class action lawsuit in the Illinois Circuit Court. The suit, *Goldstein v. Collin,* sought a preliminary and permanent injunction against the NSPA, restraining it from intentionally inflicting severe emotional harm on the survivors.[57] The Illinois courts dismissed the suit on the grounds that it was redundant to Skokie's litigation.[58] Nonetheless, it represented an important empirical claim concerning harm; and it signified the burgeoning success the survivors were enjoying in socializing their claims, as the suit was the first time the Federation had taken a position that conflicted with the traditional quarantine policy.[59]

Only in late January and February 1978, did the courts begin to hand down definitive rulings against Skokie. The ordinances case was not finally decided on appeal until June 1978, after which Jewish leaders finalized plans for a massive counterdemonstration to confront the NSPA.

Mobilization and socialization efforts gained momentum during the first half of 1978, as it became increasingly clear that the legal efforts on behalf of the survivors would fail. Resisters built on the groundwork which had been laid during the period of legal hiatus in the second half of 1977. We will look more closely at Skokie in the courts and at the denouement of the controversy in the next chapter. Let us now turn to an examination of survivors' strategies for socialization in the formative period of the controversy.

B. The NSPA and Fellow Travelers: Coercion

"This is war, rabbi." — Sol Goldstein to Rabbi Weiner.

Given the war-like relations between Nazis and Jews, the survivors naturally did not employ the strategy of exhortation against the NSPA.[60] This strategy would be fruitful only in their efforts to socialize the conflict and to win allies; consequently, they resorted to a strategy of coercion, which involved threatening the NSPA with violence if it invaded Skokie (a threat buttressed by the prediction that they would "lose control" of themselves in such a confrontation).[61] Sol Goldstein's testimony in the first court hearing on the Skokie injunction, on April 28, 1977, was a deft employment of this psychological tactic. As Frank Collin watched, Goldstein took the witness stand to testify about the potential reaction of survivors to an NSPA demonstration in Skokie. According to David Hamlin of the ACLU, who was present, Goldstein's powerful stare never wavered from Collin's eyes during the testimony. Rather than addressing the counsel or the court when responding to questions (from Skokie lawyer Harvey Schwartz), Goldstein directed his answers to Frank Collin. Hamlin maintains that Collin "squirmed" under Goldstein's glare.[62] The following segment of the testimony illustrates the technique:

> Q. And in your opinion, based upon your opinion of the mood as you have described it, Mr. Goldstein, what will occur in the village of Skokie in the event that the National Socialist Party does rally in the village on that day?
>
> A. There will be victims, there will be bloodshed, it will be damage of individual and property. I don't know what it will be. It will be loss of lives maybe. These are people that lost their parents, their children, their wives, that, you know, [is] what . . . the swastika [means] to them. They promised

the dead that a swastika won't appear any more. They promised their children. They came here to a country, to a free world, to live, at least, a peaceful life and they cannot do it for the sake of their children. That again will be threatened . . . [by the] swastika.[63]

The survivors would risk their lives, if necessary. Irrationality is suggested, as the unimaginable might occur: "I don't know what will happen." And there is *no choice* in the matter, as survivors are *obligated* to the dead and their children to take a stand. Such obligation to third parties serves to enhance the threat of coercion, as it eliminates choice and the ability to compromise.[64] The "promise"[65] to the dead creates an unabridgeable communal pact which one must be willing to protect by risking one's life. In his interview, Stephen asserted that survivors decided that "only over our dead bodies will they come to our city." And on the day that police stopped the NSPA in the nick of time at the Skokie border, the throng of survivors waiting in front of village hall was prepared to make the ultimate sacrifice. Erna Gans said that "they didn't care if they would be killed." Eileen contended that "In the Skokie issue, I honestly believe that my father didn't care if he was killed. He said there was no way he was going to let Nazis march in a community where I was living."[66]

The Jewish Defense League's entry into the conflict contributed to deterrence through coercion, as the JDL struck a highly visible posture of uncompromising resistance and the willingness to use violence. Non-survivor leaders viewed the JDL's presence with alarm, for the legal status of the NSPA's July 4 demonstration remained in doubt when Kahane first came to town. Upon arriving, Meir Kahane made his group's intentions public. "We intend to bloody the Nazis should they try," he proclaimed at a press conference. "I am not predicting violence — I am promising violence." He then castigated the Jewish establishment (ADL and Jewish Federation) for meekness in the face of an historic foe. "I can understand the Jewish leaders [in Europe] who had no precedent and they made a tragic error. But now we find people have learned nothing from it."[67] Although survivors generally dissociated themselves officially from the JDL, the JDL's threats resembled the survivors' threats. Survivors used the JDL as an extremist ally to fortify their own threats against Collin. Later in the controversy Erna Gans publicly invited the JDL to attend the final counterdemonstration.[68] And Alex told me that the JDL's intervention gladdened the survivors because they knew they could use the JDL as a front for their own claims.[69]

The survivors' commitment to not losing "face" also contributed to the strategy of coercion and confrontation. According to Muir, "the nastier one's reputation, the less nasty one has to be."[70] Past defeats at the hands of Hitler escalated the stakes of "face" and necessitated a strong resistance if Collin were to be deterred. Interviewees stressed the importance of the proper face, in the context of imagining a face-to-face struggle. Sol Goldstein affirmed that the presentation of toughness was the most important meaning of the Skokie resistance: "It is not so much Skokie, but the idea what was Skokie—the first one to stand up and to tell the Nazis, 'You won't do it!'" In repudiating the quarantine policy and those who counseled "turning one's head" rather than confronting the Nazis, Erna Gans fulminated, "When you turn your head it doesn't happen? That's a sign of weakness recognized all over the world!" These sentiments echo the JDL's militant slogan, "Never Again." In the end, the threat worked, as Collin cancelled his Skokie plans after his legal victories.

C. Strategy Toward Leadership Allies and the Public

1. The Use of Coercion. As we have seen, the survivor community was well organized before the Nazi incident—a necessary prerequisite to political influence. But it also possessed an *a priori* legitimacy in society which many minority groups lack. Accordingly, the "threshold" level of public recognition and acceptance which the survivors had to attain to be effective was comparatively low (even though the survivors portrayed themselves as an isolated minority at the start of the conflict).[71] So survivors viewed their potential allies ambivalently. On the one hand they distrusted them; on the other, they reached out to them.

The need to resort to coercion against their allies erupted early when village and area Jewish leaders proposed the quarantine policy. Survivors gave Jewish leaders a "terrible beating," according to Ab Rosen (Rosen "had his head handed to him on a platter," according to one source).[72]

Survivor sources openly discussed their initial distrust of their erstwhile allies, and why they resorted to coercive tactics. Stephen asserted:

> We realized that our problem was not only the Nazis, but most of the problem is the public opinion, and most of the problem is the government, and most of the problem is the Jewish establishment, is the B'nai B'rith . . . And we realized that we are up against a wall. And if we don't *do something* about it, it will be a disaster.

Allied leadership's obtuseness necessitated the threat of violence *against Collin,* for which allies would share responsibility. On April 25, 1977, three days before Skokie went to court for the first time to obtain an injunction in the name of "preventing violence," a survivor rose to address the Board of Trustees:

It has come to my attention that on May 1 there is going to be a Nazi parade held in front of the village hall. As a Nazi survivor during the Second World War, I'd like to know what you gentlemen are going to do about it.[73]

Skokie corporate counsel Harvey Schwartz replied that the village was considering legal action (which ensued three days later) "if that is appropriate," and that the survivors should "rest assured" that the village leadership would protect their interests. The survivor's response reveals the gulf of distrust between the survivors and local government.

May I also remind you, Mr. Schwartz, there are thousands of Jewish survivors of the Nazi Holocaust living here in the suburbs. We expect to show up in front of village hall and tear these people up if necessary. We cannot let happen again, what happened during World War II. We cannot let these people just come into our midst, into our community wearing their Nazi uniforms and swastikas. We cannot let this happen again, sir.

This survivor utilized the *threat of violence* against the NSPA to pressure the village government to take action and to ally itself with the survivors; and he reinforced the threat of violence with the commands of obligation: "We cannot let this happen again." Schwartz countered by claiming that the village leadership had to proceed prudently out of its responsibility to a wider constituency than the survivors. It was responsible for "the best interests of all, which includes, first and primarily, *all* the residents of the village of Skokie."[74] Yet survivors met Schwartz's advocacy of a moderate, consensus-seeking posture by upping the ante with a starker threat of irrationality and violence. A woman survivor took over the microphone. Her powerful, yet trembling, message (which evokes Arendt's thesis about the "two worlds" of survivors) triggered an explosive applause from the audience:

We don't want to wake up May 2 and find out nothing was done. You must understand our feelings. We might do things we don't know yet. *We are a special breed of people, people who went through unbelievable things.* History doesn't even know the things that happened to us. We cannot even explain our feelings right now. I appeal to you once more. This thing should not happen in our village [pounds the table]. They might not be able to control themselves. I appeal to you once more. We want to know what is going to be done!

Other speeches followed which included threats of violence juxtaposed with "expertise" ("You don't know what we went through and are therefore capable of doing"). Schwartz's articulate, self-possessed efforts to preserve calm proved futile. At that point the avuncular Mayor Smith intervened to quell the rancor. To do so, he created his own *emotional* appeal which proved more effective than the lawyerly, rational appeals of Schwartz. Smith, a Catholic who had been mayor of Skokie for sixteen years, pleaded for peace, the general interest, and the rule of law which he had taken an oath to uphold. He affirmed the commonness of survivors and non-survivors and assured the survivors that he would do "everything possible" to protect them. At the same time, he scolded them for impugning the good faith of the village board. It was a masterful speech made at the right time, and it supports the view of many commentators that Mayor Smith was the political force that kept Skokie's Jewish and non-Jewish communities from splitting apart during the controversy.[75] He demonstrated empathy for the survivors' moral claims, yet refused to honor their baser natures — leadership at its best. Nonetheless, the survivors' coercive pressure did indeed succeed, as Skokie went to court three days later seeking an injunction to keep the Nazis out. The coercive threat of violence, the last resort of groups who consider themselves powerless, worked.[76]

Yet village officials did not take the survivors' threats completely seriously until the near confrontation with Collin on April 30, 1977. On that day survivors substantiated their threats by turning them into action.[77] The city manager of Skokie (Matzer), the village's corporate counsel (Schwartz), and a trustee of the village board (Conrad) each told me that the counter-demonstration of April 30 was a turning point for him in terms of his support of the survivor community.[78] "At this point I realized that First Amendment theory grossly underestimated the impact on these people," said Schwartz. "The presence of these symbols was literally an assault." "I didn't appreciate the psychological effect until now," said City Manager Matzer. "There is no question that for survivors it was a reliving of the whole thing, and I changed my attitude." Trustee Conrad concurred and referred to another form of coercive power the survivors possessed: the vote. "As a politician, when those ordinances came out, if I had voted 'no,' my chances of re-election would have been slim or none." These conversions were just what survivors intended. "Schwartz was forced to change his position," Alex claimed. "Up to April 30, we didn't change the position of the village until action was shown." "That Saturday incident made them realize violence can erupt," Erna Gans asserted.

Potential allies in the Jewish Federation downtown also felt pressure to join the survivors' cause. Powerful survivors like Sol Goldstein moved the Federation. Rabbi Weiner of Skokie, who represented the moderate camp of survivor allies in Skokie, pointed out that:

> The Federation has become all important as Israel has grown after World War II. Now it calls itself the "Jewish Community." Goldstein is a great Jew,

a great man, a very gifted man. He's also a wealthy businessman and a fund-raiser. So it's easy for him to have prominence in the Jewish Federation.

Goldstein's methods appear to have been decisive in turning the Federation around, according to Eugene DuBow. The Federation was loathe to act because no consensus over the issue had been achieved. By compelling the Federation to back the survivors, Goldstein helped prevent the JDL and other radical groups from dominating the counterdemonstration policy.[79] While Goldstein was the major local survivor link to the Federation, he also played a role locally by speaking at public meetings and working with Mayor Smith.[80] Rabbi Laurence Charney of the Northwest Synagogue Council pointed out that Goldstein rose up at an early meeting that was a "turning point" and "took the meeting over."[81]

In addition to the more direct coercive pressure put on potential allies, survivors also appealed to *the public* for moral support. Although such appeals were not directly coercive, they put pressure on Jewish leadership to join the survivors in response to public opinion. According to Erna Gans, "It [the media] made it possible for us to give our message across the world. It woke up the conscience of the world, which is important not today or tomorrow, but down the road fifteen years." The conscience of the world must be awakened because favorable public opinion can then be used to put pressure in the future on potentially supportive leadership and against one's enemies.[82] "They [government] were actually convinced by the majority of the community here that they would have to do something against it," said Alex.

2. Exhortation. Erna's statement reveals that survivors also exhorted potential allies to join their cause by appealing to the allies' moral sense. Rabbi Weiner, the leader of the moderate faction at Skokie and a dedicated civil libertarian, depicted how this appeal affected non-survivor Jewish leaders at an early strategy meeting held in Rabbi Charney's synagogue:

> Goldstein's plans were obviously pre-arranged with the mayor. He got up and said he had heard all the recommendations for calm, and said "You may stay away, but I will confront them. I lost my wife and my family." This carried the day. It was very moving. My rational feeling was that it would be impossible to avoid this reaction . . .
>
> Besides civil liberties, the *real issue* was seen in a characteristic phrase: "Jewish dignity demands that before the world we face them. We won't hide behind the curtain . . ." All the congregations had a good number of people who had a conscience. We all live under the shadow of the Holocaust and guilt. Therefore, in the face of any survivor and his claims, it is hard to re-

spond any way but emotionally and almost blindly. We say "What do we have to do?"

Students of survivor psychology point out that many survivors project the sense of obligation onto others in order to relieve themselves of the sometimes oppressive burden of guilt that obligation carries; they want to be taken care of by others.[83] In addition, they dread being abandoned by others, as this is what happened to them in Europe.[84] "Six million died. Nobody did anything. And now it is going to happen here in the U.S.," Alex lamented. But Rabbi Weiner's observation on the non-survivor Jews' sense of obligation to survivors indicates that this obligation is not merely a psychological quirk, but also a natural state of mind for non-survivor Jews given the circumstances. Many non-survivors (especially Jews) identify with survivors and feel membership in a common cause.[85] Eileen, the Auschwitz survivors' daughter who founded the Children of Holocaust Survivors group in Chicago, pointed out that this process of identification was "a call to arms" for the "American-born Jews"; it "revolutionized" their thinking about their "Jewishness."

3. Extraordinary Knowledge: A Special Form of Exhortation. For over three decades survivors had harbored extraordinary knowledge of the evil nature of Nazism and totalitarianism. Like more articulate survivor commentators such as Elie Wiesel and David Rousset, they knew that the essence of their extraordinary knowledge could not be completely conveyed to those whose lives had not been branded by Hitler. However, exigent circumstances and the movement of time combined to compel communication.[86] When the NSPA targeted Skokie, the survivor activists were ready to come forth and present their insights into the enormity of Nazism. These insights also aided their power of persuasion and, consequently, the socialization of the dispute. Two types of insights appear to have been most important: the *sui generis* nature of Nazism as a forceful expression of evil, and the volatile potentiality of extremist groups.

We have already seen how the survivors referred to harms perpetrated against them in making their appeals to allies. Informants engaged in the same strategy in interviews. "Just think what happened to us!" Stephen implored. As the survivor at the village board meeting proclaimed: "*We are a special breed of people,* people who went through unbelievable things. History doesn't even know the things that happened to us. We cannot even explain our feelings." Such references establish the survivor as an authority on Nazism; they also engender a sense of obligation in potential allies.

The fact that these brutalities are "unbelievable" also leads to the conclusion that the evil perpetrated by Nazism is *sui generis,* or is, at any rate, an evil radically different from life in a non-totalitarian state. According to Arendt, a salient lesson of Hitler is summed up in the epigram of David Rousset: "Normal men don't know that everything is possible."[87] Allied powers did not act aggressively to save the Jews of Europe because of their inability (among other reasons) to fully comprehend the reality of the Final Solution; it lay too far beyond the putative outer boundaries of the capability of evil.[88] It was "unthinkable." Thus, Skokie survivors beseeched the citizens of normality to transfer their consciousness to the moral realm of the Third Reich and to "think the unthinkable," or to comprehend that some groups bent on persecution are so thinking. "Just *think* of what they did to us!" said Stephen. Think the unthinkable.

Survivors are acutely aware that the rest of the world "denied" the Final Solution as much as Jews did. Yet survivors paid the price for their failure to face facts, whereas their would-be saviors did not. Accordingly, when it comes to an appraisal of radical evil, the citizens of normality are not to be trusted. A poignant expression of the survivor viewpoint and its impact on non-survivor leaders is an impromptu speech Stephen made at Rabbi Montrose's synagogue in April 1977. This gathering was one of the meetings which followed the original meeting at which village leaders decided to adopt the traditional ("normal") quarantine policy. Montrose told me that this speech triggered his own change of mind, and that it influenced other leaders present:

> Even if you will not be there, you American-born Jews, to confront Frank Collin, we will be there. *Because our experience is superior to yours, and we cannot rely on your thinking.* Because we experienced and know that *all normal thinking and procedure and understanding does not apply in this situation, which is irrational, insane, and that normal normative thought process is inapplicable and ineffective.* Therefore, we know we must be there. Because it is a nightmare reborn and it must be protested while it is small enough to be protested.[89]

While the survivors rationally recognized that the NSPA did not pose a present *political* threat (though *emotionally* they *were* a threat), they understood the *potential* for danger that could exist. They considered the American public and local leaders naive for neglecting this threat. Since we will deal with this matter later, minimal citation will suffice. Erna Gans made a characteristic remark:

> Now, we have to act whenever we are able to act . . . we have to point to the danger. At one time, you know, when Hitler started, no one recognized the

danger to that extent. Now, some people might have recognized it; but for
the most part, the majority of people — *in the world,* not only the Jews — did
not recognize the kind of danger that Hitler represented . . . many people
knew but didn't want to know . . . We want to alert the society that it is
something that is there.

According to Erna, the American public was naive "because they are not
used to thinking the way we were thinking. The problem with American
society is that it is very removed, aloof, and it doesn't see reality." In this
respect, Americans lacked republican virtue, for they refused *to acknowledge harsh realities.*

This type of prudential appeal paid off in enlisting support of non-
survivor leaders. Rev. Koenline of the United Presbyterian Church in Skokie
emphasized how exposure to the survivors educated her about the Hitler
persecution:

> My earlier position was to let the Nazis come. I said this until I went to a
> community meeting and heard survivors. Then I realized there was no way
> this could be done. This issue was an educational experience for me. I never
> quite understood the enormity of the Holocaust before. So I read Elie Wiesel
> and other writers. I made it my business to gather information and to learn.
> All this was triggered by the survivors.

Rev. Koenline stressed the general educational aspects of her exposure
to the survivors. Other interviewees emphasized the aspects of political *prudence* concerning potential danger. Fred Richter, president of the Northwest Suburban Synagogue Council during the conflict, spoke about how
exposure to the survivors' claims led him to visualize the coexistence of
two realities, as it were — the two realities represented by the survivors' bifurcated world view discussed at the beginning of this chapter. Richter
changed his position

> when I began to realize that the subjective situation was as real to them as
> were the Nazis in Germany — that's a devastating fact for these people. You
> know, you're talking to Erna Gans now. But if you could have seen her and
> some of these people when that threat was real, it was an altogether differ-
> ent situation . . . It was so near . . . it focused on what took place histori-
> cally. More importantly, it brought about an awareness that the past is not
> as far away as people may think . . . Not this little group [NSPA] now, but
> it doesn't take much for the past to come back and get you . . . You became
> aware of the spectre of the past, the depth of this type of evil.

IV. Conclusion

In this chapter we have looked at the nature of the Skokie survivor community, at its reasons for resisting the NSPA, and at the bare essentials of its socialization of the issue. Though norms concerning resistance and the limits of free speech played a role in explaining the survivors' resistance, the thrust of this chapter has been explanatory, not normative. Survivors utilized normative claims to justify their resistance and to socialize the conflict.

The portrayal in this chapter suggests that survivors resisted Collin not only out of fear and the desire to protect their community, but also in order to attain ends commensurate with the republican virtue function of speech discussed in Chapter One. They reacted to protect their interests and to inform the public of important facts and issues. The same survivors who pleaded for the protective role of the law also emphasized the great political and personal gains which arose from the confrontation with Collin. This ambiguity suggests that the weighing of good and bad consequences in ensuing chapters will be difficult. But before we turn to this task, we must look at the denouement of the conflict in the courts and the public forum.

4

The Denouement of the Controversy

The display of the swastika . . . is symbolic political speech intended to convey to the public the beliefs of those who display it.—Illinois Supreme Court in *Skokie v. NSPA*

In the summer of 1920 Hitler . . . came up with an inspiration which can only be described as a stroke of genius . . . The hooked cross—the haken Kreuz—of the swastika, borrowed though it was from more ancient times, was to become a mighty and frightening symbol of the Nazi Party . . . The hooked cross seemed to possess some mystic power of its own, to beckon to action in a new direction . . .—William L. Shirer, *The Rise and Fall of the Third Reich*

I. Skokie in the Courts

A. The Injunction Cases

1. Skokie v. NSPA. After the order on June 14 by the United States Supreme Court to the Illinois courts to expedite the appeal of the Cook County Circuit Court's injunction, the Illinois appellate court modified the original injunction while maintaining its essential nature. The original injunction enjoined the NSPA from demonstrating in Skokie in uniform, from displaying or handing out any "materials which incite or promote" hatred of Jews, and from wearing or displaying the swastika."[1] On July 11, 1977, the Illinois appellate court modified the injunction to prohibit only the display of the swastika.

The court held in a *per curiam* decision that the record showed that the NSPA did not intend to distribute literature or make derogatory statements, but rather to hold a "peaceful assembly" of 30 to 50 demonstrators who would protest the Skokie Park District ordinances and would carry placards containing such slogans as "Free Speech for White America."[2] While the judges acknowledged that such an NSPA demonstration would most likely cause a riot, it relied upon the hostile audience doctrine to conclude that "As to the possibility of there being hostile audience members causing violence, the law is quite clear that such considerations are impermissible."[3] And without the distortion of vision caused by the hecklers, "no conclusion may be drawn from the record other than a planned exercise of 'basic constitutional rights in their most pristine and classic form'" (*Edwards v. South Carolina*).[4]

The appellate court made no mention (in this part of its decision) of the dyadic relationship between the hostile audience's threats and the NSPA's antecedent provocations. Yet no sooner had the court seemingly denied the less sanguine facts in the case than it backtracked. It moved on to distinguish the wearing of the storm trooper uniform from the display of the swastika. Whereas the uniform without the swastika would be "pristine speech," the uniform *with* the swastika would constitute fighting words due to the context at Skokie and the meaning of the swastika. The court did not satisfactorily explain just why context is a legitimate concern in considering the swastika but not in treating the storm trooper uniform. In the latter situation, the content neutrality rule applies:

> The evidence of record does not support a conclusion that the uniform *sans* swastika constitutes fighting words . . . Rather, the wearing of such a uniform must be considered, in the context of the instant case, as symbolic speech protected by the first amendment. Above all, "the First Amendment means that government has no power to restrict expression because of its message, its ideas, its subject matter, or its content." [*Police Department of the City of Chicago v. Mosley,* (1972), 408 U.S. 92, 95.].[5]

Of the swastika, however, the court held:

> The evidence shows precisely that substantial numbers of citizens are standing ready to strike out physically at whoever may assault their sensibilities with the display of the swastika. We feel that the subjective portion of the fighting words test has been satisfied.[6]

The appellate court managed to distinguish the swastika as fighting words from the facts in *Cohen v. California,*[7] the case which severely limited the thrust of *Chaplinsky v. New Hampshire's*[8] fighting words test (see Chapter One), by noting that there was evidence of a "direct personal insult" in *Skokie* which was absent in *Cohen.*[9] Yet the decision was plagued with a contradiction which had to be resolved in review. Either the content neutrality rule applies in both situations or in neither.[10] The Illinois appellate court's contrived distinction between uniform and swastika was perhaps an effort to compromise and buy time.

It took the Illinois Supreme Court six months from the date of the Illinois appellate court ruling to resolve the contradiction. The Illinois Supreme Court delivered its opinion on January 27, 1978. The decision rested primarily on demonstrating that *Cohen* and similar cases controlled *Skokie* in several respects: 1) display of the swastika is protected symbolic speech intended to convey the thought of the NSPA, even if it is offensive; 2) such display does not constitute fighting words; 3) prior restraints of expression must satisfy a high burden of justification which, given the above conclusions, Skokie did not meet.[11]

The court utilized *Cohen* at length in its eleven page decision. Unlike the appellate court, the Illinois Supreme Court held that the absence of a captive audience and the presence of advance notification of the NSPA's intentions were fatal to Skokie's fighting words claim.[12] In addition, the Illinois Supreme Court supported its decision by referring to the underlying free speech principles which *Cohen* proclaimed. Its lengthy quotation from *Cohen* revealed how *Cohen* had embodied most of the important theoretical and philosophical underpinnings of the contemporary free speech theory:

> The constitutional right of free expression is powerful medicine in a society as diverse and as populous as ours. It is designed and intended to remove governmental restraints from the arena of public discussion, putting the decision as to what views shall be voiced largely into the hands of each of us in the hope that use of such freedom will ultimately produce a more capable citizenry and more perfect polity and in the belief that no other approach would comport with the premise of individual dignity and choice upon which our political system rests. See *Whitney v. California,* 274. U.S. 357, 375–77 (1927) (Brandeis, J. concurring).
>
> To many, the immediate consequence of this freedom may often appear to be only verbal tumult, discord, and even offensive utterance. These are, however, within established limits, in truth necessary side effects of the broader enduring values which the process of open debate permits us to achieve. That the air may at times seem filled with verbal cacophony is, in this sense, not a sign of weakness but of strength. . . . How is one to distinguish this from any other offensive word [emblem]? . . . no readily ascertainable general principle exists [to so distinguish] . . . it is nevertheless often true that one man's vulgarity is another's lyric. Indeed, we think it is largely because governmental officials cannot make principled distinctions in this area that the Constitution leaves matters of taste and style so largely to the individual.[13]

I have quoted this part of the Illinois Supreme Court's decision (taken from *Cohen*) at such length because it so clearly and emphatically expresses the justifications of free speech we discussed in Chapter One. Nazi speech at Skokie must be protected because of the values of autonomy, self-government, republican virtue, and value skepticism. In addition, even if Nazi speech itself does not directly promote or protect these values, the court feared that a ruling against the NSPA could jeopardize more legitimate free speech claims because of the precedent such a ruling would establish. [14]

The court ignored the NSPA's antecedent acts of targeting Skokie in order to intimidate and ignored the fact that the NSPA hoped that the proposed demonstration would inflict trauma and engender a hostile crowd reaction. Though the court maintained that the display of the swastika is "symbolic political speech intended to convey to the public the beliefs of those who convey it," we have seen that this intent took backseat to the intent to win a hostage. "I planned the reaction of the Jews. They are hysterical," Collin said. "We *used* the First Amendment at Skokie." Nonetheless, the Illinois Supreme Court refused to consider these facts, choosing instead the more comfortable position of abstract doctrine. Only from this position could the court apply *Cohen*'s doctrine that "one man's vulgarity is another man's lyric" to Skokie. One does not normally associate the thrusting of a swastika into a vulnerable Jewish community with a Nazi's enjoyment of his "lyric."

David Hamlin of the ACLU rejoiced at the conclusiveness of the decision, saying that it encouraged the public to respect the ACLU's claims, [15] and Skokie did not even attempt to appeal the decision to the United States Supreme Court. According to Hamlin, village officials "pronounced themselves content to wait for the ruling of the federal court on the three ordinances." [16]

Yet even though the decision forcefully vindicated the First Amendment's content neutrality rule, the Illinois Supreme Court concluded on a questionable note which seemed to vitiate the force of its opinion. It stated that it had reached its opinion "albeit reluctantly." [17] Apparently it was not comfortable ignoring the "social aspect" of its decision.

2. Goldstein v. Collin. On the same day that it struck down the county court's injunction against the NSPA, the Illinois Supreme Court also dismissed *Goldstein v. Collin* in a one-paragraph summary order. [18] The *Goldstein* suit had been kicked around in the lower courts for months without a single decision on its substance. [19]

The suit's legal team, led by interviewee Jerome Torshen, then petitioned the Illinois Supreme Court for a rehearing in late February 1978.[20] The Illinois Supreme Court denied that petition on March 30, 1978.[21] On June 16, Torshen sought a writ of certiorari in the U.S. Supreme Court, which was denied.

Though the Illinois Supreme Court dismissed *Goldstein* on the grounds of its redundance to *Skokie*,[22] it could have distinguished the suit from *Skokie* because the suit was premised more explicitly on the trauma issue and the tort concerning the intentional infliction of mental trauma. Yet the *Skokie* injunction case had been troublesome for the Illinois courts (as evidenced by their procrastination in rendering review until the intervention by the U.S. Supreme Court). So the Illinois Supreme Court's reluctance to decide *Goldstein* on its merits is understandable.

B. The Ordinance Case: Collin v. Smith

"If there is any principle of the Constitution that more imperatively calls for attachment than any other it is the principle of free thought — not free thought for those who agree with us but freedom for the thought of those we hate." — Justice Holmes, *U.S. v. Schwimmer*

1. United States District Court. Collin reacted to the Illinois Supreme Court decisions on January 27 by announcing his intention to demonstrate in Skokie on April 28, 1978 (Hitler's birthday). Since the Federal District Court had not yet ruled on the validity of Skokie's ordinances aimed at stopping the NSPA, Collin obviously anticipated a favorable outcome in the federal arena. But though Collin in fact won in federal court on February 23, U.S. District Court Judge Decker issued a forty-five day stay to allow Skokie to appeal, and the U.S. Court of Appeals confirmed the stay on March 31, thereby aborting Collin's plans to celebrate his hero's birthday in Skokie.[23]

Judge Decker's decision ruled all three ordinances unconstitutional. He relied strongly on the content neutrality rule. At the very beginning of his discussion of "Fundamental Principles," he invoked the authority of *Mosley*:

The Supreme Court has held that "*above all else,* the First Amendment means that government has no power to restrict expression because of its message, its ideas, its subject matter, or its content." *Police Department of the City of Chicago v. Mosley,* 408 U.S. 92, 95 (1972). Emphasis added.[24]

In terms of the specific ordinances, Decker ruled that most of the permit ordinance (no. 994) was unconstitutional because the NSPA could not attain the necessary $350,000 worth of insurance. Consequently, the ordinance entailed "covert censorship," especially because of the discretionary waiver option which it left to the city manager. In reaching this conclusion, Judge Decker relied on testimony presented by a licensed insurance broker in Collin's concurrent federal litigation with the Chicago Park District, *Collin v. O'Malley.*[25] Yet Decker upheld the ordinance's thirty-day notice requirement.[26] Decker also ruled unconstitutional that part of the permit ordinance which denied permits to those groups who incite racial hatred; we will examine this part of the decision in our treatment of the "racial slurs" issue in a moment. In addition, Decker held the Military Uniforms Ordinance (no. 996) unconstitutional because the wearing of such uniforms is constitutionally protected symbolic expression and political speech.[27]

In the major part of his decision, Decker treated the sections in ordinances 994 (permit ordinance) and 995 (dissemination of racialist material ordinance) dealing with "racial slurs" together, designating them "Racial Slur Ordinances" (Part IV of his decision).[28] He declared the relevant sections of both ordinances unconstitutional because they were vague, overbroad, and (even without these detriments, which Decker viewed as inherent in such legislation) directed against the content of protected political speech. Citing Justice Brandeis in *Whitney* and other prominent pro-speech cases, he remarked that even potentially dangerous political speech (including the advocacy of violence) can be abridged only when it constitutes "a 'clear and present danger' of actually inciting the lawless actions advocated."[29] He reaffirmed the highly protective incitement test in *Brandenburg v. Ohio,* which held that an advocacy of lawless action may be prohibited only if it is "both intended to and likely to incite 'imminent lawless action.'"[30]

Yet Skokie disavowed any reliance on either the danger test or *Brandenburg* in its brief to the district court.[31] Skokie also downplayed the hostile audience issue, stressing instead that the proposed NSPA speech act would inflict trauma.[32] That is, Skokie alleged that the speech act would constitute fighting words as they had been defined by *Chaplinsky v. New Hampshire.*

Skokie also supported its case concerning fighting words by invoking the only group libel case the U.S. Supreme Court has ever considered, *Beauharnais v. Illinois,* a 1952 decision in which the Court sustained the conviction of Beauharnais for distributing pamphlets which impugned the reputations of blacks.[33] The reliance on *Beauharnais'* group libel doctrine in the context of a fighting words claim was unusual, even though group libel may be viewed as a form of fighting words.[34] Skokie buttressed its reliance on *Beauharnais'* group libel doctrine in its brief by incorporating the psychic trauma doctrine articulated in the *Goldstein* civil case. Skokie pointed out that a tort for the intentional infliction of mental suffering has been recognized by many courts, and that the existence of such a tort supported Skokie's claim that its ordinances defended an important social interest.[35] Accordingly, Skokie compelled Judge Decker to deal with a complex set of racial slur issues which involved questions about fighting words, group libel, and the development of tort law.

In terms of fighting words, Judge Decker held that Skokie's racial slur ordinances were unconstitutional despite the public interests they sought to protect. Relying on such cases as *Cohen v. California, Gooding v. Wilson, Lewis v. City of New Orleans,* and *Rosenfeld v. New Jersey,* which eviscerated the fighting words doctrine by limiting it to strictly captive situations and by the aggressive use of the vagueness and overbreadth doctrines (see Chapter One), he held that such statutes are inherently vague because

> the distinction between inciting anger with a social condition and hatred of the person or group perceived to be responsible for that condition is impossible to draw with the requisite clarity, and depends to a great extent upon the frame of mind of the listener.[36]

This is the logic of subjective value expressed in *Cohen.*

Concomitantly, Decker maintained that such statutes (and Skokie's in particular) are overbroad, thereby jeopardizing or "chilling" the speech the First Amendment is meant to protect. Skokie's ordinance dealing with the dissemination of material which incites racial hatred defined "dissemination" so broadly as

> to include such relatively passive activities as distributing leaflets and wearing "symbolic" clothing. It is clearly not aimed solely at personally abusive, insulting behaviour, as was required by *Cohen* and *Gooding.*[37]

And, Decker intimated, racial slur laws are *inherently* overbroad and vague. The law cannot fashion adequate distinctions in this area of policy:

> Plaintiffs believe that busing school children in order to accomplish integration is a threat to the integrity and quality of the public school system, and they also believe that blacks and Jews are the instigators of busing. They clearly have a constitutional right to say so, and to say so vehemently and forcefully. But at what point does a vehement attempt to arouse public anger at busing become an attempt to incite hatred of blacks and Jews? A society which values "uninhibited, robust and wide-open" debate (*New York Times v. Sullivan*] cannot permit criminal sanctions to turn upon so fine a distinction.[38]

In treating the group libel prong of Skokie's argument in support of its racial slur ordinances, Judge Decker also had to consider the constitutional status of group libel laws in relation to the status of defamatory speech about public officials in the wake of *Sullivan.*[39] Though the Supreme Court had never overruled *Beauharnais,* its status seemed questionable in light of *Sullivan,* for *Sullivan* protected the libel of public officials unless it is made with malice.

Decker concluded that even though *Beauharnais* had never been overruled by the Supreme Court, it was suspect law due to Supreme Court neglect, critical scholarly commentary, and the development of libel law in the area of public debate following *Sullivan.*[40] In addition, its thrust and potential scope seemed inconsistent with the more protective standards and doctrines of First Amendment law which have been promulgated in recent years:

> there is no doubt that the cases' basic premises are still sound: the government may punish speech which defames individual reputation, or which incites a breach of peace. However, as has been seen, a statute directed at unprotected speech may still fall afoul of the First Amendment if it is so broad or vague that it unacceptably inhibits free debate. The standards which the courts apply in determining whether a particular statute has this inhibiting effect have undergone considerable evolution since *Beauharnais,* and much of the analysis the Court employed in that case is obsolete by modern standards.[41]

The criminal statute in *Beauharnais* was based on broad legislative judgements about the *general effect* of group libel. Yet today the state must demonstrate an immediate harm in each case. Given the logic of *Sullivan* and such subsequent cases as *Garrison v. Louisiana*[42] and *Gertz v. Robert Welch,*[43] criminal group libel laws were, in Decker's view, too restrictive of speech.[44] For example, in *Garrison* the Supreme Court held that truth should be an absolute defense in libel suits involving public officials; yet in *Beauharnais,* the Supreme Court (per Justice Frankfurter) had held that the Illinois trial court was correct in not allowing Beauharnais to make the defense of truth.[45] The two cases seem incompatible.

Accordingly, Judge Decker held that *Beauharnais* is suspect constitutional law even though the Supreme Court has never overruled it. And, *a fortiori,* the Skokie racial slur ordinance was unconstitutional because "libel" is a traditional concept of tort law, whereas "racial" slurs have no settled meaning.[46]

Finally, free speech jurisprudence has protected free speech more assertively in the decades since *Beauharnais.* Whereas *Beauharnais* held that the Illinois group libel statute was constitutional because it bore a "rational relation" to the state's objective of preventing racial disorder (the standard of traditional, or normal, judicial review),[47] "the Court has since abandoned the rational relation to purpose approach to First Amendment cases, and now requires that laws which restrict free speech and assembly be *necessary* to achieve *compelling* state purposes"[48] (strict review to protect fundamental rights).[49]

Beauharnais' demise sounded Skokie's death knell. The racial slur provisions of the ordinances and the other aspects of the permit and military uniform ordinances were fatally flawed. All that was left was the thirty-day notice requirement of the permit ordinance. However, as mentioned, Decker issued a forty-five day stay of his ruling in order to give Skokie time to appeal. Although Skokie appealed the decision, participant statements and notes of the Jewish Federation's Public Affairs Committee reveal that Judge Decker's strong, scholarly opinion constituted a turning point in the controversy.[50] On March 7 and 8 the Skokie survivors and the PAC held separate press conferences to announce plans for a massive counterdemonstration against the NSPA.[51] *Collin v. Smith* cast the legal die in Collin's favor. After this point, the survivor community and their allies turned their attention to the second prong of their strategy of resistance: the mobilization of political and social support for the confrontation with Collin. The counterdemonstration in the public forum (or the "marketplace of ideas") became the new arena, and this shift from the legal to the social-political domain is, after all, what the First Amendment supports. Judge Decker reflected this position in the conclusion of his opinion. Like the Illinois Supreme Court in the injunction case, Decker acknowledged the negative social aspects of his decision. Yet he juxtaposed these harms with the benefits (actual and speculative) of free speech which, he concluded, outweigh the harms. He invoked *Cohen v. California* to support the court's pro-free speech position. I quote Judge Decker's concluding theoretical justification of his decision at length because it exemplifies First Amendment assumptions which we will critically evaluate in Chapter Eight:

> In resolving this case in favor of the plaintiffs, the court is acutely aware of the very grave dangers posed by public dissemination of doctrines of racial and religious hatred.
>
> In this case, a small group of zealots, openly professing to be followers of Nazism, have succeeded in exacerbating the emotions of a large segment of citizens of the Village of Skokie who are bitterly opposed to their views and revolted by the prospect of their public appearance.
>
> When feelings and tensions are at their peak, it is a temptation to reach for the exception to the rule announced by Mr. Justice Holmes, "if there is

any principle of the constitution that more imperatively calls for attachment than any other it is the principle of free thought — not free thought for those who agree with us but freedom for the thought that we hate." (*United States v. Schwimmer,* 279 U.S. 644, 654-55 (1929).)

The long list of cases reviewed in this opinion agrees that when a choice must be made, it is better to allow those who preach racial hate to expend their venom in rhetoric rather than to be panicked into embarking on the dangerous course of permitting the government to decide what its citizens may say and hear. As Mr. Justice Harlan reminded us in *Cohen, where a similar choice was made,* "that the air may at times seem filled with verbal cacophony is . . . not a sign of weakness but of strength." The ability of American society to tolerate the advocacy even of the hateful doctrines . . . without abandoning its commitment to freedom of speech . . . is perhaps the best protection we have against the establishment of any Nazi-type regime in this country.[52]

Leaving aside for the moment the telling fact that not a single major participant on Skokie's side even once intimated that the NSPA's speech act posed the danger of establishing a "Nazi-type regime in this country," Decker's concluding theory poses the normative theory of the First Amendment's tolerance of bad or evil speech. On the one hand, we cannot trust government to make content distinctions in this area of policy. On the other, tolerating such speech signifies strength, and may foster republican virtue.

2. United States Court of Appeals and United States Supreme Court. Immediately after Judge Decker's ruling Skokie officials made two moves. First, they contacted the Justice Department's Community Relations Service, asking the agency's help in avoiding or controlling the anticipated confrontation between survivor and Nazi forces. Second, Skokie appealed the district court's ruling on the ordinances.

On April 6, 1978, the Seventh Circuit of the United States Court of Appeals voted 6–2 to reverse Judge Decker's forty-five day stay of his order because of its negative impact on free speech.[53] Five days later, April 11, Collin mailed a renewed permit application to Skokie by registered mail; he asked for a permit to demonstrate on June 25, 1978.[54] On April 15, Skokie officials announced Collin's request to hold the demonstration on June 25.[55] This proved to be the final date set for the demonstration, as no subsequent court action would affect the NSPA's right to demonstrate on that date.

On May 22, 1978, the court of appeals upheld Judge Decker's ruling, with only one partial dissent.[56] Because the twenty-three page decision agreed with Decker in virtually every respect, it is unnecessary to examine its content here. It suffices to report that the decision, which was expected, virtually guaranteed that Collin could appear in Skokie in June, in full uniform.

Skokie appealed the decision to the United States Supreme Court. Skokie also asked the appeals court and then the Supreme Court for a stay of the appeals court's ruling. On June 5, 1978, the court of appeals denied the stay request,[57] followed by the Supreme Court's denial on June 12.[58] Finally, on October 16, 1978, the Supreme Court refused to grant *certiorari* to review the substance of the court of appeals' decision.[59] But by this time the controversy had ended. Collin had decided not to come to Skokie, choosing instead to demonstrate at the Federal Plaza in Chicago on June 25. He chose not to exercise the First Amendment right he had won at such great effort to himself and others. Let us now turn to the events that led to this anticlimactic conclusion.

II. The Denouement of the Controversy

A. The Bargaining Game with Collin

We saw above that Collin targeted Skokie in order to gain a bargaining chip in his dealings with the Chicago Park District. In return, the Skokie survivors and their allies threatened Collin with a massive counterdemonstration to meet Collin "head-on" on June 25, 1978. In addition to the counterdemonstration mobilization, the survivor community and the Public Affairs Committee of the Jewish Federation lobbied the Illinois legislature for the passage of a new group-libel statute similar to the one which had been on the books during the *Beauharnais* era. In May the legislature began holding hearings on the matter, apparently disregarding what Judge Decker had said about the status of *Beauharnais* in *Collin v. Smith*.[60] In framing his Skokie plans, Collin had to reckon with these traps being laid by the relentless opposition.

As June rolled along Collin began to get cold feet.[61] Angry Jewish groups and other militants from across the nation (and the world) planned to join the counterdemonstration. The deterrence policy of the counterdemonstration began having effect. As Jerome Torshen, head lawyer in the *Goldstein* suit, told me: "Collin has no death wish. If we could generate enough resistance to him, he would back down."

Yet Collin could retreat only on certain conditions. He would have to preserve face. So he would have to actually accomplish his original goal — namely, regaining his free speech rights at Marquette Park. If he could trade Skokie to regain these rights or find some alternative to Skokie, he could drop Skokie. The search for a "compromise" constitutes the final stage of the controversy. The Chicago *Tribune* described the nature of this game in late May:

> Frank Collin, the loudest mouth among a small group of neo-Nazis on the South Side, has in effect offered a bargain to Chicago Park District authorities: His group will "consider" cancelling their proposed march in Skokie if the Park District drops its demand for an insurance bond for Nazi rallies in Marquette Park.[62]

The NSPA's and ACLU's ongoing litigation with the Chicago Park District emerged at this point to play a decisive role. Back in July 1977, Judge Leighton of the district court had issued a preliminary order compelling a temporary halt to the enforcement of the Chicago Park District's injunction.[63] He ruled that the *amount* of the insurance requirement ($250,000) was excessive. Collin applied for a permit immediately after this ruling. Yet because Leighton had not explicitly overruled the district's insurance ordinance per se, the district merely lowered the amount of insurance required from $250,000 to $60,000. Of course, Collin could not afford this amount either, so the Skokie "deal" depended on further litigation in Leighton's court.[64] It was not until June 20, 1978, (five days before the proposed Skokie rally) that Leighton ruled, in *Collin v. O'Malley,* against the legality of *any* insurance requirement.[65] Leighton directed the Chicago Park District to allow the Nazis to demonstrate in Marquette Park at their soonest convenience without having to post any bond. Leighton's eleventh-hour decision may have been influenced by a "deal" between the Justice Department's Community Relations Service and Collin, or simply by the general fears in the Chicago area about a violent confrontation at Skokie. Leighton, the PAC, and the CRS denied such allegations, though CRS did plant press stories about possible deals, hoping to influence Collin's followers to abandon Skokie.[66] And Leighton's decision was consistent with the previous decisions against Skokie's similar insurance ordinance in *Collin v. Smith.* At any rate, *Collin v. O'Malley* dealt Collin and CRS their hands.

Meanwhile, after the appeals court confirmation of Judge Decker's ruling against Skokie's ordinances in late May, the CRS began moving into overdrive to conciliate the competing interests. Richard Salem, Midwest CRS director, was the first to propose a major counterdemonstration crowd control policy to the Jewish Federation in Chicago. More importantly,

Salem and Werner Petterson of the CRS began mediating among Collin, the ACLU, and the Chicago Park District.[67] Since Collin had already stated that he might cancel his Skokie plans were he to regain his Marquette Park rights, the CRS played its pitch to this possibility. At a meeting on May 26 in the ACLU's Chicago office, Salem and Petterson told Collin that he could reconsider his plans because he had prevailed in the courts against Skokie; and he was likely to prevail in the Illinois legislature (they would not pass group libel legislation) and in the court cases dealing with Marquette Park.[68] This meeting appears to have been a set-up for the next meeting among the same parties at the ACLU on June 1. At this meeting, Salem, who had been working closely with Skokie officials and Eugene DuBow of the Jewish Federation's Counterdemonstration Committee,[69] confronted Collin with detailed and vivid information about the potential for violence at Skokie. Salem then reaffirmed his belief to Collin that Collin would soon prevail on all his conditions (Skokie rights, Marquette Park rights, and the Illinois legislature's dropping of its group libel legislation). Then he added a hypothetical consideration which baited Collin. Salem inquired if Collin would be interested in demonstrating at an alternative site on June 25. Yes, Collin replied. Hamlin of the ACLU describes what ensued:

> Instantly, Salem began to suggest that Collin had solved the problem. If another site could be found, the confrontation could be avoided.
> In the discussion that followed, Salem and Petterson together hammered away at the wisdom of demonstrating elsewhere than in Skokie . . . Somebody suggested the plaza outside the federal court building. Collin liked that idea and Salem closed in; before I quite realized what had happened, Collin had traded Skokie for the Federal Plaza.[70]

To make sure, Salem told me that he contacted the relevant federal authorities to ensure that they would not obstruct Collin's new plans. Salem did not want anything to jeopardize the precarious solution. Yet Collin had every incentive to stick to his decision. First, he did not want to lose his life at Skokie ("the thought of snipers alone must have chilled him often," Hamlin remarks).[71] Second, some fellow NSPA members weakened Collin's resolve when they told the press in late May that they would not go to Skokie, regardless of Collin's "orders." After the May 26 meeting, Salem planted a story in the Chicago *Sun-Times* in which the CRS suggested an alternative site in the hopes of encouraging this faction.[72]

Yet the Chicago Park District had not finished playing out its hand. As mentioned, it was not until June 20 that Judge Leighton ordered the Chicago Park District to issue a permit, so Collin's agreement with the CRS was contingent upon the park district's adherence to Leighton's order. Yet, once again, the Chicago Park District proved recalcitrant. The District told CRS and ACLU that Collin would be given a permit only if he stated in his permit request that he would have seventy-five or fewer demonstrators. But Collin normally estimated the number of his supporters to be over one hundred (for reasons of "ego-inflation" and "image"). Surprisingly, Salem managed to persuade Collin to lower his estimates to the specified number, and the ACLU did not object.[73] Then Richard Troy, the district's "clever attorney,"[74] concocted two further stipulations which could justify a permit denial despite Judge Leighton's order: the NSPA could not leaflet or display signs, and the *crowd* at the demonstration would count toward the number of demonstrators attributed to the NSPA. Since the NSPA always carries signs, and since hundreds of people would be present, these new stipulations threatened the deal. David Goldberger, the ACLU attorney, naturally refused to accept these conditions. Luckily, Salem then managed to convince Troy to drop them. Collin's path to Marquette Park on July 9, 1978 (which was the date Leighton had ordered) was cleared. He was also set to hold his alternative-to-Skokie demonstration on Saturday, June 24, at the Federal Plaza. On June 22, with only three days to spare, Collin announced the cancellation of his Skokie plans.[75].

The NSPA held its Marquette Park and Federal Plaza rallies with massive police protection and audiences. The scenes were ugly. At the Plaza six thousand angry counterdemonstrators jeered and threw objects as Collin—protected by police lines and a screen and barely audible over the din of an angry crowd—shouted into his megaphone: "The creatures should be gassed."[76] At Marquette Park, on July 9, local toughs and racists vilified counterdemonstrators from Skokie and black areas; police broke up several burgeoning fights.[77]

The reader should not be misled by the "compromise" that resulted. Collin *did* give up Skokie and the *face* that went with it—but only after he had gotten everything else he wanted, including his admitted major goal, his speech rights in Marquette Park. Though he had to trade his Skokie "hostage," it paid off in spades.

B. Mobilization of the Skokie Counterdemonstration

The scenes at the Federal Plaza and Marquette Park were tame compared to what would have erupted at Skokie had Collin carried out his threat. According to reliable sources, Skokie police were overwhelmed by the prospects of controlling the tens of thousands of angry counterdemonstrators who planned to come to the June 25 counterdemonstration. North suburban and Chicago police agreed to help out, as did the governor, with a large contingent of the Illinois National Guard.[78] The Jewish Federation's counterdemonstration committee, headed by Gene DuBow and Sol Goldstein, had to arrange ambulance and first-aid service. "It was like planning for a war," DuBow told me.

The massive scale of the proposed counterdemonstration was due to the mobilization efforts of the survivor community and to the efforts of such prominent survivor allies as the Jewish Federation in Chicago, the Northwest Suburban Synagogue Council, and numerous religious groups around the area. These Jewish leaders used publicity to encourage groups to come to Skokie. One leader told me that:

> The essence of our effort was a public relations battle. We'd meet them with thousands. But I always knew inside there would be no confrontation . . . My efforts involved a shrewd effort to make an intelligent counterdemonstration position along with a big public relations effect. I made a suggestion to blow up pictures about the struggle in the press.[79]

These mobilization efforts, accompanied by scores of similar activities around the Chicago area by other groups, succeeded. Over a hundred major groups either announced their intentions to come to Skokie on June 25 or notified the Federation, Skokie officials, or the survivor groups of their intentions to come. A small sampling of groups: the Jewish War Veterans, the Ukraine Congress Committee, the Chicago and National Urban League, Operation Push, the NAACP, the Latino Institute, the Equal Rights Council, the National Conference of Christians and Jews (which issued a call for all Christians across America to wear yellow Star of David arm bands on June 25), the Martin Luther King, Jr. Coalition, as well as numerous Jewish groups.[80] Thousands of individuals and smaller groups formed just for Skokie also planned to come. One thousand supporters planned to fly out from Los Angeles alone, led by the publisher of *Israel Today*.[81] In addition, press reports, letters, and telegrams sent to Skokie reported dozens of groups planning counterdemonstrations across America and the world in support of Skokie on June 25. Skokie had become an international symbol.

Mobilization efforts on the road to June 25 also included struggles within the established Jewish community. Although these struggles were not part of the counterdemonstration plan, they were part of the politics of resistance. In 1978 the American Jewish Congress and the National Jewish Community Relations Advisory Council (NJCRAC) changed their traditional commitments to the quarantine policy concerning Nazi or hate group expression because of the issues raised by Skokie.[82] Astute politicking by Sol Goldstein encouraged the NJCRAC change of position at its January 1978 national meeting in Tucson. However, other Jewish groups, such as the National Jewish Committee and the Anti-Defamation League, refused to go along with their Chicago or Midwest branches in support of Skokie's legal efforts.[83] Nonetheless, these political actions and debates reveal the ferment that Skokie caused.

Jewish Federation spokesmen stressed the need to make the counter-demonstration as peaceful as possible. They worried that violence would harm the Jewish image and therefore prove to be counterproductive.[84] Yet spokesmen admitted that had the NSPA come to Skokie, the Federation and the law enforcement agents could not have prevented violence. Militant groups such as the Jewish Defense League, the Jewish War Veterans, and the Coalition Against Racism threatened crowd control plans. When 50,000 aroused people gather, it is difficult to manage groups bent on causing trouble.[85] The actions of the Skokie Police Department are instructive. The department was so distraught over its institutional incapacity to plan for the counterdemonstration that it promulgated a rigid policy prohibiting *any* department member from granting interviews concerning the controversy. The policy is still in effect.[86] And a police officer assigned to public relations allegedly took a leave of absence due to emotional distress or exhaustion.[87]

Indeed, the Village of Skokie also felt its image to be tarnished, even without the counterdemonstration; after the controversy, it hired a prestigious public relations firm and adopted a "Skokie Spirit" campaign to correct the public image of Skokie as a militant Jewish stronghold. This campaign, in turn, engendered charges of anti-Semitism against the beleaguered village.[88]

This campaign and the aftermath of the controversy's denouement compel us to turn to the consideration of consequences for Skokie. What good as well as harmful consequences occurred or were likely to have occurred had Collin made good on his threat? It is only after this analysis that we may consider the most important policy questions concerning the First Amendment at Skokie and in similar cases.

5

The Negative Consequences at Skokie

I. Taking Consequences Seriously

In the next chapters we will look at the harms and benefits which resulted at Skokie. We will deal with harms in two senses: 1) harms that resulted from the *threat* of the NSPA's coming to Skokie; and 2) likely harms that would have arisen had they come. Though these two aspects of harm are distinct, they are similar in terms of the First Amendment claim, for Collin's threat to come to Skokie would have been impotent had Skokie's legal measures not been illegitimate according to First Amendment standards.

Our treatment of harms is part of a general concern for the *consequences* of speech. In contrast to the American Civil Liberty Union's avowed disregard for the consequences of speech, we hold that consequences are crucial in terms of delimiting the speech right.[1] This concern for consequences, as a consideration in delimiting rights, is similar to Weber's notion of the ethic of responsibility in "Politics as a Vocation." The ethic of responsibility, which Weber contrasts with the puristic ethic of ultimate ends, is premised on the need to modify ideals and values in the face of their ethically relevant consequences in the real world.[2] As seen in Chapter One, the free speech approach taken in *Chaplinsky v. New Hampshire* is consequentialist in nature: the First Amendment protects speech which contributes to "the exposition of ideas" and "social value."[3] At the same time *Chaplinsky* honors the core of individual liberty and right to free speech. This approach is *not* the same thing as a utilitarian argument that exalts social good over rights; it simply entails a consideration of consequences in determining the proper *scope* of the speech right. Indeed, we will see later that the libertarian position at Skokie relies on its own kind of free speech utilitarianism that ignores the *rights* of survivors against targeted intimidation.

The consequentialist approach understood in this fashion can support a wide range of speech. For instance, Mill's aggressive stance in favor of

84

free speech in *On Liberty* is consequentialist in nature.[4] Our analysis of good and bad consequences at Skokie in this and the next two chapters will indeed reveal that significant good consequences did result due to the survivors' mobilization of resistance. On the other hand, significant harms resulted which pose problems for present free speech constitutional principles because of the existence of a *counter right*: the right to basic security against the intentional infliction of emotional trauma. Our further investigation of the consequences at Skokie will provide information which we may apply in later chapters to our normative analysis of the extent of the speech right of hate groups.

II. Emotional Trauma

A. Individual Aspects

My survivor interviewees did indeed experience significant trauma — *even though it appears that they were among the stronger survivors in the community.* Given my interviewees' relative strength, it is probable that the degree of trauma was even greater for many survivors whom I did not interview.

As seen in Chapter Three, the magnitude of trauma a survivor experiences in the present is partly a function of his past experiences. In addition, it is determined by the nature of a present stimulus. A psychiatrist depicts this effect:

> When some of these patients hear a knock on the door, this seems to them a dangerous portent. When they see a black limousine coming up and stopping before the door, this evokes a terror. When they see a man in uniform, they respond with panic because all this brings back memories of past horrors. These are classic symptoms of traumatic neuroses.[5]

The threat of the NSPA rally in the midst of the survivors' reconstituted community triggered just such anxiety. For them the Skokie conflict was a reliving of the past, at least at the beginning. Erna Gans pointed out:

> Yes it did terrorize us. It brought back many hours of anguish. Something we thought was left behind, all of a sudden we might be facing, sometime in the future, if not ourselves, then our children. This realization brought back a terror . . . here we are again, in the same position . . . for some it was very realistic — it is here today and I am going to kill them . . . We organized it, it is true. But it took us over . . . So, the terror is real — terror is always real in the eyes of the beholder.

Erna also linked the terror to her family—a matter of importance we will discuss shortly. Stephen stated:

> I couldn't sleep. It all came back to me . . . I went nights without sleeping. I just couldn't understand how this was possible.

Suzanne captured the meaning of the terror triggered by the swastika in words that support the psychiatrist's statement above:

> We were more nervous than before. How could we react, seeing the boots, the swastika . . . at a time like that you get so nervous. We weren't responsible. We don't know if we can control ourselves.

Alex then contributed the following remark:

> I don't know what is going on when I see such things. The thing that upsets me, that makes us wild, is to see the boots, the uniform, the swastika— this is the trigger. This does not change, even when we are surrounded by twenty thousand people.

Non-survivor witnesses corroborated these observations.[6] Perhaps the most poignant observation by a non-survivor was that of Skokie corporate counsel Harvey Schwartz, who pursued the legal cases for the village. Schwartz's observations are credible because of his sobriety and because he originally advocated the quarantine policy. His remarks refer to the survivors on April 30, 1977, the day the NSPA came as close as it would ever come to entering Skokie, only to be turned back by an emergency injunction. Survivor activists had spent the previous night at Alex's home organizing resistance.[7] Schwartz's description of the survivors that day is powerful. His observations were supported by every other interviewee who was present that day:[8]

> I knew these people well, and never recalled any conversations about their experiences in the death camps. They were regular citizens before this. On this date, however, they were changed people: fanatical, irrational, frightened, angry. No one could possibly appeal to them with any reasonable argument. When we told them at noon that Collin had been served an injunction, many refused to believe us. Many stayed until five o'clock, chanting loudly, etc. It would take a psychiatrist to understand the impact. There seemed to be different states of being: catatonia, frenzy, etc. They were possessed, some of them. It was as if they had repressed something for twenty years that was now loose. It was very disturbing. At this point I realized that the First Amendment theory grossly underestimated the impact on these people. This was not the " exchange of ideas"; it was literally an *assault*—the

presence of these symbols was literally an assault. It was different from the *Beauharnais* type of thing. No case I have read is similar. People there on that Saturday were injured, damaged — I dare say even physically.

The terror Schwartz captures was evoked in the legal suit, *Goldstein v. Collin. Goldstein* emphasized the tort of emotional trauma. The evidence also shows that harm had been caused by the mere *threat* of the demonstration. This terror constitutes the greatest harm caused by the NSPA's actions, and is a powerful reason why the survivors were unwilling to compromise and let the Nazis in. The pain was too great.

The matter is more complicated, however. David Hamlin of the ACLU told me that he considered the Goldstein suit to be hypocritical because Goldstein followed the NSPA around the Chicago area, attending its rallies in protest.[9] And Alex, Erna Gans, and Stephen told me that they, too, attended the NSPA rallies in the Federal Plaza and Marquette Park after Collin cancelled Skokie. Alex attended the Federal Plaza rally even though it took place on his silver anniversary.

Nonetheless, the claims of the Goldstein case and our interviewees are credible. First, the Goldstein case was a class action suit; so even if Goldstein and stronger survivors were not terrorized, certainly others were. There were reports of heart attacks, nervous breakdowns, and the like. Judith, for example, told me that there was an increase of over 50 percent in the number of Jews who came to the local Kaplan center for psychological counseling during the Nazi conflict.[10] Second, while our interviewees were driven by a sense of obligation and moral anger to confront Collin, they also experienced trauma (even though they were "stronger"). It is possible for trauma to coexist with other motivations. Indeed, the feeling of emotional trauma may even supplement the senses of obligation and anger in compelling survivors to actively resist, for "doing nothing" exacerbates trauma and the feeling of helplessness. As Judith told me:

> I don't know if the war taught me, or whatever — that as long as you are doing, it's okay. You don't always know what you are doing, but what I am afraid most of, is not doing . . . when you do feel helpless, you feel immobilized.[11]

Finally, there is a sociological dimension to the survivors' trauma which refutes Hamlin's contention of hypocrisy. The NSPA's presence in Skokie provokes a more traumatic reaction than its presence in Chicago or Marquette Park.

B. Sociological Aspects of Emotional Trauma

1. The Protective Community. Sociological studies demonstrate that groups are most likely to engage in violence when their turf is "invaded" (or, if they so perceive) in some respect by "outsiders."[12] The idea of turf includes such values and institutions as local control, autonomy, familiarity, family, neighborhood, and basic values—in short, the sense of community. Community in this respect constitutes the web of interrelatedness which provides an important basis of self-identification.[13] Accordingly, attacks against one's turf can be traumatic and emotionally provocative for reasons which transcend sheer individuality. This result is all the more likely when the attack includes explicit reference to the *values* and *right to exist* of that community, making it a moral as well as physical assault.[14]

Interviewee statements reported in Chapter Two also addressed the sociological aspect of emotional trauma. Recall that Alex said, "The minute somebody comes and tries to attack my home, I have to defend myself." Erna Gans remarked,

> Why should we allow Nazis free access to the community . . . to espouse their views, their political philosophy of the right of Jews to live? . . . He had a special reason to come and hurt us. You can see a breakdown of the community protection.

The "breakdown of the community protection," of course, is precisely what happened in Europe under Hitler. The Skokie survivor community was a reconstituted community. Accordingly, Nazi expressions of hate targeted at Skokie constitute a different harm from those caused by more general expressions of hate which are less targeted.[15]

It only takes contemporary *signs* or *symbols* of Nazism to trigger such fears of destruction of communality and self. The threat of the NSPA bringing its swastika into Skokie can be understood only in relation to this past experience, which comes alive once again in the form of the "nightmare reborn."[16] Many survivors have difficulty distinguishing past from present and reality from fantasy in times of great anxiety and stress.[17] "When you've been in fire, it scares you every time you see it," Judith told me. "It all came back to me," Stephen lamented.

The Skokie survivors' traumatic reactions are distinguishable from the reactions of other types of survivors (e.g., Hiroshima and Buffalo Creek).[18] For the Nazi persecution was a prolonged *personal* persecution involving a master-slave relation. On one hand, this personal form of terror in which Jews are singled out on "metaphysical" grounds for persecution leads to unique feelings of helplessness and loss of autonomy which we will examine in the next chapter. On the other hand, this terror represents a loss of communality due not only to nature or accident, but rather to an insidious *moral judgment* by the masters against the very existential validity of the slave or target of persecution (we could call this the *face* of terror, denoting personal *judgment*). This judgment can take on a metaphysical meaning, as the persecutor condemns the victim on the basis of a cosmology of race.[19]

The victim is condemned by the whole society in which he lives. The "moral community" of others (negatively defined in contradistinction to the persecuted, as was Nazi and pre-Nazi Germany)[20] aggressively, invidiously singles out the persecuted for pain or death. Because of the putatively moral nature of the persecution, a deeper aspect of self is condemned and, therefore, traumatized. Dr. Niederland, for example, distinguishes "fear" from "terror" in a manner which illuminates this difficult point:

> The coming of the Nazis, let us say to Poland, was an attack made by one organized nation upon another. But to the Jews . . . it also constituted more than a threat to their physical and personal existence . . . terror and fear are not synonymous. While the latter refers to an anticipated danger, terror relates to an experience in which the total personality is not only involved, but is actually overwhelmed or in the process of being overwhelmed. Terror is therefore an experience which is almost ineffable . . . the trauma of being outlawed, outcast, and reduced to the status unwelcome vermin (*lästiges Ingeziefer*) has to be considered in addition to the actual cruelties suffered.[21]

"Terror" in these terms cuts more deeply than sheer fear for the body, as it is directed to the very core of personality and self-esteem. Fred Richter, president of the Northwest Suburban Synagogue Council during the Skokie conflict (a non-survivor Jew), told me that what survivors feared according to his own observations was "not their lives, their existence. There is a difference between their lives and their existence." And Stephen expressed anguish at the moral condemnation society levelled at the Jews by exclaiming, "Just think of what they did to us! We were hunted by every human being, not just the Nazis."

Another aspect of existential terror due to "moral" illegitimacy may involve the fact that the Final Solution and its antecedents were perpetrated by the German *state*.[22] This historical fact appears to have been another reason that the Skokie survivors felt a "lack of community protection" to be so serious a problem at Skokie. The state—the putative institutional repository of legitimation and law[23] had officially condemned the Jew as "vermin." And as Stephen and Erna Gans told me, the German people thoughtlessly followed the state, allowing it to dictate moral values. Accordingly, survivor interviewees told me that the lack of governmental and societal support early in the controversy exacerbated their trauma. Skokie city attorney Harvey Schwartz depicted this link between trauma and the lack of government support:

> The survivors came here for sanctuary. A big problem [in the early going] was that they saw this [quarantine policy] as the acquiescence of their local government in permitting this destructive force to enter their community and inflict itself on them. While the ACLU argued for freedom of speech, their reverse argument was "How dare the government sanctify this thing by permitting this to take place on public property?"
>
> Historically, it was the government of Nazi Germany and the government of Europe that perpetrated crimes against the people. When Sol Goldstein was a young boy, as he observed local Nazi leaders, they were in many instances local governmental leaders. Here, in Skokie, it was *the leaders* who said "Let the Nazis come in and speak."
>
> Had Collin rented a private hall, we would not have taken the action we did. There would have been a confrontation, yet it would have been different. What made it different for us was the fact that *the government* was participating in the violation by issuing the permit.
>
> In America, we are taught that the public streets are for everyone — let it all hang out. Our one area of rights is public. Yet Holocaust victims see it differently. They see the government as a *protector* of rights. This is one reason why they believe in civil liberties — but here we have a paradox . . . They saw institutions meant to protect them as *not* protecting them. My legal action was meant to show the community that the government is working for them . . . Many people in Skokie I spoke to felt that the courts betrayed them . . .[24]

`Of course, the harms Schwartz depicted in this observation could be attributed to Skokie leaders rather than to Collin. But the survivors *also* viewed the libertarian interpretation of the First Amendment, which stood against the laws eventually passed by the Skokie Board of Trustees, as partly responsible for the lack of protection, and as aspects of the *national* government. The courts eventually struck down Skokie's legal obstacles in the name of the First Amendment. So survivor activists associated the courts' First Amendment position at Skokie with a lack of governmental and communal protection. As Stephen exclaimed:

The purpose for writing that amendment was not for Nazis, not for people to call to build new ghettos and new concentration camps . . . We need protection from the law because as citizens, we also have the right to be protected.

2. Breakdown of Civility. Although civility is intimately related to the protective function of community, it may be treated separately because it entails a different set of values and because its violation at Skokie constitutes a cost in itself. Civility involves the general mental and emotional *tone* of a community which is conducive to the basic respect of the dignity and individuality of others. On one hand, it entails treating others politely, with due respect.[25] On the other hand, it concerns respecting and not violating the *distance* between people who are not on intimate terms; such distance protects privacy and the individual's sense of personal sanctuary.[26] When civility and the concomitant moral tone of society deteriorate, people feel that the privacy of their inner sanctum is being invaded, or, at least, that it is jeopardized.[27] And turning one's eyes may not be enough to ward off the harm.[28]

There are two forms of mental "invasion" when civility declines. On a macro level the *general tone* of society can affect the mind.[29] On a micro level, individual acts of incivility can disturb targeted individuals. The Supreme Court accounts for the latter in its "captive audience" doctrine which allows the abridgement of speech when the speech is thrust upon an unwilling listener who is not able to avoid the speech by turning or looking away.[30] Yet uncivil (even threatening) speech may be targeted and consequently traumatizing even though it is not addressed to a captive audience in the strict sense the Court requires. Skokie was such an instance, as Collin's proposed speech act would not have been addressed to a captive audience. It was pre-announced and was to take place in a public forum which did not hold captive any particular target.[31] Yet the interview data strongly suggest that the NSPA's antecedent targeting nonetheless did (and *would have*—recall that we are dealing with the proposed demonstration and antecedent threats) inflict a sense of insecurity and incivility which was linked to the "breakdown of community protection" so upsetting to survivors.

III. The Other Slippery Slope

A related, potential harmful result should be discussed briefly even though it is speculative. Though the NSPA failed to gain adherents to its advocacies concerning Skokie (indeed, the immediate marketplace of ideas bestowed victory upon the survivors), it is *possible* that in conferring the First Amendment right upon the NSPA, the courts simultaneously conferred a subtle, hidden measure of legitimacy upon the group and its ilk. If so, the *general long-range effect* of such constitutional protection could be to confer legitimacy upon such groups. Was the late legal theorist Alexander Bickel foolhardy when he stipulated that "to listen to something on the assumption of the speaker's right to say it is to legitimate it . . . Where nothing is unspeakable, nothing is undoable"?[32] The law is a teacher,[33] and many people may psychologically associate legality with morality (even if such association is "unsophisticated").[34] If the legal right of Nazi speech subtly legitimated Nazi doctrine, it would constitute a "slippery slope" that cut in the opposite direction from the slope the ACLU and its supporters visualize in their own bad dreams. Of course, at this point we have no way of proving the new slope's existence or non-existence. And in Chapter Eight I will argue that *general advocacies* of all kinds should be protected by the First Amendment. Yet Bickel's admonition should not be ignored, as society is a seamless web of interconnectedness.

IV. The Threat of Violence

The final important harm to note is the threat of violence at Skokie. This harm has two elements. First, Collin forsook his First Amendment rights at Skokie because of the threat of nothing less than "massive retaliation." It could be argued that such a form of abridgement is not conducive to a sane, well-ordered society. Yet contemporary First Amendment doctrine, as applied to cases such as Skokie, inevitably encourages the use of such retaliation. The contemporary doctrines of the heckler's veto and fighting words allow official abridgement of speech only in the unusual case when substantial breach of the peace is imminently threatened and authorities are literally unable to protect the speaker.[35] The "danger test" is inoperable until this point. Accordingly, groups who legitimately feel assaulted usually cannot rely on the law to quiet speakers who verbally or symbolically assault them, and will be inclined to take the law into their own hands. This is one of the worst lessons the law can teach.[36]

The second element of the threat of violence is less subtle. Violence threatens lives and property. At Skokie no violence erupted because the NSPA backed down in the face of the threat of massive retaliation. Yet had they come, the scene would in all likelihood have been disastrous. Fred Richter of the NWSSC agreed with my contention that many positive con-

sequences resulted from Skokie's confrontation with the Nazis. But then
he paused for further reflection and amended his conclusion:

> Yeah. But that's because everything turned out rosy. It wasn't a confronta-
> tion. Old ladies didn't get killed. So examine that argument and see what
> you come up with. Based on what you said, that's a good conclusion . . .
> taking the circumstances . . . But changing the end of the movie . . . there
> are a lot of high costs involved.

The evidence supports Richter's conclusion. It may be alleged, therefore,
that present First Amendment doctrine poses a serious cost to society in
this regard because it encourages vigilante-like behavior in retaliation to
assaultive speech.

V. Conclusion

The major harmful consequence at Skokie was the infliction of mental
trauma on the survivors. This infliction entailed the NSPA's intentional
triggering of painful memories in the survivors as well as the threat of an
attack on the protective community. Survivors felt exposed to hostile forces
from which, they felt, a civilized society (and government) should protect
them. Accordingly, their trauma appears to have involved both personal
and communitarian dimensions. They also construed their trauma as a
breakdown of civility.

In addition, the possibility of an NSPA demonstration in Skokie (made
possible by the First Amendment doctrine endorsed by the courts) threatened the community with serious counterdemonstration violence. While
this violence would have been detrimental to Skokie, it also threatens other
communities which could find themselves in similar circumstances in the
future.

These harmful consequences challenge the present constitutional doctrine governing political speech because that doctrine limits the ability of
relevant governments to protect the individual and communitarian interests at stake. But the findings in the next two chapters pull in the opposite
direction. Let us now investigate the positive consequences.

6

Benefits for Survivors:
The Theory and Practice of Mastery

> I would suspect that in many ways that this was a growth experience . . .
> Collin was to some extent created by the survivors. In order to overcome
> something, one must have a feeling of mastery over it. The very fact
> that Collin existed allowed this mastery.— Judith, Skokie survivor

The Skokie affair did not simply result in negative consequences. As Mill,
Brandeis, and others would have hoped, significant benefits in terms of
political education and republican virtue did arise out of the conflict. Mill
had unusual insight into the way in which conflict spurred by free speech
can lead to clarification, commitment, and self-development. In this respect his theory of free speech resembles the arguments of other theorists
who discern the social and individual benefits of certain types of conflict.[1]

In the next two chapters we will look at the favorable consequences in
terms of two groups: the survivors and non-survivor participants at Skokie. We will see that the benefits (and the limits of these benefits) were
different for the two groups.

I. Survivors: Mastery and Political Participation

A. The Theory of Mastery

One of the major justifications of free speech is the knowledge and truth
which may result from its practice.[2] Yet the survivors, it might be argued,
already possessed all the knowledge they would ever need of the central
element in the controversy: the nature of Nazism.

Because the survivors were already experts on Nazism, we must look elsewhere for beneficial consequences in their regard. One of the benefits is the attainment of mastery. This mastery is related to another First Amendment value, what Emerson, Mill, and others call "self-development" or "realization."[3] Simply stated, mastery is the sense that one has some adequate measure of control over important matters in one's life. Erik Erikson defines "active mastery" as

> the individual's need (central to the function of his ego) to experience fate as something which he chose and in which he was active even if this means to have chosen or caused, invited or accepted annihilation or persecution and exile.[4]

Erikson further distinguishes *patiens,* or the state of being exposed from within or without to "superior forces," to *agens,* which is "an inner state of being unbroken in initiative and of acting in the service of a cause which sanctions this initiative."[5] That is, *patiens* entails the passive and disintegrated state of mind that follows *submission* to outside forces, whereas *agens* pertains to the *active,* integrated state of mind that one possesses when he actively confronts outside forces and exercises autonomy. The *result* of such action is less important than the attitude and mental state that *agens* engenders and signifies. *Patiens* can be a result of either early character formation or an overpowering event which renders one helpless and ego-defunct.[6] The devastation may be all the worse when the fate to which one submits is not that of nature, but that which is perpetrated by man.

Before we look at the role of mastery at Skokie, it must be asserted that the following analysis is somewhat speculative. Unlike the evidence concerning harms, the evidence pertaining to mastery is indirect; it is derived from statements dealing with matters other than mastery, per se. It is a matter of interpretation. Thus, the analysis of mastery is meant to be persuasive rather than conclusive.

B. Mastery and Holocaust Survivors

Many survivors of the Hitler persecution suffered from having been rendered helpless and ineffective. Many feel that their survival was simply a matter of fate having nothing to do with masterful actions on their part. "I have dreams, I cannot get rid of them. It was fate that I survived. I was not better than my brother [who died]," Stephen said.[7] (This sentiment should be juxtaposed with the fact that some survivors *did* survive because of legitimate initiative or sometimes less legitimate animal cunning and/or collaboration with the Nazis.)[8] In addition, there is the collective shame of having "gone like sheep." According to Henry Krystal, the editor of *Massive Psychic Trauma,*

> Many survivors have a perpetual need to atone for cowardice or other "failures." There is either real personal shame or assumption of collective shame for the failure of the Jews to fight the Nazis.[9]

There are not many antidotes to the condition of *patiens,* which often results in a state of stagnation and withdrawal. Yet resolutions can be found, especially if in the subsequent course of one's life one is able to rebuild a competent existence and a meaningful communality. Such an existence, which is probably more likely to develop if the state of *patiens* is not due to an early character formation but rather to a condition imposed upon an antecedently competent character,[10] provides a positive basis upon which to take subsequent masterful action. The distinction between strong and weak survivors is important in this regard, for only the former may be in a position to actually regain mastery that was surrendered to the Nazis.

Another resolution is what Erik Erikson calls "totalism" or a "totalistic ideology." Totalism is an absolutist, rigid belief system or cause to which one can attach oneself. The commitment to a totalistic cause (which is akin to the notion of extremism discussed in Chapter Two)[11] can offer a means of personal salvation, a means of propelling the self out of the torpor of *patiens* into the more positive state of *agens.* Yet while providing a solution to the throes of negativity, this solution does not bring true independence because it entails the uncritical attachment of self to cause. In a sense, the totalist substitutes one form of necessity for another.[12]

The Skokie survivor resistance appears to have entailed measures of both *agens* and totalism. Mastery could be regained by re-encountering the Nazi foe on a more propitious basis than in the past. Erna Gans stated in Chapter Three that the Nazis must be faced "now, when we are free to stand up." "Standing up" denotes the willingness to actively resist, to move toward independent action. "Now we must be strong and not be silent. We cannot afford to be weak. We have got to fight," asserted Stephen.

Stephen's proclamation about fighting is not of merely rhetorical significance. It signifies an important element in the psychology of mastery. In order to attain a deeper understanding of this matter, it is helpful to briefly consider Hegel's theory of bondage and the master-slave relationship in *The Phenomenology of Mind.* We will limit our use of Hegel to the ways in which his theory of bondage casts light upon the mystery of survivor motivation and growth.

According to Hegel, the psychology of the master-slave relationship cuts to the very center of the will and the sense of identity. Self-certainty requires the willingness to risk life in danger. There is a relation between self-certainty and the esteem granted by others: "it [consciousness] *is* only by being acknowledged or recognized."[13] Defeat, especially cowardice, in the eyes of another can be debilitating to self-certainty so defined. To retreat in the face of a necessary struggle is to lose self-certainty, as Hegel explains:

> The relation of both self-consciousnesses is in this way so constituted that they prove to themselves and each other through a life-and-death struggle . . . And, it is solely by risking life that freedom is obtained; only thus is it tried and proved that the essential nature of self-consciousness is not bare existence, is not the merely immediate form in which it first makes its appearance, is not its mere absorption in the expanse of life . . . the individual who has not staked his life, may, no doubt, be recognized as a Person; but he has not obtained the truth of this recognition as an independent self-consciousness.[14]

Hegel distinguishes between "person" or "bare existence" and selfhood based on "independent self-consciousness." The former is the sheer natural existence of the self, unmolded and undeveloped by acts of discipline and courage which conquer the instinct of self-preservation. True autonomy (and Hegel's philosophical project is preeminently about autonomy)[15] involves not only a requisite mastery of the external world (nature or being), but also mastery of the self and fear of death.[16] Consequently, when one gives in to the natural inclination to avoid danger, one may gain one's "bare existence," yet one loses one's "self-certainty" in the process. A related political consequence is a loss of self-esteem and the respect of others. European Jews and quiescent American blacks in the nineteenth century were unable to gain respect without standing up for their manhood.[17] A. I. Melden points out that blacks gained self-respect only when they stood up *themselves* for their rights; they lacked this respect under the Abolitionists' policies, for these policies made them only the *passive* recipients of rights. It is

> the distinctive moral requirement imposed upon the victims of injustice that they assert their authority as persons with rights, failing which they acquiesce in the wrongs they suffer and continue as before to go about in fear and trembling as if they were devoid of any rights.[18]

"Passive" (*patiens*) responses to claims of rights engender "fear and trembling." Yet *agens* effectuates moral and personal autonomy.

Many survivors of the Nazi persecution did not make a fight, or at least psychologically feel that they did not. In the end of *that* struggle they were liberated by the Allied forces; yet, as in Melden's depiction of the Abolitionists' treatment of blacks, they were in most cases not *themselves* responsible for their liberation. The fear and trembling created by persecution are not conquered by such salvation by outside forces. Consequently, the return of the Nazi menace triggers not only the terror of physical annihilation ("bare existence"), but the loss of spiritual autonomy ("independent self-consciousness") as well. Recall Fred Richter's statement concerning Skokie survivors, "You know, there is a difference between their lives and their existence."

German theorists of race before and during Hitler often distinguished the "spirituality" of the "true," "courageous" German from the "base materialism" of the Jew.[19] That is, the German was naturally a master, the Jew a slave. This interpretation provides a means for understanding the paradox which we have encountered at Skokie: why many survivors were simultaneously terrified of and committed to confronting the Nazis. According to Hegel and the theory of *agens, terror is not only a function of the fear of death, but, interestingly, of the very submission to this fear.* The *manner* in which the Jews allowed themselves to be taken into the camps, above and beyond the sheer brutality, exacerbates what Melden calls "fear and trembling," for trembling is a function of failed mastery over the natural inclination of self-preservation (a form of "base materialism"). Bruno Bettelheim observed that those *political* prisoners who actively resisted Hitler and who formed "democratic resistance groups of independent, mature, and self-reliant persons" in his concentration camp experienced the least psychological disintegration in camp.[20] Their active resistance fostered *agens*.

Some critical depictions of the psychological dilemma in colonial relations cast light upon this issue. Albert Memmi, in his essay on the psychology of French colonialism in Tunisia, argues that the "colonized" are reduced to a state of inferiority and a status of mere objects (mere "person," in Hegel's terms) by the colonizers:

> He is hardly a human being. He tends rapidly toward becoming an object
> . . . Willfully created and spread by the colonizer, this mythical and degrad-
> ing portrait ends up by being accepted and lived with to a certain extent by
> the colonized.[21]

Memmi and Frantz Fanon, who writes in a similar vein about the colonialism in Algiers, portray a psychology of ego-regression or disintegration which is similar to that of the Nazi-survivor relationship. In both cases the oppressed party adopts a negative identity due to the loss of mastery over the situation (they also depict aspects of "identity with the aggressor"). Yet Memmi and Fanon also point out a resolution to the crisis which was not available to the incarcerated Jews of Europe: revolt. Fanon advocates revolt as a means to regain the "full stature of a man" and a positive communality; note the use of the term "sets on foot," which symbolizes the movement from *patiens* to *agens*:

> The conflict, by reinstating the down-trodden, sets on foot a process of re-integration which is fertile and decisive in the extreme. A people's victorious fight not only consecrates the triumph of its rights; it also gives to that people consistence, coherence, and homogeneity. Armed conflict alone can really drive out these falsehoods created in man which force into inferiority the most lively mind among us and which, literally, mutilate us.[22]

Because Jewish survivors of Nazi persecution were treated more brutally than most colonized people their psychological crisis is deeper. According to Krystal, "problems of identification with the aggressor are ubiquitous, " and "when an entire population is reduced to an inferior status such as that [created by Nazi Germany] . . . the individual's self-respect is damaged in ways not repairable by himself."[23] Since many of these survivors were freed by Allied troops,[24] they did not have the opportunity to engage in a major revolt that might salvage *agens*. Erna Gans described the subsequent process of Americanization in terms which suggest a continued *patiens,* at least concerning politics and public life (of which she is an exception):

> Many survivors are less educated than other Jews. The American immigration organizations told us to get to work to build independence and self-esteem. Many did well in business, but always feel shy and can't express themselves in public. They feel pampered, and pamper their children.

Fred Richter and Harvey Schwartz agreed that before the Nazi conflict, survivors were inconspicuous in terms of public participation. Because appearance in the public realm requires at least a measure of courage,[25] the reluctance of certain survivors to enter the public realm is itself a sign of the lack of self-confidence and mastery or *agens*. At the same time, however, Erna's statement also suggests that in non-public respects many survivors *had* developed a sense of autonomy; so, presumably, they would be capable of furthering the project of *agens* at some opportune time in the future.

The eruption of the Skokie resistance indicates that the time for further action had arrived. Sooner or later certain survivors may feel the need to reclaim mastery vis-a-vis the source of its original loss, and will be ready to engage in revolt in a Fanon-like fashion. Precedents are provided by instances of Jewish resistance in the post-Hitler world which preceded Skokie.

C. The Regaining of Mastery

1. Past Events. In his book *The Faith and Doubt of Holocaust Survivors,* Reeve Brenner theorizes that both the Eichmann trial and the Six Day War of 1967 provided survivors with the opportunity to reenact past travails on a new propitious basis. He maintains that these events provided needed outlets for pent-up emotions that had long been mute. Based on numerous interviews with survivors in Israel, Brenner constructs a composite statement about the psychological meaning of the Six Day War for survivors:

> Something happened to our psyches during the breath-taking weeks before the Six Day war in June 1967. It was *deja vu,* as though we had been there before. We all felt the long-buried, smothered but still smoldering emotion rising to the surface of our consciousness . . . Once again we were stripped naked . . . the *selector* of *life and death* standing before us . . . But suddenly like a dream, the nightmare was transformed into a lovely fantasy, a shared vision, in which we were advancing cloaked in military uniform and armed and proud — and *self-reliant* don't leave that out . . . Since the Six Day war — a day for each million, I wonder? — I've been more at peace with myself. I'm whole again; I find I am kinder, less moody, freer of speech, admitting to faults previously denied. It was years of psychotherapy concentrated in a few short days and weeks . . . I'm a new person, really.[26]

If Brenner is correct, the Six Day War meant reliving the past on new terms: as a beneficial reconstruction of the confrontation between master ("the selector of life and death") and slave ("self-reliant," "proud warriors"). This transformation allows one to reinterpret one's character in relation to the past. Brenner suggests that a similar process went on during the Eichmann trial in Jerusalem in 1961. While that did not appear to have provided for the regaining of *agens* (Eichmann was no longer an active selector or enemy), it did offer an opportunity for the release of pent-up emotions. Brenner calls it a "public psychodrama" in which the past was reenacted.[27] And according to Harold Rosenberg, who covered the trial for *Commentary,* the trial was "the first collective confrontation of the Nazi outrages" that "represents a recovery of the Jews from the shock of the death camps, a recovery that took fifteen years and which is still by no means complete."[28]

2. Skokie and Mastery. Skokie may have furthered the completion. For this to occur, the NSPA and Frank Collin would have to be infused with a symbolic importance that linked them to the Nazis of Germany; in Hegel's terms, the conflict would have to be, to some extent or in some manner, a life-and-death struggle. Perhaps this is one reason Eileen's father "honestly didn't care if he was killed" while standing up to a Nazi "invasion" of Skokie.[29] While the NSPA threat reignited inner fears for many survivors, the *elevation* of the Skokie struggle to a life-and-death status could also (simultaneously) be a means of setting up a situation in which *agens* could be regained in the struggle with the very foe who had taken it away decades earlier.

Rabbi Weiner, the "moderate" leader who sought so hard to maintain a consensus of Jewish and non-Jewish opinion and policy at Skokie, certainly believed in this mastery thesis. He told me that, in his estimation, survivor activists fought the Skokie issue on two planes: the "real Skokie," which is a cosmopolitan community with Jewish and non-Jewish traditions and lifestyles, and the "symbolic Skokie," which was "the battlefield between the glorious knights and the devil." Weiner maintained that the "symbolic Skokie" represented survivor activists "refighting World War II." For example, in an important Jewish Federation Public Affairs Committee policy meeting called to discuss strategy for the proposed final counterdemonstration on June 25, the major survivor leader, Sol Goldstein, rebuked Weiner's suggestion that the counterdemonstration not be held by proclaiming, "But you don't understand! This is war, rabbi!"[30] In addition, Goldstein's statement to me about the political meaning of the survivors' resistance at Skokie suggests that Weiner's "refighting World War II" thesis is correct:

> It is not so much Skokie, but the *idea* of what was Skokie [that was important]. The first one to *stand up* and to tell the Nazis, "You won't do it."

Yet the elevation of the Skokie conflict to a higher plane of significance was not limited to the survivor activists. Israeli Prime Minister Menachim Begin visited Skokie near the end of the conflict, and Skokie's Mayor Smith was presented with a key to Jerusalem on an expenses-paid trip to Israel.[31] And such Jewish dignitaries as Simon Wiesenthal, Elie Wiesel, Israeli diplomats, and Meir Kahane of the Jewish Defense League came to Skokie and spoke of its symbolic and political importance.[32]

Many other comments made by survivors support the mastery hypothesis. I select only the most illustrative, those which stress the importance of self-reliance and strength before the enemy. Erna Gans:

We are not going to let ourselves be in that position anymore [that survivors were in under Hitler]. No sir, no more. And when you cannot protect us, we will protect ourselves.

Stephen:

This is what they would like to do, that we should break down. That's what Hitler did. They like to break us. We have to be strong now. *We cannot go back.* We cannot be silent. We have to fight back. We cannot afford to be weak. We have to unite . . . We called meetings, we explained to people, and the response was tremendous.

The present confrontation must be fought on the higher grounds of *agens.* At the near-confrontation of April 30, 1977 (the turning point in the mobilization of allies), Stephen told me that he stood up and challenged the other resisters (in Fanon-like terms):

Nobody should move. It's now or never. We stay until we find out they are not here . . . But we found out you can succeed if you are determined, if you are fighting the right cause.

Other interviewees concurred. I conclude by simply reporting the remarks of two insightful interviewees, Judith and Eileen. The quotations speak for themselves. Judith (recall she is a psychological counselor):

I would suspect that in many ways this was a growth experience, if for no other reason than that people found that there were resources within them, that they go and act and that there are frames of reference, that there is a group of people that they can attach themselves to and that people are listening to them. *Collin was to some extent created by the survivors.* In order to overcome something, one must have a feeling of mastery over it. The very fact that Collin existed allowed this mastery. As an analogy the children of survivors, mine included, often feel they have to prove themselves and do dangerous things to get mastery. They will create handicaps . . . I really think that in this way, very subconsciously, the Skokie thing was an exercise in mastery. All this is very subtle; no one goes around thinking of it this way. At the time you think of it as an event that takes place . . . With Collin there was more room for the imagination and for interpretation. Very few people will tell you that he was really a tremendous threat.[33]

Eileen (speaking of her father):

As you said, he was reconstructing the German situation . . . This [Skokie] was the question of whether he'd be capable again. He still looks at himself as someone who was a D.P. [displaced person] or concentration camp person, which means incapable. But it [Skokie] may have really given them a feeling that, "Yes, my feelings are accepted in the community" . . . He's not the docile survivor that a lot of other survivors are. He has come to a lot of our association meetings and stood up and talked about it. I don't think he would have done that before the [Skokie] Nazi thing, I really believe that . . . I don't know if he would have come to meetings and stood up and spoken . . . He was always very self-conscious about his English, which is very good, by the way. But he was always afraid that his speech wouldn't be good. But after that [Skokie], I haven't heard that, in the last three or four years.

3. Mastery and Trust: Ingredients of Political Education. Some theorists of free speech and politics maintain that participation in politics and the public realm develops courage and appropriate trust in the world (aspects of republican virtue).[34] The expression of mastery at Skokie seems to confirm these hopes for the benefits of free speech. In the last quotation Eileen states that her father gained the confidence and trust to enter the public realm. Elsewhere, Erna Gans stated that

> the other survivors don't take part too much in public issues . . . In this issue they overcame this kind of fear because they saw there was nobody else to carry the banner . . . They were available to speak publicly, and they still are.

Stephen also emphasized the gaining of trust due to participation:

> We had to go [to public meetings], and we did. We called meetings, we explained to the people, and the response was tremendous. This is the good I would like to bring out . . . The first time that I felt that we are getting strength, that we are getting sympathy and support, [was] when we met with non-Jewish people . . . I would like to emphasize strongly that we succeeded by having the support of the non-Jewish community, and not only from Skokie, but from all over . . . It strengthened my conviction that the American people are different.

Stephen's remarks demonstrate the link between mastery (*agens*) and participation in a communal enterprise based on trust. As Bettelheim points out in his essay on politics in the German concentration camps, self-reliance was buttressed by the formation of support groups "in which every member backed up in all other members, the will to resist."[35] This type of communal reinforcement appears to have prevailed to a significant extent at Skokie. Survivors gained strength through the political action compelled by the threat of the NSPA's presence.

Yet there are limits to the mastery gained. These limits concern the point made above about "totalism." While the survivor interviewees do seem to have gained some sense of mastery and trust in their resistance to Collin, they nonetheless appear to have remained bound in certain respects by a negative, totalistic sense of community. Their resistance efforts brought them closer to others (and vice versa), but the boundaries of the negative gemeinschaft were not entirely broken.

II. The Limits of the Mastery Thesis

A. Political Education and the Tragic Perspective

The first limit of the mastery thesis is obvious: it applies only to the more autonomous survivors whom I interviewed and who participated in the controversy. Indeed, most sources agreed that there were only about thirty to forty full-time survivor activists during the controversy, which is less than five percent of the Skokie survivor community (though many more played active secondary roles; most sources estimated their number in the low hundreds).

A second limit is more subtle. Realistic trust in others is one earmark of autonomy and political education because it represents an ability to see reality for what it is rather than "projecting" one's own fears onto reality.[36] One hoped-for consequence of free speech is the development of a greater sense of reality and its complexity in contrast to a rigid, pre-determined world view characteristic of the notion of "totalism" or "prejudice." The totalistic mind bifurcates the world between polar opposites of good and evil and "we" versus "them." A community constituted by such bifurcations and distrust is a "negative gemeinschaft," or a community premised on the exclusion of outsiders who are excluded because of their failure to be "loyal" to the single-issue (or otherwise narrow) community.[37]

This type of community opposes the hope that free speech will lead to a more balanced, realistic view of the political world (another aspect of republican virtue). One way to express this opposition is to distinguish between public and private interest. Political education should entail thinking about political issues from the perspective of the public good; membership in the body politic means the "subordination of the private for the public interest."[38] (This subordination, of course, need not preclude private interest when that is appropriate, or the utilization of private interest to achieve public policy ends.)[39] According to Tocqueville, political participation draws one "from the circle" of his "own interest," and exposes him to the larger scheme of things, "the close tie which unites private to general interest."[40]

Another way to express the movement from a negative gemeinschaft to a more open one (one, therefore, with more "mastery") is to distinguish simplistic (or reductionist) world views from complex depictions of reality. Weber's differentiation of the ethic of absolute ends from the ethic of responsibility involves this distinction. The latter views reality as complex and tragic, whereas the former sees things more simplistically and moralistically. Weber endorsed a "tragic" view of reality as opposed to a simplistically moralistic view because a tragic view is both more realistic and more responsible. The tragic view entails the recognition of the limits of moral absolutism. According to William Ker Muir, Weber's tragic perspective avoids the polar pitfalls of immature absolutism and amoral Machiavellianism by endorsing the virtues of "passion and perspective" — that is, moral commitment balanced by an objective assessment of the validity (or invalidity) of competing interests, values, and concerns in a complex world. In Weber's terms, the "professional politician" possesses "the knowledge of tragedy with which all action, but especially political action, is truly interwoven."[41]

B. Skokie Survivors

To the extent that Skokie survivors gained a measure of relative trust toward Americans during the controversy, they appear to have moved away from the negative gemeinschaft which characterized their previous stance. Such a view appears realistic (Americans, after all, are solidly anti-Nazi);[42] and in structural terms, it came about as a result of the wider contacts survivors made with allies outside the survivor community. An observation of Rev. Koenline, of Skokie's United Presbyterian Church, portrays this movement toward trust; Rev. Koenline was talking about a meeting she attended in April 1978, which addressed the plans for the final counterdemonstration:

> There were five Christian clergy there in a hall packed with Jews. It became clear that it was a Jewish effort to deal with a Jewish problem. But one man was very pleased to see us there and went to the podium and announced all our names. The entire crowd applauded and stood up, and we had to go up on the stage and make speeches. People [survivors] said publicly, "This is the first time we felt that we were not alone. There is support we didn't know we had."

According to psychiatrists, this type of trust signifies a propitious development in the psycho-therapy of survivors.[43]

Yet in some other important respects the survivor interviewees did not transcend the negative gemeinschaft of narrow interest. Attitudes about two issues demonstrate the problem: 1) survivor attitudes about the ACLU's actions on behalf of the First Amendment in general and ACLU lawyer David Goldberger in particular; 2) survivor attitudes about the Jewish Federation, other elite allies, and the counterdemonstration planned for June 25, 1978. Each of these issues concerned the relation between the survivors' position and wider yet competing legitimate interests; to the extent that they failed to adopt a more reflective, "tragic" perspective about these issues, their political education fell short of the First Amendment ideal.

1. The ACLU, the First Amendment, and David Goldberger. Aryeh Neier and David Hamlin of the ACLU both contend that a strong First Amendment is among the best long-range policies for protection of minority rights in America.[44] Their contention is persuasive; at the very least, a strong First Amendment is vital to the promotion of views which minority groups rely upon to influence the political system.[45] Accordingly, Jews who sought to limit the reach of the First Amendment should view their quest in tragic terms—that is, to exhibit a sense of reluctance or irony in their commitment to the cause. They might, for instance, worry about the detrimental effects a favorable court ruling would have on the right of free speech. Or they might discern analogies (however tenuous) between their desire to suppress the Nazis and the desire of, say, white southerners to suppress Martin Luther King. In addition, one would expect them to regret any negative consequences accruing to the ACLU, as the ACLU provides the foremost institutional support for the First Amendment in the land.

For the most part, survivor interviewees did not exhibit such a tragic perspective. Characteristically, Judith was the only exception, though even she dropped her ACLU membership because of Skokie. Most of them saved their greatest wrath for David Goldberger, the Jew who defended Collin; they also refused to acknowledge that the ACLU had a legitimate concern. Stephen stated that David Goldberger was:

> A rotten person and an opportunist. And I'm pretty sure, I can visualize it. If he had lived in my time, during the Nazi era, I know how his stand would be. We had people like that. They were collaborators. I had a friend, he did collaborate with the Gestapo. When I was hiding, he knew where my hiding place was and he came with them . . . these collaborators, there was Quisling, there was Lavall in France, they got paid. David Goldberger is that type of a person . . . He's the greatest opportunist. He is scum . . . If I were to

have a choice, Frank Collin and David Goldberger, the first one to go would be David Goldberger.[46]

Stephen's intense view of Goldberger reveals very little effort to confirm one's view by reality testing; it utterly disregards the nature of Goldberger's commitment (see Chapter Two) and is wildly speculative. The other survivor interviewees (excepting Judith) made similar, though less virulent, remarks. Erna Gans' comments indicate a closed mind on the issues of the ACLU's policy and role at Skokie:

> Now when you're talking about the ACLU, that's a different kettle of fish. Because the ACLU's position was totally wrong, is totally wrong. And Mr. Goldberger, especially, to me he is the personification of all the Judenräte put into one man, and that's Mr. Goldberg (sic) . . . I'm still waiting for the downfall of Mr. Goldberger, and I'm hoping that someday he'll get paid back.

Can one who possesses the tragic perspective maintain that the ACLU's position was "totally" wrong? I doubt it. Judith appears to have been correct when she said that survivors projected onto or "invested" Goldberger with anxieties about their own pasts.[47]

It is interesting to compare the survivors' more hostile views to those of non-survivor Jews. The results are mixed. On one hand, leaders in the Anti-Defamation League, the American Jewish Committee, and the Jewish Federation whom I interviewed expressed a more balanced, "tragic" position. Ab Rosen of the Anti-Defamation League was most representative: "My summary of the conflict is that it was a contest between the good and the good, the ACLU and Skokie."[48] Rosen and the other "institutional" Jews balked at supporting the survivors at the start of the controversy precisely because of their long-standing commitment to the First Amendment (this commitment constituted one reason for adhering to the quarantine policy). Given their institutional roles, one would expect such a stand.[49]

On the other hand, other elites such as Skokie trustee Morris Topol and Jerome Torshen (Torshen directed the *Goldstein* suit team) execrated the ACLU in interviews with me and during the controversy. Topol told the press that the ACLU was the "real villain" at Skokie,[50] and told me that he wished he had belonged to the ACLU so he could have withdrawn. Torshen labeled Goldberger a "neo-Nazi counsel" in the *Goldstein* suit; and according to ACLU's Hamlin, Torshen hoped for the ACLU's demise simply because of its defense of Collin's speech rights at Skokie.[51] Other stories are instructive: psychologist David Guttman, who testified in federal court on behalf of Skokie, wrote a letter to Franklyn Haiman (national secretary of the ACLU) in which he engaged in what Haiman considered "character assassination."[52] And Rabbi Montrose told me that he mocked Goldberger's commitment to free speech when they both appeared on the "Phil Donahue Show" during the controversy:

> I mocked Goldberger. He responded poorly, muttering over and over again, "free speech, free speech, free speech." He just kept muttering, "freedom of speech." He wouldn't answer any of our questions.[53]

While Montrose's complaint is valid in certain respects, it also reveals a disconcerting disrespect for the principle of free speech and for those who take risks to support it. Montrose's actions were duplicated by Jewish leaders who made public pleas to turn the conflict into a litmus paper test of "Jewish loyalty." Jews who supported the ACLU were "traitors."[54] What is important in this regard is not one's policy position, but rather *the way* in which that policy position is held. A more tragic, balanced view of Skokie would have included a tension between commitment to free speech and the survivors.

To be fair, the Skokie conflict was unusually divisive. Family members were set against one another. David Goldberger was denounced at a worship service by his own rabbi.[55] Ab Rosen told me that no organizations filed *amicus curiae* (supporting briefs) in the Skokie litigations because all major groups were reluctant to commit themselves to one side in the controversy.

2. Elite Allies and the Counterdemonstration. Survivor interviewees resented the early procrastination of the ADL, the Jewish Federation, and other Jewish groups, scoffing at the notion that these groups had conflicting responsibilities. They also remained more militant at the end of the controversy, refusing to empathize with the Federation's and village's concerns about the potential violence threatened by the counterdemonstration. An insular, single-issue focus remained at the end, signifying the continuance of a negative gemeinschaft. For example, when I asked Erna Gans if she had developed a wider view of the establishment groups' responsibilities, she replied:

> I would not say that I had changed my mind because I couldn't. And I couldn't understand them. And I felt that their responsibility is to understand us, or the issue, and not to hide like an ostrich, to turn your back "and it will go away." This is a sickness. So they changed their minds . . . It was a long battle with the ADL, to change their minds. [I then asked, "What about ADL's greater responsibilities and pressures?"] Responsibilities? Fine. But pressures? Forget it! But there is no change as far as I am concerned, about the basic issue.

In a similar vein, Stephen and Alex stated that the survivors sometimes viewed the established Jewish leadership as actual enemies. Stephen was more emphatic in this regard. Stephen distrusted Sol Goldstein all along because Goldstein was associated with the Federation and the village government. He also disliked the Federation's counterdemonstration plan because it was based on keeping the survivors and the masses away from the NSPA's presence in order to preserve peace — it was "compromise," a copout. Accordingly, the Federation was a traitor.

> When you talk about the Jewish Federation, I think they are too naive. We went through that in our time, they put us to sleep. History repeats itself. ["You put them in the role of the Judenräte?" I asked.] Yes. They don't understand. It's just like what happened in World War II right here in the United States. When they had to speak up, they were afraid to speak up.

While Stephen's remark is praiseworthy in terms of the need to recognize the existence of evil, it is also unrealistic and extreme in other respects. A more authentic view would have exhibited more of a tragic perspective; it would have combined the assertion to be vigilant with a more realistic appraisal of the Federation's role in America (as Stephen stated earlier, America after all, is not Nazi Germany). And it would have included a greater appreciation of the potential consequences of this type of stand for the First Amendment.

III. Conclusion

In this chapter we have seen that survivors may have gained a sense of mastery as a result of their participation in the Skokie controversy. In some respects the attributes of mastery entail the elements of republican virtue: courage, reasonable trust, activism, and the willingness to confront painful yet politically relevant evil. In this sense, the highest hopes of the First Amendment were met because of the purposive reactions of the targets of bad speech.

At the same time, political education as a realization of a tragic perspective does not appear to have resulted for our survivor interviewees. In the respects discussed, they remained bound to a single-issue negative gemeinschaft. Yet this limit appears to be inherent in the mastery hypothesis itself. Since the will to mastery for the survivors involved a psychological imperative that included reconstructing a past life-and-death struggle, it is perhaps only natural that any mastery gained would overpower the sensitivity required for a tragic view to emerge.

A background development occurred which we did not discuss in this chapter: the gain in knowledge about Nazism and how to mobilize against it. Though the survivor activists certainly shared in this gain (and contributed to it), it was more important for other participants because they are the ones who man the institutions of resistance. Accordingly, we turn to this benefit in the following chapter.

7

Republican Virtue:
Benefits for Other Participants

If there be time to expose through discussion the falsehood and fallacies, to avert the evil by the processes of education, the remedy to be
applied is more speech, not enforced silence. — Justice Brandeis in
Whitney v. California

Democratic societies are accustomed to think in liberal, pragmatic categories; conflicts are believed to be based on misunderstandings and can
be solved with a minimum of good will; extremism is a temporary aber-
ration, so is irrational behaviour in general, such as intolerance, cruelty,
etc. The effort to overcome such basic psychological handicaps is im-
mense. Each new generation faces this challenge again for experience
cannot be inherited. — Walter Laqueur, *The Terrible Secret*

I. Knowledge

A. The Nature and Reality of Nazism

In Chapter Three we saw that the survivor mobilization strategy entailed
imparting knowledge about the exceptional (even *sui generis*) nature of
Nazism and anti-Semitism. The gaining of such knowledge constitutes a
benefit because such knowledge informs its holders of uncomforting politically relevant reality which they might otherwise ignore, thereby enabling
them to deal with that reality more responsibly. The republican virtue justification for the First Amendment stresses this type of learning and responsibility. The evidence suggests that the Skokie controversy transmitted
such knowledge; and this knowledge would *not* have been transmitted had
the First Amendment doctrines governing free speech not provided a real-

111

istic opportunity for the NSPA to socialize the conflict in the courts. Aryeh Neier agrees with this assessment in his interesting book on Skokie:

> The best consequence of the Nazi's proposal to march in Skokie, is that it produced more speech, a great deal more. It stimulated more discussion of the evils of Nazism and of the Holocaust than any event since the Israelis captured Adolf Eichmann in Argentina in 1960 and brought him to Jerusalem to stand trial for war crimes.[1]

Neier's remark pertains to the speech engendered across the Chicago area and the nation. In this section, however, we will focus primarily on the ways in which immediate or active participants gained such politically relevant knowledge.

The process of "conversion" to the survivors' cause came about on a one-to-one and group basis. Participants changed their minds after being exposed to the survivors and their vehement claims. "First it was on a one-to-one basis. You had to convince that one person," said Erna Gans. "Then they were starting to convince others, so then it spread somehow." For non-survivor Jews, the conversion process entailed a modifying or deepening of perspective with an accommodation to the reality depicted by the survivors. This conversion process was the flip side of the "mastery" some survivors came to experience as they acted in the public arena at Skokie. It signified the way in which survivor allies in the Jewish community learned *from the survivors*. Eugene DuBow, the organizer of the final counter-demonstration for the PAC, depicts how the process worked for him:

> I don't feel about Nazis like Goldstein and the survivors. My mother was not thrown into a well. There are two realities to the situation. To me, they were 20 clowns. To Goldstein, the NSPA represented Hitler and his Nazis. But Goldstein said that "Hitler started with seven." And this is a reality, too. I decided to go with his reality, or I'd have to get out of the whole thing. But I got more insight. I can sort of see how he felt. In "rational" American terms, it was an overreaction. But not in the survivors' terms.

Fred Richter, head of the Northwest Suburban Synagogue Council during the conflict, protrayed the conversion process more graphically. His language is that of republican virtue (the willingness to face disturbing facts):

> They [the survivors] added a dimension far beyond any dimension I believed could take place. When I started realizing that the subjective situation was as real to them as the Nazis in Germany, that's a devastating fact for these people. You know, you're talking to Erna Gans now, but if you could have seen her and some of these people when that threat was real, it was an al-

together different situation. It was so near [Nazi Germany], that it became a reality right in front of your eyes. And I knew it was only a handful of guys. It was like nothing anyone had ever experienced. I don't care how much experience you had . . . It focused on what took place historically . . . It brought about the awareness that the past is not as far away as people may think. Not for this little group now. But it doesn't take much for the past to come back and get you — it's the spectre of the past, the depth of this type of evil.

The other leading non-survivor participants expressed similar views. Skokie trustee Charles Conrad (a non-Jew) spoke in a representative vein:

> Their fears and their terrors were very real in their minds. See *War and Remembrance* — incredible things happened that these people went through. You can't imagine . . . I argued I didn't think it's fair to draw an analogy between fascist Germany and democratic America. But you can't categorically say, either, that it couldn't happen here. I had a learning experience this way, though I'm not sure it worked the other way.[2]

B. Political Mobilization

> "Even if the received opinion be not only true, but the whole truth; unless it is suffered to be, and actually is, vigorously and earnestly contested, it will, by most of those who receive it, be held in the manner of prejudice, with little comprehension or feeling of its rational grounds. And not only this, but . . . the meaning of the doctrine itself will be in danger of being lost or enfeebled." — John Stuart Mill, *On Liberty*

1. Institutional Features. Another important benefit accrued to the participants, especially the Jews: knowledge about mobilization against anti-Semitism. Though the survivors shared in this benefit, I include it here because it mainly concerns the larger Jewish community. As we have seen, Skokie mobilization was massive, as thousands of people and groups from all over the country planned to come to Skokie to confront the Nazis. In this section I will examine this result in relation to the major Jewish political groups.

In *The Functions of Social Conflict* Lewis Coser develops and elaborates on sixteen propositions concerning the benefits of social conflict.[3] His propositions and conclusions parallel Mill's arguments in favor of free speech in many respects. This point is important as the Supreme Court has held that the "discord" caused by some speech is often beneficial for society.[4] The most relevant propositions for our purposes are the following, which I have derived from Coser's work by a process of codification:

1) conflict helps groups define themselves and their boundaries, increasing their internal cohesion and adjusting policy to reality; 2) concomitantly, conflict can create a heightened commitment to value; 3) conflict can lead to the beneficial creation of associations and coalitions.

The Skokie conflict engendered controversy and debate within major Jewish groups, some of whom changed their policies concerning anti-Semitism and Nazi demonstrations. Many also joined the Skokie counter-demonstration coalition. The local (Midwest) ADL, the National American Jewish Congress, and the National Jewish Community Relations Advisory Council (NJCRAC) revised their established quarantine policies in favor of selective confrontations designed to support the community.[5] Interviewees who prominently participated in the debates over Skokie and the quarantine policy in the national conventions of the NJCRAC, American Jewish Committee, American Jewish Congress, and ADL reported that the issue played a substantial (even dominating) role at these meetings.[6]

The American Jewish Committee and the NJCRAC did not support Skokie's *legal* efforts, but they did adopt new counterdemonstration policies. For example, a year after Skokie, a California Nazi group obtained a permit to hold a rally in Walnut Creek, a suburb about ten miles east of Oakland. The East Bay American Jewish Committee community relations head, Bob Jacobvitz, worked in concert with local Jews and political leaders to plan support systems and to defuse the Nazis' impact. Skokie had taught them two lessons, according to Jacobvitz. First, that the issue cannot be simply ignored. Second, that *too much* publicity may play into the Nazis' hands (at Skokie, of course, the Jewish leaders aggressively utilized publicity because by the time they became involved the issue had *already* been highly publicized). In response to the lessons, the committee advocated quarantining the actual demonstration, while it sponsored numerous meetings before the demonstration in order to promote support for Jews outside the immediate demonstration arena. This policy represented a compromise between the old quarantine policy and the Skokie counterdemonstration plan. Jacobvitz also worked with the press, not asking it to censor itself, but rather to exercise responsibility in its coverage of the issue and the actual demonstration. According to Jacobvitz, this strategy worked.[7]

As a result of the education provided by Skokie, Jewish groups had the institutional means of resistance and public education in place. Fred Richter of the Northwest Suburban Synagogue Council told me that Skokie "improved channels of action"; it "proved it [action] can reach down deep into the community and across the country and effectuate change." Skokie is "a verification of the fact that that vehicle is in place." This result certainly constitutes a beneficial consequence, for it means that Skokie compelled the Jewish establishment to arm itself more adequately against the potential threat of targeted, assaultive anti-Semitism. As we have seen, the establishment was conservative at the start of the Skokie controversy, stuck in the rut of the quarantine policy which was, in many respects, rather comfortable to live with.[8] The Skokie issue put pressure on the establishment to revise its policies and rededicate itself to Jewish interests by formulating more active plans to deal with threats in the public forum. This result is a victory for republican virtue.

To the extent that the Skokie conflict engendered knowledge and mobilization among Skokie leaders, the Jewish establishment, and the public, free speech for Nazis is supported on utilitarian grounds because it compelled the reaction under discussion. Without the spur of Frank Collin's provocation in speech, these difficult-to-achieve benefits would not have been realized. The results appear similar to those which the ADL discovered in a study of previous outbreaks of anti-Semitic acts. *Swastika 1960: The Epidemic of Anti-Semitic Vandalism in America* addressed the consequences of anti-Semitic acts of vandalism in the New York City area in 1960. On one hand, the authors found that publicity about such acts encouraged further acts. On the other hand, publicity triggered outpourings of support for Jewish rights:

> In addition to informing the public that the incidents had occurred, the media also published reactions to the outbreak — and the reactions were uniformly negative. Religious, civic, and political leaders alike condemned the incidents in the strongest terms. Regardless of the actual level of anti-Semitism the epidemic represented, it called forth a unanimous denunciation of religious intolerance and a public reaffirmation of the principles of brotherhood. We do not know what long-range effects the reiteration of this public morality may have. It is possible that once the crisis passed, the feelings passed also . . . But it is also possible that because of the crisis itself, new agencies of cooperation were created, dormant patterns of collaboration were reactivated, and the Jewish community was reassured about the good will of its neighbors . . .
>
> Just as the epidemic may have taught some to be anti-Semitic, it may have taught others not to be.[9]

Whether or not this result occurred in New York in 1960, the evidence emphatically indicates that it did in the Skokie controversy. Perhaps the activism which ensues from such dramatic episodes is not permanent in the scheme of things. But no episode in the American politics of anti-Semitism caused the revision of the quarantine policy until Skokie or such an outpouring of resistance. The evidence suggests that the impact of Skokie will be substantial.

2. Deterrence. The last type of benefit to the Jewish community is the establishment of the deterrence factor against anti-Semitism and racialist threats. Deterrence signals to hate-mongers that the targets of their hate will protect their dignity and interests. It is also an indication of the willingness to take action (to engage in mastery), and it informs potential allies that support may be expected sometime in the future. A successful deterrence policy requires the mobilization of support for two reasons: 1) it creates a resource which the protest group may use to gain more powerful allies in the fight against the foe;[10] 2) it contributes more directly to the display of force or power against the foe. At Skokie, survivors generated enough power and support to gain favorable legislation and the allegiance of elites. For example, by the end of the controversy, the Springfield legislature almost passed a new group libel law. In addition, the survivors and the Jewish community mobilized enough support to compel Collin to back out of his Skokie plans. Though the threat of violence at the counterdemonstration must be viewed as a harmful consequence, the concomitant success of the Jewish community's mobilization and the message it must have given to potential anti-Semitic groups must be viewed as a positive consequence. As Sol Goldstein and other activists stressed, the message was that the Jewish community would no longer sit back and acquiesce in directed attacks against its dignity and security. In the politics of hate, the presentation of this resolve is valuable, however regrettable its necessity may be. Stephen's son, John, is an activist lawyer in Jewish affairs; he told me that he actually welcomed the controversy because he knew it would compel activism in the name of deterrence.

> I know that that particular confrontation (with Collin) I welcomed, because I felt that there would be some good out of it. I thought that it would awaken people to a real danger that I still think exists. The problem in Europe was that people were not always aware of it. I felt a very similar feeling that I feel when Wiesenthal finds another one of these criminals in society, completely hidden and then he's exposed for what he was. I think there's an element of justice there, an element of identifying and delineating what has really happened. And I think that a Collin trying to march in Skokie after the Jews — it's not a good thing, I'd rather have it not *occur* — but as long as there are people thinking that way, *there's something good about them coming out and saying it.*[11]

II. Debate About Free Speech: Paradoxical Benefit

A final aspect of public debate should be touched on, even though it is outside the main purview of my analysis of benefits, which has focused on the political education concerning Nazism and resistance and on the development of republican virtue. This other aspect is debate about free speech. Undoubtedly Skokie spawned a great deal of discussion among participants and the general public about the *meaning* of free speech.

Some ACLU spokesmen complained that most of the commentary to which they were exposed (in the press, at meetings, over the phone, etc.) was of a poor quality. While Aryeh Neier proclaimed that the level of public debate over the First Amendment constituted a major beneficial consequence of the Skokie controversy,[12] the Illinois ACLU spokesmen I interviewed were much less sanguine. Illinois executive director David Hamlin bemoaned the lack of sophistication in the public discourse concerning the First Amendment. He alleged that the press stressed the "social" (the resistance) as opposed to the "legal" issues, and that they continuously misstated the facts in the case and in First Amendment precedent.[13] He also maintained to me that Skokie and the PAC missed the opportunity to provide legal education in the courts because they reacted too quickly and forcefully. "Had the issue been handled subtly, it would have been a marvelous education in the courts — had they not come at it with a goddamn baseball bat!"

Hamlin's comments are hard to evaluate because of the complex and subtle nature of the data. But a look at some of my interviewee statements above and at the *reporting* (as distinct from the editorializing) of the press appears to partially confirm his allegation. For example, as late as June 1978 the Chicago press still talked about a Nazi "march through" Skokie, even though the NSPA never intended to "march through" anything, but rather to demonstrate just in front of village hall.[14] And *if* one were to accept Hamlin's terms and view a pro-Skokie position as "unsophisticated" (as it is allegedly "undemocratic")[15] then the public opinion polls taken during the controversy bear him out. Two polls taken of public opinion in Illinois and in Skokie near the end of the controversy found that substantial majorities felt that the First Amendment *should* not allow *any* public demonstrations by American Nazi parties, either in Skokie or elsewhere;[16] and another poll of Illinois residents taken in May 1978 found that 57 percent of 436 Skokie residents polled felt that the constitution *did not* grant the Nazis the right to "march in Skokie," even though the state and federal courts had previously confirmed such a right in resounding fashion.[17]

Yet the matter is not so simple. First, as David Goldberger of the ACLU affirmed in his interview, the *editorial* content of the major Chicago newspapers was consistently of a high intellectual quality:

> The media handled the issue very superficially, to sell papers. I wrote a speech to criticize the media, but said "Fuck it." I had enough enemies as it was. But the editorials were good, even those who disagreed with us were thoughtful about the constitutional issues.[18]

Second, even assuming that survey polls adequately capture the meaning of respondents' views (a rather dubious assumption), they cannot be said to adequately portray the level of political education about free speech itself which took place. One of the most interesting features of the Skokie conflict appears to be the way in which participants related the free speech issue to the "social question" or the *context* of the application of the right. This process is of the utmost importance because constitutional policy must always address the context of rights if it is to be responsible. Indeed, conceptions of reality and morality cannot be grasped adequately without recognition of the social environment within which they are embedded.[19]

We have seen that interviewees discussed both the First Amendment and the "social" issues in the controversy. Other interesting examples are found in an article by John J. Camper in *The National Jewish Monthly* about Skokie and the poll taken by Northwestern University on the question of the Nazis' constitutional rights. As seen, 57 percent of Skokie respondents said that the Nazis did not have such a right. Yet Camper interviewed some Skokie residents himself and discovered that many gave rather interesting and legitimate reasons for their anti-free speech position. One (a shoe clerk) made both legal and social arguments in a statement that shows how exposure to the "social" question made a person with racist tendencies a bit less racist:

> There's a fine line between the right to assemble and incitement to riot. I heard one of those Nazis on a talk show. His speech really got me aggravated. He said the Jews and colored are subhuman. That's going too far. I don't like the colored too much, but that speech really made me anti-Nazi.[20]

Another (a secretary) said:

> It's horrible. It should never be allowed. It makes me ill. I don't think that means I'm against free speech. The Nazis are against what we believe in. People came to this country to be free from that kind of thing. Now we have it marching right down the street. I'm not Jewish, but I despise anyone putting people down.[21]

These remarks are suggestive for two important reasons. First, they show how the social issue cannot be separated too much from the First Amendment issue.[22] Second, they suggest (as do many of the comments made by interviewees) that the "social" question at Skokie cannot be relegated to a secondary status *precisely because it invokes a principle which is just as fundamental as the principle of freedom of speech*: the right to be treated with the respect due free citizens, which means not to be targeted by vilifying speech. The ACLU's legalistic position disparaged the "social" issue at Skokie because it never could escape from the perceptual and intellectual limitations of the "heckler's veto" doctrine: all hostile resistance to speech is a mere "heckler's veto" and (as Judge Decker argued in *Collin v. Smith*) there is no way to distinguish justified from unjustified resistance or vetoes. However, Camper's interviewees (like my interviewees) believed that Skokie resisters were not simply reacting viscerally to speech that they *happened* to find "offensive" (the term used by Judge Decker), but rather because the NSPA threat violated a democratic principle that is coeval with the principle of free speech.[23]

This claim will provide the normative basis for our constitutional analysis in Chapter Eight. Yet I raise it in this final chapter on beneficial consequences because it helps to reveal that the public debate about free speech generated by the Skokie conflict was indeed both sophisticated and beneficial, even though most of the public surveyed disagreed with the First Amendment position defended by the ACLU. There is no question that a great deal of debate about the *limits* (or delimitation) of the First Amendment in relation to its context and application[24] occurred at Skokie. Such debate is clearly as valuable in our society as debates in favor of the First Amendment's absoluteness or extension.

In this respect, Ab Rosen's statement that the Skokie conflict involved a "contest between the good and the good" provides a basis for understanding the final beneficial consequence of the controversy. When all is said and done, Skokie boiled down to a debate over fundamental or first principles of liberal, constitutional democracy. That is, it embroiled its participants in a form of political action and participation which required them to engage in political theory. Thomas Kuhn's theory of "scientific revolutions" is analogous in some respects. Kuhn maintains that new theoretical "paradigms" arise when fundamental controversies or crises erupt over the inadequacy of previously accepted theory to account for new facts.[25] A similar process occurred at Skokie in the political and constitutional realms. Such a renewal of fundamental debate is essential in a free society that evolves and changes while maintaining a commitment to its most basic principles. Astute theorists of social and political conflict have pointed out that such conflict is often good because it facilitates the adjustment to change and renews the understanding of (and commitment to) fundamental values.[26]

This conclusion leaves us with an irony, however, for this debate over fundamental principles was due to the very libertarian doctrine of the First Amendment that the Skokie resisters challenged. Had the courts upheld Skokie's legal barriers, the great debate may not have taken place. It is for reasons such as this that free speech has been given a "transcendent value" by the courts and libertarian theorists.[27] Accordingly, this final benefit of the Skokie conflict must be viewed ambivalently. On one hand, it supports the libertarian position of Mill and Brandeis because free speech for Nazis at Skokie spurred this fundamental debate; on the other hand, the content of the debate suggests that this very position should be questioned.

III. Conclusion: The Task of Chapter Eight

The process of free speech at Skokie contributed to debate about the nature of Nazism and about the principles and limits of free speech itself. These results are praiseworthy and consistent with the norms of republican virtue. When the result of mastery is added to these consequences, a strong case for positive consequences can be made. At the same time, however, the content of the debate over the free speech principle poses the normative policy question: did the speech right extend too far at Skokie despite the beneficial results we found? For as we saw in Chapter Five, the controversy also generated substantial harms, such as emotional trauma, the breakdown of civility, and the threat of massive violence.

The analysis of harms and benefits, including the analysis of the debate over First Amendment and democratic principle, has been fraught with the central tension with which this study began: the tension between procedural and substantive justice. Participation in the process of debate at Skokie led to important beneficial consequences which are hoped for by such free speech advocates as Mill, Brandeis, and Meiklejohn. Yet significant harms also resulted which invoke other, counter-principles of democratic society. As will be elaborated in Chapter Eight, the most relevant counter-principle entails equality (of which dignity and respect are constituent parts) and the right to be protected against unjustified intimidation. These principles are substantive. In essence, the Skokie conflict can be reduced to the following issue: to what extent does the speech of hate groups suggest the substantive limits of procedural justice (when do the principles of substantive justice outweigh the principles of precedural-participatory justice?). That is, to what extent does the Skokie conflict suggest the minimal reconsideration of the First Amendment's content neutrality rule, which has been grounded on the principles of procedural justice?

8

Assaultive and Non-Assaultive Racialist Expression

Terror as we know it today strikes without any preliminary provocation, its victims are innocent even from the point of view of the persecutor. This was the case in Nazi Germany when full terror was directed against the Jews, i.e., against people with certain common characteristics which were independent of their specific behavior . . . it is decisive that they are objectively innocent, that they are chosen regardless of what they may or may not have done.—Hannah Arendt, *The Origins of Totalitarianism*

I. Introduction

The purpose of this chapter is twofold. I want to show why the harms of the NSPA speech threat outweighed the benefits at Skokie, however substantial the latter may have been, and I intend to demonstrate that *the type* of speech act at Skokie engenders harms which justify a reconsideration of the present constitutional law of the public forum outlined in Chapter One of this work. In making this demonstration, I will show how *targeted racial vilification,* such as that which took place at Skokie, is fundamentally different from other forms of racialist speech and targeted expression concerning racial issues. I hope to refute a central assumption in Judge Decker's decision in *Collin v. Smith*: that "A society which values 'uninhibited, robust, and wide-open' debate cannot permit criminal sanctions to turn upon so fine a distinction"[1] as mine. We will see that Judge Decker ignores the difference between *targeted* hate messages and non-targeted forms, and thereby fails to account for the difference between speech which is inherently or directly assaultive and speech which engenders tension but is not *inherently* assaultive. Finally, I will show how such harmful expression violates the basic values of constitutional democracy.

122

II. The Harms Outweigh the Benefits:
Skokie-like Cases and the Principle of Harm

We saw in the last section that substantial benefits such as mastery, mobilization for deterrence, republican virtue, and political education were achieved at Skokie in reaction to the NSPA proposal, and that these benefits were similar in important respects to those hoped for by pro-free speech theorists. At the same time, we saw that significant harms also resulted: the survivors were terrorized because the NSPA threat caused them to relive their past nightmares. We confront an enigma in weighing harms and benefits.

The enigma is resolvable by two means. First, by recognizing (perhaps surprisingly) that there are other, similar cases which actually could pose more severe harms than those that arose at Skokie: the type of harm inflicted by the NSPA at Skokie can be seen as an instance of a general class of harms engendered by assaultive speech. This is important because we are now concerned with constitutional policy, which means that we must consider all cases arising within the general class of Skokie-like speech acts. Second, the enigma may be solved by applying a weak version of the Kantian principle of ultimate ends, which maintains that individuals shall not be treated as the means of other people's ends. A corollary of this principle is the distinction between direct and indirect harms which provides the basis for distinguishing assaultive from non-assaultive speech in terms of legitimacy.

A. Skokie and Similar Cases

1. Equity versus General Rules. Non-survivor interviewees who were active in the Skokie conflict told me that one irony (or limit) in their legal stand against free speech was the fact that the Skokie case was *sui generis*: the harm was special because the survivors (who *made* Skokie an issue) were exceptionally vulnerable. Fred Richter told me that "the funny thing is that in a few years, when the survivors are all dead, this kind of case probably won't happen again." At the same time, however, Richter and others argued against granting First Amendment protection to the general class of racialist speech, especially when directed against the community of the object of the racism. Some interviewees actually confused these two approaches, calling for special consideration for Skokie at one time, and for general laws against racial vilification at other times.[2]

These two prongs were expressed in the legal cases. On one hand, the

Skokie injunction and the *Goldstein* tort case were predicated on the twin principles of equity and special relief;[3] each case began in the equity courts of Cook County. Equity involves the principle of individualized and natural justice;[4] claims of equity are made when individual cases arise which cannot be resolved by the existing general rules without causing injustice (the *sense* of justice is violated). On the other hand, the Skokie ordinances were directed to the general class of racialist vilification.

Though the evidence presented in earlier chapters supports the equity claim concerning the survivors' uniqueness, it is better to address the issue from the other perspective. First, the rule of law is better protected by the reliance upon general rules than upon equity because general rules do a better job of providing predictability concerning the legal consequences of one's actions; accordingly, it is advisable to respond to the claims of equity by modifying and revising the rules rather than to sanction exceptions in court.[5] This method is especially advisable in the free speech area, for the unpredictable nature of equity decisions would threaten the same chilling effect that vague and overbroad laws threaten.[6] Consequently, we should address the general class of racial vilification rather than consider Skokie a special, unrepeatable case. In addition, evidence reveals that the Skokie case is *not sui generis*.

2. Skokie and Other Harmful Cases. Although Skokie *was* an especially difficult case because of what the ACLU called the "social" issue (the survivors' vulnerability), in other respects it actually represents an *easier* case in "social" terms than some other cases of its class. After all, the traumatized survivors gained the overwhelming support of the community and they galvanized this support into a substantial resistance front. While the NSPA played on the "sociology" of terror in the beginning at Skokie, the sociological circumstances at Skokie also provided the basis for ensuing support. The "mastery" hypothesis, in fact, relied upon this community of support.

Harder cases arise when the targets are less highly organized or are more isolated from a community of support. In recent years hate groups, in particular Ku Klux Klan and Nazi groups, have systematically engaged in targeted intimidations of more or less *isolated* racial or ethnic minorities within majority-race areas or neighborhoods. The Southern Poverty Law Center keeps a constant watch on Klan and Nazi activity and publishes a bimonthly *Poverty Law Review* which includes a *Klanwatch Intelligence Report.* In its May/June 1982 edition, the center reported that the Klan is increasingly engaging in symbolic acts designed to intimidate minorities and to generate publicity:

Nationwide, while the Klan currently does not appear to be making great strides in recruiting, Klan members themselves are engaging in a wide variety of publicity-seeking activities, ranging from road blocks to cross burnings. In addition, acts of racially-motivated vandalism, harassment and intimidation by groups and individuals influenced by the militant right continue to occur with alarming frequency.[7]

Most of the acts of intimidation involve physical destruction or entering of property which go beyond the symbolic and speech acts protected by the First Amendment. Yet some involve the wearing of hoods or other hate symbols in front of homes or in the targeted neighborhood, thereby evoking fear in the targets of hate. The California Fair Housing and Employment Commission held extensive hearings in late 1981 on the disturbing frequence of hate group vandalism and intimidation in Contra Costa County, California. The county sheriff told the commission that the Klan used symbols

> for harassment value . . . what they are trying to do is scare the people . . . and it's very, very, effective. The KKK is a very scary organization . . . using those things, whether or not they are involved themselves with the KKK, is going to throw some fear into the neighborhood, that's exactly what they meant to do.[8]

Though the targets of this type of speech normally lack the exceptional antecedent psychological vulnerability of the Skokie survivors, their sociological circumstances are often less propitious. For example, the first black family to move into a white neighborhood would normally feel vulnerable to such intimidation. If targeted racialist vilification or intimidation is inherently traumatic (as I hope to demonstrate below), then such targets are as entitled to constitutional protection as Skokie survivors.

B. The Kantian Principle of Ultimate Ends and the Principle of Direct Harm

1. Kant and Assaultive Speech. In the *Groundwork of the Metaphysics of Morals,* Kant articulates the moral principle of ultimate ends:

> Now I say that man, and in general every rational being, *exists* as an end in himself, *not merely as a means* for arbitrary use by this or that will: he must in all his actions, whether they are directed to himself or to other rational beings, always be viewed *at the same time as an end* . . . The practical imperative will therefore be as follows: *Act in such a way that you always treat humanity, whether in your own person or in the person of any other, never simply as a means, but always at the same time as an end.*[9]

Kant's principle of ultimate ends counsels against the undue sacrifice of the individual's interest in the name of the greater societal good. In this respect, it underlies the theory of individual rights and is a major premise of constitutionalism.[10] Yet it may pose the same problem of absolutism as Weber's depiction of the ethic of ultimate ends, at least as long as one pursued it without reservation. Kant's moral theory is "categorical" in the sense that it is not contingent upon empirical consequences or the demonstration of actual harm. Consequently, the Kantian principle of ultimate ends is absolutist in nature. For example, pure Kantian principle would not allow one to distinguish speech acts in terms of the nature of the harm they caused. Hadley Arkes, who adopts a Kantian view on racialist expression, maintains that general racial defamation that does not directly cause the harm of intimidation is just as unjustified and abridgeable as racialist expression that *does cause* such a harm. Arkes rejects merely singling out direct harms for abridgement because "the estimate of material harms often depends on empirical evidence and conjectures, and on propositions of a statistical nature. It rests, in other words, on what we would have to call 'contingent truths,' rather than the kinds of truth or principles that 'cannot be otherwise'."[11]

Yet we will see later in this chapter that laws against *all* racialist expression or group libel threaten First Amendment rights, and that many forms of racialist expression do not inflict direct and substantial harm. Indeed, we have seen that Skokie itself witnessed even *beneficial* reactions to the NSPA's expression. Thus, the strict Kantian position in this area seems incompatible with what Frederick Schauer calls the "free speech principle," which holds that free speech is so fundamentally and independently important to democratic life that it merits special constitutional protection on a systematic basis.[12] When the principle of ultimate ends collides with the free speech principle, a judge must make a prudent yet principled choice among values which a strict Kantian would be loathe to make. Respect for the free speech principle demands that a balance be struck in the spirit of Weber's ethic of responsibility, which governs a tragic world. This balance should clearly accommodate free speech. Accordingly, I suggest the following rule for the balancing of values: *the more substantial and direct the harm, the more compelling the principle of ultimate ends.* This is similar to the Supreme Court's balancing of speech versus societal interests under "strict" judicial review (in which the societal interest must be "compelling" in order for a narrowly tailored speech restriction to be valid).[13] This use of the Kantian maxim is *weak* rather than *strong,* for it tolerates a prudential (yet principled) balancing of values based on consequences which the strict Kantian position would not allow.[14]

This approach serves as a tool to distinguish justified from unjustified resistance to free speech. There is a difference between a speech act that appeals to reason and the conscience and one which is primarily assaultive; the former treats listeners or targets as rational, autonomous agents, whereas the latter clearly treats them, in Kant's words, "merely as a means for arbitrary use by this or that will." Kant's maxim concerns the *willful* use of individuals as means.[15] In our discussion of fighting words and the speech acts of "extremist groups," we saw that such speech treats targets as victims or as means to bring about disruption and publicity, and that the NSPA consciously targeted Skokie for these reasons. Their behavior at Marquette Park and other areas indicates that the vicious treatment of others as means constitutes the very *modus operandi* of the NSPA.

One means of applying the weak principle of ultimate ends may be derived from Charles Fried's analysis of the distinction between direct and indirect harms, a distinction I will use as a standard for delimiting the right to free speech. Fried compares two hypothetical cases: 1) plunging a dagger into someone's heart; 2) revaluing the currency with the foreseeable result that wheat will be less available for famine relief, which would result in greater hunger abroad, perhaps even starvation. Fried maintains that if we could not say that the former act constituted a special harm that is morally more grievous than the latter, "then our whole position as free moral agents, our status as persons, would be grievously undermined," because we would jeopardize the notion that concrete persons as "particular entities" are the basis of the moral order.

> If the person is to remain at the center of moral judgment, this link to the concrete must be maintained by the very form of our moral norms. We must avoid what I shall call disintegrating universality.[16]

Fried's theory of disintegrating universality is useful in distinguishing forms of speech and in balancing the Kantian principle of ultimate ends. Speech acts which directly and purposely harm others, those which "by their very utterance inflict injury" (to use *Chaplinsky*'s language), are morally less justifiable than those which result in harm as a secondary consequence, but which are primarily meant to appeal to reason or the conscience. In addition, speech that is threatening in content but is *not directed at* a particular target would not constitute a direct harm (this is a *strong* application of Fried's harm principle, for here the *motive* is bad — as it is *not* in unpopular appeals to the conscience or in revaluing the currency — yet the *effect* is not tangibly or directly harmful). The Supreme Court has correctly held that political speech is not sheerly cerebral, that it can be passionate, provocative, and upsetting as well, and that the First Amendment protects it despite this consequence. In *Terminiello v. Chicago,* Justice Doug-las stated that "A function of free speech under our system of government is to invite dispute. It may indeed best serve its high purpose when it in-duces a condition of unrest, creates dissatisfaction with conditions as they are, or even stirs people to anger."[17] The courts relied on similar logic in the *Cohen* case and in the Skokie cases.

These cases express the view that discord, tumult, and the stirring of anger are side effects of the core purposes of the First Amendment as those have been classically stated in *Chaplinsky.* In Fried's terms, they are in-direct harms (at worst — conflict can also be beneficial to groups and the system, as Douglas affirms in *Terminiello*).[18] Yet when the *primary purpose* of speech is not communication, but rather the infliction of harm, and that purpose is successful, we can no longer construe harm as secondary, and the principle of disintegrating universality does not apply. In a 1978 com-mercial speech case, *Ohralik v. Ohio State Bar,* the Supreme Court ruled that a state may forbid in-person solicitation of clients by lawyers because such speech is not consistent with the purposes of the First Amendment, which involve rational political or public discourse. Although in-person solicitation is different from assaultive speech, the Court's logic is relevant:

> In-person solicitation by a lawyer of remunerative employment is a busi-ness transaction in which speech is an essential but subordinate component. While this does not remove the speech from the protection of the First Amend-ment, as was held in *Bates* and *Virginia Pharmacy,* it lowers the level of ap-propriate judicial scrutiny. A lawyer's procurement of remunerative employ-ment is a subject only marginally affected with First Amendment concerns.[19]

Ohralik addresses the distinction between primary and secondary harm, and, concomitantly, the primary and secondary purposes of speech. The primary purpose of racial vilification is assaultive, as we will demonstrate. Indeed, *a fortiori,* if speech is secondary in in-person solicitation, it is sec-ondary in targeted racial vilification; for in such cases, the harm is inflicted for more vicious ends.

The Court has fashioned a similar normative approach in the area of libel. On one hand, it has held that the First Amendment protects the libel of *public* officials (unless made with malice) because the First Amendment needs "breathing space."[20] Judge Decker utilized this logic to overturn Skokie's ordinances in *Collin v. Smith.*[21] These cases espouse the standard that *sometimes harmful (or potentially harmful) speech must be protected in order to ensure the protection of potentially beneficial speech.* On the other hand, the Court has allowed liability if the libel of a public official is made with malice (e.g., with knowledge that it is false, or with reckless disregard of its falsity)[22] and its treatment of the libel of *private* figures shows its concern for competing values. In *Gertz v. Robert Welch,* the Court held that libel of private figures is not protected, even if it is non-malicious.[23] Such speech is less associated with (or less a by-product of) valuable speech than is libel of public officials. And it *harms* its targets more because they have fewer resources of retaliation or refutation and (more importantly) because they have not voluntarily exposed themselves to public scrutiny as have public officials. That is, *the speech is less valuable, and its harm is both greater and less justifiable given the status of its targets.* So private figures are subject to the principle of ultimate ends as modified by the principle of direct harm.

Skokie survivors claimed a similar status. Frank Collin and the NSPA purposely sought to traumatize Skokie Jews and survivors. Skokie survivors felt symbolically assaulted. Collin told me: "I caused the reaction of the Jews. They are hysterical." And to columnist Bob Greene: "I hope they're terrified. Because we are coming to get them again."[24] Moreover, the NSPA left thousands of vile anti-Semitic leaflets on doorsteps of North Shore residents at an embryonic stage in the controversy.

Compare these actions to those of demonstrators in *Cox v. Louisiana,*[25] *Edwards v. South Carolina,*[26] and *Williams v. Wallace* (the Selma case),[27] cases discussed in Chapter One. In these cases, no direct harm was intended in the manner of the NSPA at Skokie. Civil rights demonstrators appealed to the conscience and reason of the audience, stressing the injustice of racism. They were not "extremist," as we have used that term. Though the Selma case certainly involved a substantial hostile crowd reaction (whereas the crowds in *Cox* and *Edwards* were less threatening), it is distinguishable from Skokie because of the nature of the speech. The cause of Martin Luther King (the major Selma activist) was fundamentally different from the cause of Frank Collin. To be sure, King's Selma strategy *was* designed to *provoke* a strong reaction in order to create a major public issue. According to David Garrow, King, like Gandhi,

> came to appreciate more and more the view of coercion which Reinhold Niebuhr had articulated . . . What Niebuhr wrote of Gandhi in 1932 is equally applicable to King: "He came finally to realize the necessity of some type of physical coercion upon the foes of his people's freedom, as every leader must."[28]

Yet none of the leaders at Selma made racial *threats.* They simply engaged in public demonstrations to protest the denial of their right to vote. They knew a hostile crowd would meet them, but they did not provoke the crowd by prior intimidation or racial vilification as did the NSPA at Skokie.

A comparison of Collin's writings in the Nazi publication *New Order* with King's famous "Letter From a Birmingham Jail"[29] supports this distinction. Whereas Collin's "writings" exhibit pathological hate and vilification (recall the discussion of *New Order* in Chapter Two), King's letter exhibits love of justice and the willingness to engage in civil disobedience to promote justice. King also explicitly refers to the *humanity* of the opposition while Collin refers to their *inhumanity*. Whereas King's politics represent the more or less selfless dedication to justice of classic civil disobedience,[30] Collin's politics represent utter selfishness and manipulation of others for the party's own ends. In Walter Berns' terms, King practiced "moral anger,"[31] whereas Collin immorally incited anger in vulnerable targets. To be sure, Collin and the NSPA do engage in speech and "moral anger" about such racial public policy issues as busing, forced integration, and affirmative action. Judge Decker emphasized this point in *Collin v. Smith*. Such discourse is clearly entitled to First Amendment protection. But Decker did not pay sufficient heed to all the expressive acts of intimidation which accompanied or preceded these more substantive policy proclamations at Skokie. He ignored (in legal terms, at least) the unmistakable primary intent of the NSPA to inflict trauma in order to hold Skokie hostage, and he ignored the success of this intent.

So King's speech act at Selma, though coercive, is reconcilable with the principle of ultimate ends, whereas Collin's speech concerning Skokie is not. The court decisions in the Skokie cases reveal those courts' supra-legal recognition of this difference, even though they supported the NSPA's speech right. But while the Illinois and federal courts in the Skokie cases apologized for their decisions, thereby tacitly acknowledging the incongruity between justice and law in their decisions (see Chapters One and Four), U.S. District Judge Frank Johnson explicitly predicated his decision concerning the Selma march on the sense of justice:

> There must be in cases like the one now presented, a "constitutional boundary line" drawn between the competing interests of society. In so doing, it seems basic to our constitutional principles that the extent of the right to assemble, demonstrate and march peaceably along the highways and streets in an orderly manner *should be commensurate with the enormity of the wrongs* that are being protested and petitioned against. In this case, the wrongs are enormous. The extent of the right to demonstrate against these wrongs should be determined accordingly.[32]

2. Substantive Justice and the Content Neutrality Rule. At the time it was decided, U.S. Attorney General Nicholas Katzenbach called Johnson's Selma decision "unusual," stating that Johnson "had to interpret existing doctrine imaginatively in order to give the march from Selma to Montgomery the protection of a court order."[33] Yet such a decision would be unusual under the reign of the current content neutrality rule (which ascended the throne after Selma) for another reason: it takes the substantive justice of the speech claim seriously. Given Johnson's logic, Collin would have lost at Skokie, for the historical "enormity of wrong" had been committed by Nazis against Jews, not vice versa. Like the victims of libel, Skokie survivors and Jews did not deserve the injuries inflicted upon them by vicious parties. Judge Johnson's logic in the Selma case would have accounted for these facts. Yet given the content neutrality rule, Johnson's logic (the "commensurity theorem")[34] is illegitimate because it takes the ends and substance of the speech claim seriously.

It seems that the type of speech practiced by Frank Collin and others is distinguishable from speech about racial and other political matters which is not directly assaultive but is nonetheless either provocative due to its controversial nature or is assaultive in content but not directed at a target. But if we are to endorse a change in constitutional policy in this area, we must establish the nature and extent of the harm of targeted racial vilification more concretely. A *compelling* societal interest must be demonstrated, and the nature and limits of this interest must be established. The discussion of Fried's principle of direct harm in this section has shown that speech acts may be morally culpable when they are made with bad motives *and* when they directly harm (the strict Kantian position expressed by Arkes stresses motives alone). Thus, the perpetration of direct, substantial harms in which persons are treated as means rather than ends forms the basis of our investigation.[35] We must now find out whether racial vilification constitutes such harm, and if so, under what circumstances.

III. Application of the Free Speech and Harm Principles to Skokie and Similar Cases

In this section we will analyze actual and hypothetical cases in order to demonstrate why *targeted racial vilification* inflicts a harm which is substantial enough to give rise to a compelling state interest in the abridgement of the expression. Targeted racial vilification is *derogatory reference*

to race directed at a predetermined target for the purpose of intimidation.
My method in this demonstration is twofold. First, I will show how targeted racial vilification inflicts a special kind of harm which is clearly distinguishable from the harms caused by other forms of unpopular, disputatious speech. Second, I will show how such speech is inconsistent with
the basic liberal values and justifications of the First Amendment, as well
as with a balanced principle of ultimate ends.

A. The Basic Values of the First Amendment

The free speech values we will utilize in the following analysis are a codification of the free speech justifications discussed in Chapter One: self-
government (which includes republican virtue) and autonomy. Alexander
Meiklejohn provides the most powerful theory of free speech as self-
government. His theory utilizes the concept of autonomy in relation to
political participation and deliberation over political issues. According to
Meiklejohn, the citizenry is the ultimate governor of the polity. When it
comes to the question of what politically relevant ideas shall be offered
and accepted in the public forum, the people must be allowed to decide
for themselves which ideas are good and which ideas are bad. If the government censors or punishes such ideas because of an *undifferentiated* fear
of their acceptance, the government usurps the process of intellectual and
moral autonomy and responsibility which constitutes the heart of self-
government.[36]

While the autonomy principle forms a constituent part of the self-
government principle, its adherents also apply it to forms of expression
which lie outside the domain of "political" speech. For example, Mill's notion of liberty in *On Liberty* makes no distinction between political and
non-political speech (though most of his examples, significantly, concern
political matters or moral disputes that clearly impinge on politics). Mill's
liberty-autonomy principle is defined and endorsed in Thomas Scanlon's
influential essay, "A Theory of Freedom of Expression." Scanlon maintains
that the "Millian principle" means that:

> Certain consequences of speech cannot be grounds for abridgement if the
> resultant harms are: a) harms to certain individuals which consist in their
> coming to have false beliefs as a result of those acts of expression; b) harm-
> ful consequences of acts performed as a result of those acts of expression,
> where the connection between the acts consists merely in the fact that the
> act of expression led the agents to believe (or increased their tendency to be-
> lieve) these acts to be worth performing.[37]

Scanlon maintains that the Millian principle protects the value of *autonomy* in the making of decisions concerning beliefs, values, and truths; it entails intellectual freedom, as it were.

> I defend the Millian Principle by showing it to be a consequence of the view that the powers of a state are limited to those that citizens could recognize while still regarding themselves as equal, autonomous, rational agents.[38]

Scanlon's interpretation of Mill's autonomy principle may be summarized as follows: *speech may not be abridged on the grounds that harms to the individual or society may result due to the individual's acceptance of the validity of the speech*; he must be given the freedom to make the decision, (though he may be punished if his *acts* violate the law). This normative position entails Brandeis' notion in *Whitney v. California* that "if there be time to expose through discussion the falsehood and fallacies, to avert the evil by the processes of education, the remedy to be applied is more speech, not enforced silence."[39] Brandeis' standard suggests that there is a temporal (and perhaps spatial) component in the *structure* of autonomy and self-government. This standard provides another means of bridging the autonomy and harms principles: *speech-related harms which occur after having been filtered through the process of deliberation are different — in nature and in First Amendment terms — from harms which are caused directly by the speech itself.* This distinction separates fighting words, which are direct verbal assaults, from the advocacies of harmful doctrines, which threaten indirect harms.

In the following analysis it will be shown that the First Amendment principles of autonomy and self-government are inapplicable to targeted racial vilification. First, such expression is not a part of self-government. Second, such expression violates autonomy rather than honoring it. Third, these principles are superceded by the *harm* principle and the principle of ultimate ends as balanced by the right to free speech. Finally, targeted vilification violates a constitutional principle that is coeval with self-government: the right to be treated as a person, entitled to equal dignity. Let us now turn to that demonstration.

B. Cases

1. Organization for a Better Austin v. Keefe. We start with a very important case which poses a serious hurdle for our analysis: *Organization for a Better Austin v. Keefe.*[40] *Keefe* is important because it convincingly establishes the standard that verbally coercive speech directed at selected targets may indeed be entitled to First Amendment protection. I will attempt to show that *Keefe* was correctly decided, leading us to distinguish between different *contents* of targeted speech. This demonstration will dramatically illustrate the difference between targeted racial vilification and other forms of speech. And, by supporting the *Keefe* decision, it will show that my position is meant to be limited to only extreme cases.[41]

In the *Keefe* case, the Illinois Circuit Court had issued an injunction against the Organization for a Better Austin (OBA), prohibiting it from distributing leaflets or similar literature in the city of Westchester, which borders Chicago. The leaflets criticized Keefe, a real estate broker, for engaging in "block busting" and "panic peddling activities." Panic peddling occurs when a real estate agent (or some other interested party) induces home owners to sell their homes by spreading rumors that the quality and value of their neighborhood and homes will soon be diminished because of the entry of racial minorities into the neighborhood or because of some other cause. The agent then reaps a windfall profit in commissions. A group of whites and blacks responded to Keefe's panic peddling efforts by forming OBA. They targeted Keefe by passing out the leaflets, which apprised the recipients of Keefe's activities, at Keefe's church and throughout his neighborhood. They resorted to the leaflets because previous attempts to dissuade Keefe had failed. OBA did not call for a segregated neighborhood (after all, blacks as well as whites belonged to OBA), but rather for a "racially balanced" neighborhood. The evidence suggested that their primary motive in leafletting was to put pressure on Keefe in order to coerce him to stop his activities, which threatened their hopes. Keefe's legal actions reveal that the leaflets upset him. Does this understandable reaction to targeted expression justify the abridgement of the speech? We will see that it does not, despite the fact that Keefe felt vulnerable.

Chief Justice Burger's opinion for the Supreme Court, setting aside the injunction against OBA, stated

> This Court has often recognized that the activity of peaceful pamphleteering is a form of communication protected by the First Amendment. [The] claim that the expressions were intended to exercise a coercive impact on respondent does not remove them from the reach of the First Amendment. Petitioners plainly intended to influence respondent's conduct by their activities; it is not fundamentally different from the function of a newspaper. Petitioners were engaged openly and vigorously in making the public aware of respondent's real estate practices. Those practices were offensive to them, as the views and practices of petitioners are no doubt offensive to others. But so long as the means are peaceful, the communication need not meet standards of acceptability.[42]

Burger's opinion entails the following propositions: 1) the intentional targeting of individuals is acceptable First Amendment behavior as long as the targeting is peaceful; 2) free speech is not limited to the pristine expression of ideas bereft of any coercive impact. As Holmes (and Meiklejohn) has stated, "every idea is an incitement." Indeed, often the controversy surrounding speech is an indication of the speech's importance, for strong repressive emotions are often aroused by the advocacy of change or the pointing out of questionable behavior.[43]

So targeting of an individual is not per se an abridgeable speech act. However, such acts may raise serious problems in other situations; these problems include both the content and the context of the speech (the nature of the target). A slight modification of the facts in *Keefe* raises thorny First Amendment problems.

Before we turn to this modified case, we should note the ways in which the *Keefe* case concerns the self-government and autonomy functions. The primary reason for the leafletting appears to have been to gain support: the OBA sought to *socialize* the issue by making Keefe's neighbors and fellow worshipers aware of his actions in the hope that this awareness would compel Keefe to change his views.[44] OBA did not desire to simply enlighten the public, but rather to gain a strategic advantage in the battle over panic peddling. Keefe's actions had important negative social and economic consequences; and if the citizens of the republic are to be part of the self-government process, they must possess the right to influence action within civil society by targeting speech acts to other relevant members within civil society. To restrict such targeting to the government (i.e., allow OBA to complain or petition to the relevant governmental or judicial body which would then take discretionary action) would be to limit the self-governing powers of what Meiklejohn calls "We, the rulers."[45]

2. "Kike Keefe" Hypothetical. But did not Frank Collin also desire to effectuate a strategic advantage? To see how his speech claim differed from OBA's let us take the same basic set of facts as in *Keefe,* but change the content of the leaflets. Let us assume that Keefe is Jewish. What if the leaflets read, *Jew Greed Pockets Another Commission: Kike Keefe Cashes in on Families' Homes*! Would we feel as comfortable granting speech rights to this type of leafletting? If not, what factors are different in the two cases?

I would suggest two major differences which are interdependent. First, as is obvious, the leaflets now refer to Keefe's ethnic origin or race, and in quite an intimidating fashion. Second, because of the racialist content of the pamphlet, we may *assume* that Keefe possesses a greater vulnerability in this case than in the real *Keefe* case. Why? Because OBA's (hypothetical) reference to Keefe's race or ethnic origin *changes the very nature of the speech act from a criticism of Keefe's economic practices to a vilification of something over which Keefe has no control.* The racial vilification constitutes more than a reference to Keefe's character. Had the leaflet said something like "Keefe is a scoundrel who sucks profits from innocent homeowners," the charge *would* have referred to Keefe's moral character, and would have been much less odious than the reference to race or ethnicity, even if it may have been unfair. It could still be labeled a verbal assault, yet it seems at least a potentially *justified* verbal assault because of the alleged harms which Keefe has attempted to perpetrate. Yet the reference to race or ethnicity seems uniquely noxious and nefarious. Why is this so?

First, race and ethnicity are characteristics over which a person has no control. They do not represent roles or chosen lines of action, but rather unchangeable facts of nature for which no individual is responsible. By linking Keefe's actions to his Jewishness, the hypothetical OBA leaflet, in effect, accuses Keefe of being Jewish. It also assumes that race or ethnic background *causes* immoral action: it ironically denies the very autonomy of will upon which responsibility rests and, less ironically, upon which the moral conception of constitutional and human rights rests.[46] Second, the qualities of unalterability and race heighten the intimidation of the message. This is so not only because there is nothing Keefe can do to alter his ethnicity, but also because targeted racialist speech is inherently vicious and *assaultive.* The history of racism in this and other countries suggests so, as racism has led to the greatest inhumanities. And, as we saw in Chapter Two, racism represents an extremist psychological state which is intrinsically irrational[47] and which evokes highly emotional responses.[48] Targets naturally interpret racialist speech as vicious and intimidating. Skokie survivors and other Jews reacted so vehemently to the NSPA's intimidations partly because they understood the denotative meaning of the NSPA's racism; they understood the way in which that racism questioned the legitimacy of their very lives. These trauma-evoking factors are among the reasons that racial classifications in the law are "immediately suspect," according to the Supreme Court.[49]

Another hypothetical modification in the content of the *Keefe* leaflet will further illuminate and substantiate these contentions. Suppose that Keefe were a member of the Libertarian Party, and the leaflet read, *Libertarian Advocate Keefe Unmasks Capitalism's True Face: Real Estate Shark Devours Home Life.* Is this remark as assaultive and disturbing as the hypothetical reference to race in the last modification? I think not. What constitutes the difference? I propose that there is a difference between the reference to Keefe's political and economic roles and his race or ethnic origin. Unlike race, economic and political roles are alterable and freely chosen and may indeed be related to one's political and economic actions. When one criticizes the alleged link between such roles and one's action, the allegation may be incorrect, yet it does not deny in principle the moral autonomy of the target.

To be sure, some serious commentators have maintained that we do not actually choose our most basic beliefs and political theories, that value choices spring more or less spontaneously from subliminal sources deep within the self.[50] But this view seems exaggerated. Value choices are no doubt less autonomous than many rationalists assume, yet this fact does not necessarily mean that they are totally unfree. Freedom of the will is not an all or nothing proposition. We are certainly more free in our determinations of political and economic values than we are to change our race or ethnic origin, as evidenced by the conversions people often make to new parties, ideologies, or principles. Indeed, the criminal law is predicated on the assumption of moral choice and autonomy concerning actions, though the state often bears the burden of proof in establishing such autonomy (or specific intent).[51]

In addition, criticism of a target's political or economic actions or memberships, divorced from the irrational consideration (or accusation) of his race, is not inherently irrational; it is normally directed to real, objective actions in the world with important consequences. Indeed *Chaplinsky v. New Hampshire*'s "two level" or "definitional" approach to free speech assumes that speech about politics is presumptively rational (see Chapter One). Criticism or vilifications directed to the *moral character* of a target due to his political or economic actions are fundamentally different from racial or ethnic vilification, even if the former involve hate or anger.

Another way of illuminating or clarifying this difference is to compare the treatment of race as a matter of vilification and such treatment as a matter of what behavioral psychologists call "realistic group conflict." Realistic group conflict is not due primarily to irrational psychological displacement of inner tensions upon racial targets, but is rather a function of the more objective or tangible conflictive relationships that can exist between or among groups. In some areas of the country, for example, whites might have valid reasons independent of race to be angry at certain blacks (or vice versa) or to be in dispute with them. Such social phenomena as threats to personal safety, neighborhood security or quality (an issue in the actual *Keefe* case), and the conditions in schools *may* be relevant examples of realistic racial conflict.[52] Many Marquette Park residents may fit this category of conflict. Yet the NSPA strives to turn any realistic group conflict there into the psychopathology of racism. In the latter case, the racial vilification exists for its own sake, independent of objective phenomena and associations (of course, many racists find *post hoc* "objective" reasons for hating, and objective phenomena may turn a non-prejudiced person into a prejudiced person — yet the basic distinction between realistic conflict and racial prejudice is still valid).

To vilify one's race is to allege that one's race is a causal factor in one's behavior. It is to deny the very humanity of the target, for the notion of humanity inalienably includes moral autonomy distinct (to some threshold extent) from what Kant calls "necessitation," or the compulsions of passion and unfree will.[53] We saw that one feature of the survivors' "mastery" motivation at Skokie may have been a function of the way their Nazi persecutors in Europe denied their moral autonomy in the name of a racist metaphysics which attributed causal behavioral powers to race. A similar reduction of character to race is depicted by observers of colonial master-slave relations and totalitarian racism.[54] One explanation for the virulence of the Skokie survivors' reaction to the NSPA was their need to have taken purposeful action "in the face" of this type of accusation. Fanon and Memmi maintain that militant revolt is required psychologically to purge the victim of the sense of inferiority racism engenders. The Skokie survivor reaction appears to have been motivated by a similar drive. Targets of racial vilification react with a depth of emotion which signifies the inherent irrationality of the relation between speaker and target. "You cannot have . . . these people with the same ideas as those who killed my people or my parents [coming into Skokie] because they are protected by the Constitution," Stephen asserted. "We cannot afford to be weak. We have got to fight." "Why should we allow him access to the community, to flout his obscene ideas in our faces?" Erna Gans asked.

The difference between the speech act of targeting in the *Keefe* case and in Skokie and our racial vilification hypothetical reduces to the issues of autonomy, assault, and rationality. Targeted racial vilification is inherently traumatic and assaultive, so it perpetrates a substantial direct harm which counters the free speech principle and the principles of self-government and autonomy. It is a form of direct intimidation (or fighting words) so the autonomy and self-government principles do not apply because of our application of the Kantian principle of ultimate ends to cases of direct harm. Any long-range benefit that might result from targeted racial vilification cannot justify its expression because of the direct harm which results. Furthermore, its very nature is inconsistent with the rationality principle of *Chaplinsky*. As one commentator states:

> group-vilifying speech directly addresses the subconscious needs of the overtly or latently prejudiced hearer, including the needs to externalize self-hatred and anxiety, to project repressed desires, and to stereotype the target group in order to avoid uncertainty.[55]

A final difference between our cases must be mentioned. In the real *Keefe* case, the primary *intent* of the OBA leafletters was to modify Keefe's economic practices. In our "Kike Keefe" hypothetical, the only imaginable motive of the use of the ethnic vilification is to intimidate and emotionally injure—otherwise, why employ the racial vilification? The use of the vilification is independent of the economic issue at stake and constitutes an unjustifiable harm *despite* the justice or truth of the economic claims. Thus, as in a libel case, the coexistence of the assaultive speech with true and justified speech does not render abridgement due to the harmful speech constitutionally impermissible. The *Sullivan* and *Lando*[56] cases involving the libel of public officials entail the judicial investigation and determination of intent; if false statements are made with malice, they are liable to civil action and are not saved by the First Amendment because of any true statements that accompany them. In other words, the "mixed utterance" doctrine (i.e., that bad speech must be protected if it coheres to good speech) *loses its validity once it is determined that false statements (even those mixed with true statements) have been made with malice.* The same principle should apply to racial slurs.

3. Third Case: Silent Symbolic Intimidation. Let us imagine that OBA has failed to influence Keefe with its pamphlets. Consequently, it changes tactics and targets the homes of black families. At eight o'clock in the evening a group of twenty OBA members stand silently on the sidewalk or edge of the street in front of a black family that has just moved into the area (this action would be unlikely due to the actual racial mixture of OBA, but let us imagine it for purposes of analysis). Hadley Arkes refers to a similar situation in his essay on group libel laws. The example is analogous to actual occurrences in Cicero, Illinois. Arkes describes the situation this way:

> No violence arises; no rocks or bottles are thrown. The crowd merely stands there, chanting in a low tone, and as it stays on through the night, it makes almost no sound at all. There is no breach of the peace, or even anything

that fits our usual notion of a public disturbance. The crowd simply stands in silence through the night, intimidating by its presence.[57]

Arkes points out that no *physical* danger or disorder is posed or threatened here (i.e., the danger test is inapplicable), and that the speech act (which is more symbolic than expressed) of the whites is intended to induce or coerce a consequent action by the blacks (to *move out*). Indeed, let us say that OBA is "merely" striving to achieve the same ultimate end it strove for in *Keefe,* to slow down the process of blacks moving into the neighborhood. Yet once again salient features exist which qualitatively distinguish this case from *Keefe.* These features boil down to the difference between intimidation designed to trigger *immediate emotional trauma* (can anyone say this speech act is not *intimidation* by its very nature?) and verbally coercive speech (to use Burger's term in the real *Keefe* case) designed to apprise the public and the target of the negative consequences of its actions. In *Keefe,* OBA targeted the person who was allegedly responsible for panic peddling, and made no references of any nature to Keefe's ethnicity; in Arkes' hypothetical, they target blacks who simply exercised their right to buy a home, and the racial reference is implicit. But what if the OBA crowd carried signs that said, "Property values drop when blacks pour into neighborhoods"? This statement is certainly "political speech," which *Cohen v. California* protects fully,[58] and the statement is quite possibly *true.* In libel cases of public officials, truth is an absolute defense, according to *Garrison v. Louisiana.*[59] Thus, true political speech made in the public forum is normally granted full First Amendment protection. The problem is that the accompaniment of OBA's speech act here by true political speech *does not lessen the intentional intimidation.* The essential nature of the speech act — the intentional infliction of emotional trauma upon an innocent and vulnerable party — is not modified by its being true and authentic political speech.

The factor of race which is present in this act of symbolic intimidation distinguishes this type of targeted expression from picketing cases, which otherwise resemble it. Since *Thornhill v. Alabama* in 1940, in which it was ruled that a broad statute banning all labor picketing was unconstitutional because the Court considered peaceful picketing a form of freedom of speech, the Supreme Court has progressively given less First Amendment protection to picketing.[60] In *Milk Wagon Drivers Union v. Meadowmoor Dairies,*[61] the Court upheld a general injunction against picketing based on past violence which justified the anticipation of future violence. In later cases, the Court concluded that even peaceful picketing is different from pure speech because it involves more than communication.[62] Of course, so did the leafletting in *Keefe* and the speech acts in many other cases discussed above, so the Court's treatment of *peaceful* picketing seems inconsistent with its protection of speech in other cases. It seems particularly inconsistent with the incitement test developed in *Brandenburg v. Ohio*: speech advocating disorder may be abridged only if it directly incites an imminent unlawful act.[63] And it seems inconsistent, therefore, with the autonomy and self-government values we have discussed. Nonetheless, because picketing often poses the potential of disorder, and because it often advocates actions "contrary to state policy in a domain open to state regulation,"[64] the Court has treated it as a special form of expression entitled to less First Amendment protection.

Both picketing and Arkes' symbolic case involve "inducements" to perform certain acts (legal or illegal).[65] Yet Arkes' case and our "Kike Keefe" hypothetical go further: the factor of race (whether explicit or implicit) transforms the expressive act in each case into an act of intimidation. To be sure, labor picketing and other forms of picketing *may* involve intimidation; but they are not *inherently* intimidating. The burden of proof should be on the government to prove intimidation. Arkes' targeted symbolic act, however, *is* inherently intimidating for the same reasons we discussed in our analysis of the "Kike Keefe" hypothetical. Those who target people in this fashion are presumptively *attempting* to intimidate. Consequently, the burden of proof should cut the other way.

Moreover, in these hypotheticals *the issue of the truth and falsity of such speech is again extraneous to the nature of the harm*. OBA's truthful reference to property values does not change the nature of the intent or the concomitant harmful impact. Similarly, the inherently assaultive nature of a Nazi speech act that targeted a Holocaust survivor would not be altered by the astute Nazi's use of a sign that read "Hitler killed six million Jews." The truth of this statement does not magically transform the inherently assaultive nature of the speech act. The *independent status* of truth-testing and assault in these cases draws the line that marks the limit of the autonomy and self-government values. Truth-testing is certainly something that must be resolved by "we the listeners" (Meiklejohn) in the public forum. As Brandeis (*Whitney v. California*) and Decker (*Collin v. Smith*) maintain, the best antidote to false or bad speech is often true or good speech; Mill's defense of free speech is similar. But psychological assault constitutes a harm that *cannot be answered*; it is *inherently* not remediable by "more speech."[66]

This conclusion reveals that we should not judge speech solely on the grounds of its truth value, as Mill often does in *On Liberty*. Truth and morality are not always the same things, even though political regimes which seem dedicated to the denial of truth also fare poorly on the morality scale.[67]

Parallel limits exist in the areas of obscenity and privacy. Obscenity poses a harm in certain cases not simply because it poses a speculative clear and present danger of incitement to sexually deviant or dangerous behavior (the evidence does not prove that it does); it can also be "patently offensive."[68] That is, like fighting words, it cannot be mitigated or answered by counter-speech. Any truth which accompanies its expression does not change its effect. Similarly, as Arkes points out, courts have found that a speech act invading privacy may give rise to liability in tort even when the speech act exposes the truth. For example, in *Brent v. Morgan*, the defendant placed a sign in his window which read: "Notice. Dr. W. R. Morgan owes an account here of $49.67."[69] Arkes concedes that skepticism about the invasion of privacy tort has grown in recent years,[70] but he nonetheless supports the tort in a manner relevant to my argument:

> I feel, however, that we would still like to uphold the plaintiff in *Brent v. Morgan* and, if so, we would seem to be conceding in principle that, in certain contexts not yet precisely defined, some things are so insulting or harmful — inflict such hurt — that there should be no justification for publishing them, even if they contain a residue of truth. This is the rationale behind the old view that truth alone is not sufficient to justify publication; one must show, in addition, good motives or the absence of malice.[71]

As pointed out above, racial vilification such as Collin and the NSPA directed at Skokie utterly lacks good motives; the NSPA acted with malice by intentionally inflicting emotional trauma on survivors. "He came [or wanted to come] to Skokie for a certain reason. He knew that there was a concentration of survivors, and he had a special reason to come and hurt us," Erna Gans correctly pointed out.

Another important issue is posed by Arkes' hypothetical: the nature of a captive audience in the act of targeting. The Supreme Court has repeatedly held that the First Amendment does not give a speaker the right to thrust his views on an unwilling listener.[72] In order to protect free speech as much as possible, however, the Supreme Court (and concurring libertarian theorists) has chosen to apply a test of captivity which requires the target's interest (often a private interest) to be "substantial." Once again, Justice Harlan's standard for captivity in *Cohen v. California* has been influential:

> The mere presumed presence of unwitting listeners or viewers does not serve automatically to justify curtailing all speech capable of giving offense . . .

the ability of government, consonant with the Constitution, to shut off discourse solely to protect others from hearing it is . . . dependent upon a showing that substantial privacy interests are being invaded in an essentially in-
tolerable manner.[73]

Geoffrey Stone points out that the *Cohen* captivity test requires four
considerations: 1) the nature of the privacy interest in a particular case;
2) the "substantiality" of this interest; 3) the extent to which the person
is indeed captive; 4) whether the state can find ways to protect this interest
that are "less restrictive" than abridging speech.[74] The substantiality of the
privacy interest is a function of the nature of the relevant unwanted speech
and the availability of avoidance. The more intrusive, undesirable, or assaultive the speech, the more substantial is the privacy claim. At the same
time, in terms of the captivity issue,

the true measure of an individual's privacy in this context consists, not in
his total protection from initial exposure to unwelcome ideas but, rather, in
his ability to avoid continued exposure to those ideas once he has rejected
them.[75]

If we apply Stone's logic to Arkes' hypothetical (which is based on past
activities in Cicero), it is clear that captivity exists. The privacy interest is
obviously substantial. First, the sanctity of the home has always been supported by the Supreme Court in speech-related and other cases.[76] Second,
the racial intimidation in the symbolic expression is emotionally assaultive, making it presumptively highly undesirable. Third, such home dwell-
ers are clearly captive according to even *Cohen*'s and Stone's standards,
which are weighted in favor of free speech. Though the residents could turn
their eyes or shut their blinds, they would probably continue to be intimidated because the group would still be outside. Indeed, their fears would
linger even after the "demonstrators" left, for intimidation of this sort does
not easily wear off. Fourth, no means short of abridgement or punishment
appear to exist by which the state could protect the privacy interest at stake.
So racialist intimidation, expressed or symbolic, inflicts a substantial harm
when directed at the home or a similar domain. Skokie, unfortunately, poses
a problem, for there the NSPA gave advance notice of its plans and would
have appeared on the steps of village hall, which exists in a commercial
area. Later, however, we will see that this difference should not distinguish
Skokie from the cases discussed in this chapter.

Compare our conclusion about captivity here to the conclusion that
would follow from the ACLU's Franklyn Haiman's standard of captivity.
Haiman, an interviewee and national secretary of the ACLU during Skokie, would not allow the content or motivation of the speech act to influ-

ence the determination of captivity; nor would he allow the form of presentation of the speech to matter. The result is a surprising disregard of the right not to be assaulted by targeted expression:

> I would start with the basic proposition that the concept of captivity should be narrowly and literally understood to refer only to situations in which an audience is unable to get away from communication stimuli it finds offensive. This would exclude all circumstances where only the initial impact of communication is in question, and it would also exclude all settings in which avoidance of *continued exposure* to the communication is physically possible by averting one's eyes . . . Certainly captive audience doctrine should protect us, as we sit in our homes, from the continual din of singing, chanting, or yelling picketers on our front sidewalk. The question becomes more difficult, however, if the picketers march silently up and down. Here I would suggest that the presence or absence of captivity is dependent on how long the demonstrators remain. If they are there for an hour or so, *it would be just as easy for the residents of the home to avoid looking out the window or to pull their shades as it would be to throw away a piece of mail or hang up a telephone.*[77]

The insensitivity of Haiman's view is highlighted by asking some simple questions: What if the "picketers" carry signs saying "No Blacks Here!" and the family inside the house is black? What if they simply behave as in Arkes' hypothetical? Would it really be "just as easy" for the targets to avoid looking out the window as it "would be to throw away a piece of mail"? By now the answer should be obvious. Haiman ignores the subjective mental state by focusing exclusively on eye or ear contact as the only element of captivity. Alexander Bickel's view that "what is commonly read and seen and heard and done intrudes upon us all, want it or not"[78] may go too far in terms of establishing captivity, but it more adequately takes account of the psychological reality of man. If Haiman's psychological view makes him blind to the captivity and intimidation in cases such as Arkes' hypothetical, he is also blind, *a fortiori,* to the claims of Skokie survivors. Indeed, in his interview he told me:

> The Skokie case was no different from what we [the ACLU] had done in the past. It was routine, no different from the old Rockwell defenses. We do not believe that the composition of the audience at Skokie makes a difference. There is no difference *in principle* from Jehovah's Witnesses in New Haven in the 1940s.

Just how this equation works is difficult to fathom, unless the content and context of speech is ignored.

It should also be noted that Arkes' hypothetical differs from a case such as *Gregory v. Chicago,* in which blacks marched around Mayor Daly's home protesting Chicago's desegregation policies. The difference is analogous to the difference between the actual *Keefe* case and the "Kike Keefe" hypothetical: in *Gregory,* the target of the protest was allegedly involved in action objectively tied to a policy. Yet in Arkes' hypothetical, the targets are held accountable for their race. In addition, Daly was a public official, and such exposure goes more with the job; whereas the residents in the hypothetical have not voluntarily put themselves in such a position (recall the difference from *Gertz* in this respect). Had the *Gregory* demonstrators vilified Daly's ethnicity, the "Kike Keefe" hypothetical would then control.

4. Beauharnais v. Illinois, Collin v. Smith and the Delimitation of Targeting. Before we draw our conclusions from our consideration of cases, we must look at an actual case which requires us to draw the line between forms of racialist expression and vilification. My treatment of *Beauharnais v. Illinois* will demonstrate that laws against general, non-targeted racial vilification (such as Skokie's "racial slur" ordinances and other "group libel" laws) *should* be held unconstitutional because they violate the self-government and autonomy principles and because the harms caused by such expression are less direct and substantial than those caused by targeted vilification. Hence, the treatment of *Beauharnais* reveals the prudential balancing of the principle of ultimate ends in favor of free speech in cases in which speech of bad content does not directly cause a harm.

Beauharnais was convicted under an Illinois statute which closely resembled the Skokie racial slur ordinances. The statute made it a crime to:

> Manufacture, sell, or offer for sale, advertise or publish, present or exhibit in any public place in this state any lithograph, moving picture, play, drama or sketch which publication or exhibition portrays depravity, criminality, unchastity, or lack of virtue of a class of citizens, of any race, color, creed or religion which said publication or exhibition exposes the citizens of any race, color, creed or religion to contempt, derision, or obloquy or which is productive of breach of the peace or riots.[79]

Skokie modeled its racial slurs ordinance on this statute, which Illinois revoked years prior to the Skokie case.[80] As the critics of group libel laws assert, the statute appears to be excessively vague and broad.[81] No mention is made of the intent or the virulence of the vilification; the statute would provide grounds for punishing such works as *Huckleberry Finn* and *The Merchant of Venice,* as these works fictitiously portray racial and ethnic characters in an unfavorable light. Important works such as *Mein Kampf* could also be affected by the law, even if published or taught for educational purposes designed to teach the evil of Nazism. Nor does the act specify the context of the speech act. The mere publication of racialist expression could be punishable even if no individuals were shown to have been harmed by it.

As president of the White Circle League, Beauharnais organized the random distribution in 1950 of leaflets which (like Collin's plea at Skokie) were cloaked in the form of "a petition" to the mayor and the Chicago city council. The leaflets beseeched the Council and mayor "to halt the further encroachment, harassment, and invasion of white people, their property, neighborhoods and persons, by the Negro—through the exercise of the Police Power." The leaflets, which Beauharnais distributed randomly at street corners, went on to vilify blacks and exhort

> one million self-respecting white people in Chicago to unite under the banner of the White Circle League . . . if persuasion and the need to prevent the white race from becoming mongrelized by the negro will not unite us, then the aggressions . . . rapes, robberies, knives, guns and marijuana of the negro, surely will.[82]

Justice Frankfurter upheld Beauharnais' conviction in the only group libel case ever decided by the Supreme Court. Frankfurter held that the alleged truth of Beauharnais' derogatory statements about blacks was immaterial to his speech right, and that the Illinois legislature's determination of possible *long-range* social violence due to such defamation was enough constitutional justification for punishing Beauharnais' expression. The absence of imminent or clear and present danger was not deemed to invalidate the law.[83]

This type of balancing has been criticized[84] in the years since *Beauharnais* for two basic reasons: 1) it is not based on clear guidelines or principles, so it results in either undue judicial discretion which "chills" speech or in undue judicial deference to legislative judgments;[85] 2) it represents paternalism by allowing legislatures to abridge speech because of its possible effectiveness (it violates the self-government and autonomy values).[86] As a result, the Supreme Court has replaced this type of balancing with strict judicial review in cases involving political speech. According to the standards of strict review, the state must now demonstrate an imminent danger or other compelling interest *in each case* in order to abridge the speech right. Given this new approach, Judge Decker found *Beauharnais* no longer valid in the Skokie case, *Collin v. Smith.*

Decker's position on *Beauharnais* and Skokie's racial slur ordinances is correct. The self-government and autonomy principles seem to apply in cases of racial slurs which are not directed at a chosen audience. To be sure, Collin *did* target Skokie; but the Skokie racial slur *ordinances* were general, applying to broad areas of such expression regardless of the context and the particular facts in the case. Accordingly, these ordinances must be treated in the same fashion as the Illinois group libel statute in *Beauharnais* (even though Collin's speech act was different from Beauharnais'), for in First Amendment cases, the nature of the statute supercedes the nature of the speech act as far as the constitutional question is concerned.[87] If the statute is vague, overbroad, or "chilling," it is declared unconstitutional even if the defendant's speech act could constitutionally be punished under a properly drawn statute.

Targeting is the essential difference between Beauharnais' speech act and that of OBA and Frank Collin. Beauharnais' leaflets were vile and libelous in a group sense; yet they also constituted pleas concerning public policy and matters of race. In Decker's terms, they were mixed utterances (at best). But more importantly, *no evidence was adduced showing the infliction of a harm to any individuals or definite group.* In *Cohen* (the "Fuck the Draft" case), Justice Harlan found that "No individual actually or likely to be present could reasonably have regarded the words on appellant's jacket as a direct personal insult."[88] The same conclusion applies to Beauharnais' speech act, though the content of his speech explicitly singled out blacks for ridicule, whereas Cohen merely execrated the draft. The key point is that neither Cohen nor Beauharnais intentionally directed his speech to definite targets, so their speech acts were less assaultive than the speech acts of Collin, OBA in the "Kike Keefe" hypothetical, white groups in Cicero, and the Klan intimidations in Contra Costra County, California. Had Beauharnais passed his leaflets out in front of black homes or given them directly to blacks in similar settings, the very nature of his speech act would have been transformed from a racialist plea into an act of intimidation. General group libel and racial slurs, in contradistinction to targeted group libel or racial vilification, do not normally constitute the same type of harm as a direct verbal assault; it leaves the public forum intact for counterarguments because the mental state necessary for counterargument (see Brandeis' formulation in *Whitney v. California*) is not destroyed by the direct infliction of an emotional assault. Beauharnais' speech act, in other words, is conducive (however problematically) to the self-government and autonomy principles. The state should not abridge his views because of the *anticipated* fear of their results, as did the Illinois legislature.

A brief comparison of Beauharnais' speech act to another Nazi case with which Arkes deals in his analysis illuminates these conclusions. In *Chicago v. Lambert,* a Chicago branch of the American Nazi Party (an affiliate of George Lincoln Rockwell's national party and later a competitor in Chicago with Collin's NSPA)[89] headed by Lambert passed out vile, verbally assaultive leaflets in front of a downtown Chicago theatre which was showing a film featuring Sammy Davis, Jr. The leaflet, which they distributed to passers-by and to people emerging from the theatre (many of whom were blacks or Jews), read as follows:

> Niggers! You Too Can Be a Jew . . . I'ts Easy: It's Fun . . . Sammy-the-Kosher-Coon Shows You How . . . In Ten Easy Lessons . . . Be One of The Chosen People . . . Here's some of the Things You Learn: Jewish Customs and traditions such as how to force your way into social groups . . . How to make millions cheating widows and orphans . . . How to Hate-Hitler and get believing he killed six million of us even though we are all over here living it up on the dumb Christians.[90]

Recipients of the pamphlets gathered into an angry mob of about two hundred people. Police testified in court that about forty to sixty people threatened to attack Lambert unless the police moved in and took him away; the police asked Lambert and his group to leave, and arrested them when they refused.[91] Their conviction for defamatory leafletting and criminal libel in the trial court was upheld by the Illinois Appellate Court.

Lambert shows the anger which can result when the vilifying leaflet is targeted at a particular group of people in a sensitive context. To be sure, the targets appear to have been more angry than intimidated, making the case less vicious than some of the cases discussed above. But, as our analysis of Skokie showed, anger and intimidation may coexist and be elements of a "fighting response." As the Skokie survivor interviewees stressed, the law should protect innocent citizens from unprovoked verbal assaults.

Yet *Lambert* is different from *Beauharnais* because there was no such targeting and direct infliction of injury in *Beauharnais* (though the charges in *Lambert* were similar to those of *Beauharnais*). In this respect, I disagree with Arkes' conclusion that *Beauharnais* and *Chaplinsky* deal with the same types of speech, that group libel (general racial slurs) is per se "fighting words." This distinction reveals the importance of *context* in determining fighting or assaultive words; and the context is a matter of the *form and content* of the expression.

Finally, because general racial slurs such as Beauharnais' do not pose the same harm as targeted racial slurs or similar forms of expressive assault, the problem of institutional incapacity in the application or implementation of the law is a more legitimate concern in assessing such legislation than it is in cases of more direct and substantial harm. Group libel laws are subject to abuse in application because of their vagueness and the discretion they therefore give prosecutors and courts. Though implemental problems could accrue to laws against targeted racial vilification, these problems are not determinative in two respects. First, the greater level of harm in such cases outweighs the implemental problems we will examine in a moment (the harms principle overrides the "chilling-of-speech" claim). Second, the requirement of targeting in these cases would eliminate most potential litigations, for most racial vilification is not targeted in the ways we have discussed; consequently, the potential for abuse of free speech is less in this area than in the area of general racial slurs or group libel legislation.

There is a large literature on the implemental problems of group libel laws. In an influential article on group libel published in 1950, Joseph Tanenhaus pointed out some standard flaws in such laws. Even if a group libel law is tightly drafted so as to avoid the endemic problem of vagueness, Tanenhaus asserts, the defendant in a trial may succeed by: 1) proving that the statements he made are true; 2) proving that he "reasonably and honestly *believes* them to be true," even if he cannot prove them to be objectively true; 3) proving that he did not act with the intent to create ill will, even if he cannot prove the status of his beliefs. Given the availability of these defenses, which Tanenhaus claims will generally be available (though Frankfurter and the lower court did not allow them in *Beauharnais*), convictions for group libel will be difficult for prosecutors to attain. And trials (successful prosecution or not) will tend to turn into public forums for the defendant, as did Hitler's trial over his Beer Hall *Putsch*.[92] Commentators have pointed to such a result in litigation under the authority of the 1965 Race Relations Act in England.[93]

Finally, Tanenhaus points out that group libel laws could harm self-government and the interests of groups attacked:

> Group libel legislation, no matter how carefully drafted, would tend to discourage discussion and criticism, the backbone of democratic government. If improperly applied, even the use of legitimate discussion and criticism might be prosecuted. The very groups which the legislation was passed to protect might be hurt. Hate-mongers if convicted would become martyrs, if acquitted would, in effect, have had their allegations justified. The publicity caused by prosecution might be far greater than that afforded the actual propaganda. The public might well resent the attempt of particular groups to use the law as

a means of attaining special protection and privileges. Group libel laws could, in addition, hamstring the efforts of groups to discredit their attackers.[94]

Given these implemental problems, which have been found in both America and in English enforcement of the Incitement to Racial Hatred provision (Section 6) of the 1965 Race Relations Act,[95] general group libel or racial slur laws are not a good idea. This conclusion is reinforced by the fact that the harms such expression normally poses are indirect and long range, thereby rendering the expression amenable to the self-government and autonomy values. For these reasons, we must distinguish *Beauharnais* from the cases of targeted vilification discussed elsewhere in this chapter (*Collin, Lambert,* "Kike Keefe," Contra Costa County, Cicero, etc.). And because Skokie's racial slur ordinances were similar to the statute in *Beauharnais,* the federal courts were correct in ruling them unconstitutional, even though Collin's speech act qualified for abridgement because of its assaultive nature.

IV. Conclusion:
Targeted Racial Vilification and Substantive Justice

The major aim of this chapter has been to demonstrate that certain forms of racial vilification pose harms that are distinguishable in terms of severity from other forms of vilification and speech pertaining to either race or other matters of social importance. It has been shown that targeted racial vilification is qualitatively different from non-targeted racial vilification and racialist speech as well as from targeted and "coercive" speech pertaining to a person's alleged political or economic actions. Whereas the latter forms of speech are congruent with the values of self-government and autonomy, the former type of expression is not.

In demonstrating the validity of this conclusion, the following factors were highlighted concerning the special harms caused by targeted racial vilification: (1) such expression is inherently assaultive. (2) Intent and motive are significant factors. As seen in Chapter Two, Collin's main intent at Skokie was to inflict trauma in order to cause disruption that the media would publicize; such a motive treats targets viciously and as means to the illegitimate ends *of the speakers.* And the targeting of racial vilification is presumptively intentional. (3) Intimidation can occur in contexts that fall outside the narrow definition of captive audience endorsed by extreme libertarians like Franklyn Haiman, as well as the test in *Cohen,* which did not apply to Skokie. (4) Any valuable or worthy speech which accompanies targeted racial vilification does not justify protecting such speech by the First Amendment because such speech does not compensate for the harm committed. The weak version of the Kantian principle applies in a slightly different respect to this issue: such harms cannot be justified by the social utility of the speech *because then the targets would be treated as the means of large societal First Amendment ends.* (5) Targeted racial vilification is a particularly virulent and intimidating form of fighting words.

These findings direct us to the issues raised in Chapter One concerning the content neutrality rule and the evisceration of *Chaplinsky*'s fighting words test. We saw there that in the wake of the civil rights movement, and, more particularly, *Cohen v. California* and its progeny in the area of fighting words, that the content neutrality rule had nullified *Chaplinsky*'s notion of fighting words. Skokie challenges this result because the principles and standards of *Cohen* appear inapplicable to the *facts* of Skokie and similar cases. Yet to accommodate the facts at Skokie, the courts would have to take content seriously once again (e.g., racial vilification), at least in relation to the context of targeting. This policy would constitute a partial return to the basic principle of harm in *Chaplinsky*.[96]

In the final chapter, I will make my own modest proposals about Skokie and assaultive political speech in the public forum. These proposals are meant to implement the conclusions reached in this chapter. My proposals are not meant to be definitive, but rather to point out the direction in which we must travel to regain a sense of civility and substantive justice in the constitutional law of the public forum.

But before we turn to this task, I must briefly discuss a final point which has emerged from the analysis in this chapter: that the right to protection against targeted racial vilification is consistent with the fundamental principles of constitutional democracy. This is so in more than one respect. First, as the analysis of our "Kike Keefe" hypothetical demonstrated, racial vilification treats others as if their race caused their actions, thereby implying (or explicitly asserting) *in principle* that they are *not* the autonomous moral agents that liberal democracy assumes citizens to be.[97] Second, such expression inherently and directly "inflicts injury by its very utterance" (*Chaplinsky*'s terms) without cause, thereby violating the Kantian principle of ultimate ends (as we have employed it).

Finally, each of these applications or interpretations of principle constitutes part of a more fundamental principle which underlies the constitutional order: the equality premised on the essential dignity of the individual and his right to be treated in accord with this dignity. This fundamental principle has different levels of meaning. To begin, it *must* apply to the *essential nature* of man (his soul or spirit, as it were) even if it does not pertain to his material resources.[98] Unless he *does something* to forfeit his basic claim to dignity, the individual is entitled to be "treated as an equal" in terms of being accorded basic respect, even if he is not entitled to "equal treatment" (e.g., an equal distribution of resources or output).[99] Some theorists apply this basic right to the citizen-state relationship, whereas others stretch it to public relations among citizens in civil society.[100] Yet the basic principle of individual dignity grounded in essential equality is the same for each. Walter Berns expresses this essential equality in terms of the political principle of the consent of the governed.

> While the United States recognizes no religious truth, it is founded on the "self-evident" philosophical truths respecting the natural freedom and equality of all men. Being free and equal with respect to natural rights, and however unequal they may be according to any religious doctrine or in any other respect, no man may justly rule another without his consent.[101]

A similar logic has prevailed in the Supreme Court's treatment of legislative racial classifications in Fourteenth Amendment equal protection adjudication. Joseph Tussman and Jacobus ten Broek demonstrate the ways in which unjustified racial classifications in the law violate the fundamental principles of constitutional democracy and equal protection in a 1949 article that foreshadowed the judicial activism that was to ensue in this area:

> The assertion of human equality is closely associated with the denial that differences in color or creed, birth or status, are significant or relevant to the way in which men should be treated. These factors, the egalitarian asserts, are irrelevant accidents in the face of our common humanity. To these differences in the supplicants before her bar, Justice must be blind. Such traits should not be made the basis for the classification of individuals in laws.[102]

Whatever the debate over the magnitude and scope of the right to equality, the right to be treated and respected by the state as an equal individual without regard to race is essential to constitutional democracy. At this basic level, the conflict that arises between liberty (freedom) and equality[103] (when the claim to equality becomes more distributed) is absent.

Though the commentators above discuss the natural right of equality in terms of the state's treatment of its citizens (state action),[104] the principle of equality under discussion should also apply to the state's regulation of public speech. As seen in Chapter One and in our discussion of harmful consequences at Skokie, one of the most basic and important functions of community and government is to protect its citizens from assaultive speech and marked incivility. Berns stresses the relation between equality and the formation of a government based on consent in the state of nature. Yet one reason for the formation of that government was the protection of citizens against unjustified acts of intimidation (the protective function of community). Skokie survivors clearly understood the nature of this function of government. And so did the Supreme Court in *Chaplinsky v. New Hampshire,* in which the Court limited the speech right in order to honor the egalitarian principle of constitutionalism. *Chaplinsky*'s doctrines concerning fighting words and the social values of speech distinguish rational speech which respects the essential equality of its targets from speech which violates this equality (e.g. Martin Luther King versus Frank Collin).

It could be argued that the principle of equality under discussion is mainly procedural, for "treatment as an equal" means essentially that each citizen be given due process.[105] Indeed, as seen in Chapter One, the due process revolution in administrative and civil liberty law was based largely on egalitarian logic. Yet the value of equality we are treating is also substantive, in the sense that it concerns a basic right which should not be abridged by even a fair hearing governed by the most meticulous due process. If it is "due process," it is "substantive due process." According to Tussman and ten Broek,

> There is here a possible parallel between the equal protection and the due process clauses. The latter in its "substantive" development is interpreted to say that there are some rights which legislatures cannot impair by any process.[106]

The substantive nature of this right to equality is strengthened when it is applied to the First Amendment, for such an application requires taking the *content* of speech as seriously as its *form*. Targeted racial or ethnic vilification directly and substantively violates the most basic values of the constitutional order.[107] Accordingly, when speech includes the *context* of targeting and the *content* of racial or ethnic vilification, it should be constitutionally abridgeable in the name of substantive justice.

9

Reform Suggestions

Political freedom does not mean freedom from control. It means self-control . . . Self-government is nonsense unless the "self" which governs is able and determined to make its will effective . . . dependence upon intellectual laissez-faire [e.g., the marketplace of ideas], more than any single factor, has destroyed the foundations of our national education, has robbed of their meaning such terms as "reasonableness" and "intelligence," and "devotion to the general welfare." It has made intellectual freedom indistinguishable from intellectual license. — Alexander Meiklejohn, *Political Freedom*

I. The Direction of Reform

We saw in the last chapter that group libel or racial slur laws like Skokie's and the Illinois legislature's in *Beauharnais* pose constitutional problems because of their vagueness and breadth, because they violate the principles of self-government and autonomy, and because they do not distinguish direct and substantial from indirect and less substantial harms. Accordingly, the definition of targeted speech must be more specific and limitable than the simple distribution or utterance subject to abridgement in *Beauharnais*.

At the same time, our considerations of the Skokie case and similar cases in the last chapter have demonstrated that targets may be intimidated even when they are not strictly "held captive" according to the criteria of *Cohen v. California* or other libertarian doctrines. This conclusion is especially important when the targets of intimidating speech are relatively isolated in the community (in which case they are sociologically or situationally more vulnerable than Skokie survivors). Consequently, it makes sense to think of targeting in terms which lie between the narrow doctrine of captivity and the open-endedness of *Beauharnais* (in which the context of the

154

expression was irrelevant to the constitutional status of the speech act). To find targeting, something more than the sheer expression must be found (*Chaplinsky*'s "very utterance").[1] Yet a strictly *captive* target need not be present either.

In the following analysis I will indicate what targeting looks like, and how it should be defined by legislation. Before I do so, however, it is necessary to define what type of *content* constitutes sufficient intimidation to allow abridgement if targeting is also found.

II. The Content of Speech: Vilification and Intimidation

Expression causes a serious harm if it explicitly vilifies because of race; yet intimidation can occur even if expression is not explicit, as in the Cicero case discussed in the last chapter. Accordingly, we must concern ourselves with both the explicit and the tacit or connotative meaning of speech in order to protect the values of fundamental equality and security which are at stake.

Our analysis in the last chapter revealed that targeted racial or ethnic vilification causes harm because it is inherently assaultive or intimidating. Expression is assaultive when it seriously injures the dignity or self-esteem of a person; it is intimidating when it threatens a person's sense of security. Targeted racial or ethnic vilification commits both of these harms, so it is assaultive and intimidating content that concerns us. Assaultive and intimidating racial vilification may appear in the following forms: 1) accompanied by threats of violence; 2) when racial or ethnic slurs or degrading epithets are directed at targets without explicit threats of violence; 3) when the substance or content of the targeted expression is not explicit, but rather implicit, tacit, or symbolic. In the first case, the expression is clearly intimidating. In the latter two instances, intimidation may be present, depending on the context (e.g., the "Kike Keefe" hypothetical or the silent vigil in Cicero).

A. Threats of Violence

1. The Content of the Threat. The clearest case of harm exists when racialist expression is accompanied by a threat to harm. The NSPA's leaflets that started the Skokie controversy are one example of this type of threat. Had Beauharnais' leaflets been given to blacks and read "The marijuana and crimes of the Negro prove his inferiority. We advocate the slaughter of the Negro," they would have taken on a similar threatening meaning, even though there may have been no immediate "objective" reason to fear for the target's physical security. Both Collin's and these hypothetical leaflets cause *psychological* insecurity. Both a *direct threat* and *the advocacy of death or violence* against the target constitute intimidations. Both should be abridgeable. Survivor interviewee Erna Gans expressed the psychological harm caused by even the *general advocacy* of death:

> It is not Collin that is a danger. We aren't fighting him, but the ideology, those who advocate killing. No one should have a right to advocate killing. This is not a civil liberties issue. The KKK? It is all the same. My limit is killing. Beauharnais' speech was subject to arguing and truth-testing. But to kill is final, unanswerable. I am not after Collin. I want to be sure that no one should advocate killing, that no one should advocate it, anywhere, not even in Chicago.[2]

The abridgement of such speech should be limited, however, to situations of targeting, even though the general (non-targeted) advocacy of death or violent action against others poses serious problems to the value of civility. When such advocacy is targeted, it is more harmful; and we have seen that giving due weight to the free speech principle requires drawing the line of abridgement at the point of direct harm. Limiting abridgement to instances of targeting would guard against an undue "chilling effect" on speech (a concern which gains in importance the less serious and direct the harm becomes).[3] In addition, the act of targeting provides evidence of another important factor in our recommended policy; in conjunction with the content of the speech, it provides *prima facie* evidence of the *intent* to harm.

    2. The Legal Doctrine. I suggest the following legal doctrine to cover racialist expression accompanied by threats of violence: *When expression pertaining to matters of race or ethnic origin is accompanied by the advocacy of death or violence against members of that race or ethnic group, and is targeted at such members, it is constitutionally subject to abridgement.*

B. Racial Vilification Without Explicit Threats of Death or Violence

    1. The Content of Vilifying Speech. In some of the cases (actual or hypothetical) discussed in the last chapter, targeted racialist expression may harm without explicitly advocating violence. In recent years, as the *Goldstein* tort suit at Skokie pointed out, some courts have recognized a tort action for the intentional infliction of emotional trauma.[4] More to the point, a tort action for racial insults, epithets, and "name-calling" has been supported by some courts, though the progress of this tort is uneven and uncertain, especially after Skokie[5] (though the federal courts in *Collin v. Smith* dealt with *group* libel and *general* racial slurs rather than the question of the constitutional status of a tort for racial insults directed against individuals). Nonetheless, some courts have held that such expression is tortious on one or more of the following grounds: 1) the tort of outrage,[6] 2) assault and battery,[7] 3) intentional infliction of emotional distress,[8] 4) defamation,[9] 5) the statutory provisions of federal civil rights law (if the speaker is a state official).[10]

Though such torts appear to be legitimate given the analysis and conclusions of the last chapter, we are not concerned with tort law, per se, but rather with the manner in which the principles of tort law in this area support the constitutional reform doctrines I am suggesting. In addition, though *Collin v. Smith* did not reach the issue of the tort of racial slurs, its position on the First Amendment protection of racial slurs could indeed limit or even invalidate the tort of racial insult, just as *Sullivan* limited the tort of the libel of public officials.[11] Accordingly, my analysis does bear on the status of such torts, though that status is beyond our purview. Simply stated, targeted racial vilification is harmful because (to use the terms of tort law) it constitutes the intentional and assaultive infliction of outrageous emotional distress. In his article on the tort of racial insults, Richard Delgado addresses the First Amendment question by invoking *Chaplinsky*; in so doing Delgado also mentions some of the terms which constitute vilification:

> The government also has an interest in regulating the use of words harmful in themselves. In *Chaplinsky v. New Hampshire,* the United States Supreme Court stated that words which "by their very utterance inflict injury or tend to incite an immediate breach of the peace" are not protected by the First Amendment. Racial insults, and even some of the words which might be used in a racial insult, inflict injury by their very utterance. Words such as "nigger" and "spick" are badges of degradation even when used between friends; these words have no other connotation.[12]

2. The Legal Doctrine. Words which are *commonly accepted as vilifying or derogatory* (such as the epithets Delgado mentions) would qualify as abridgeable under our standards. So would expression that meant the same thing. The governing test should be objective, not subjective: Is the content of the speech vilifying (and therefore assaultive) to a "reasonable person" of the general community? Delgado offers a sensible legal standard in the tort which may be extended to the constitutional law governing expression in the public forum:

> Language was addressed to him or her by the defendant that was intended to demean through reference to race; that the plaintiff understood as intended to demean through reference to race; and that a reasonable person would recognize as a racial insult. [13]

The only major difference between our policy and Delgado's in this regard is that we should substitute the words "targeted at a definable audience" for "addressed to him or her."

C. Implicit or Symbolic Threats

Arkes' example in the last chapter of a group of whites standing outside the home of blacks in Cicero reveals that targeted expression may be harmful even when it is not explicit or does not use *verbal* forms of vilification or threats. Indeed, it is at this level that speech in the public forum may differ most clearly from tortious expression, for the latter normally involves "language" (see Delgado's code) or words that explicitly vilify. Yet expression in the public forum often involves symbolism or expression which is intimidating only on an implicit, connotative level, as Arkes' example shows. At Skokie, the NSPA intended to stand in front of village hall — replete with storm trooper uniform and swastika — and distribute leaflets that simply stated the broad goals of "White Power." *The NSPA foreswore any intention of engaging in explicit racial slurs.* Yet our analysis has clearly shown that the implicit, connotative meaning of the proposed NSPA expressive act at Skokie was precisely to intimidate (especially in light of the leafletting and statements in the press which preceded the Skokie controversy). Once the hate-monger has grabbed the attention of his target, he can accomplish his goal of intimidation by more subtle, symbolic means. Accordingly, targeted symbolic expression should be abridgeable even though it is not explicitly vilifying. The legal standard should be the *intent to demean or intimidate* (as mentioned, targeted vilification both demeans *and* intimidates) *as determined by a reasonable person of the community.*

The issue of symbolic expression highlights a factor that must be demonstrated in the other areas of more explicit vilification and intimidation as well: the factor of intent to assault or intimidate. Let us consider the factor of intent separately, as it is independent of the issue of content, though it is also related to that issue.

III. Intent

Intent to harm (intimidate) should be present before an abridgement of the speech right is justified. Yet given the criteria of harm I have stressed, intent would normally be easy to establish, for the very targeting of vilifying or intimidating expression (be it explicit or symbolic) establishes clear evidence of intent. In a criminal prosecution, the jury could decide the issue of intent in either of two ways: 1) on the basis of the facts, such as the content of the expression and its form of presentation, is intent established beyond a reasonable doubt? 2) given the prior finding of intimidating or vilifying content *and* the act of targeting, the jury could *presume* intent, with the burden of proof then shifting to the defendant to demonstrate a lack of intent to vilify or to intimidate. Because my policy presumes that targeted vilification is *inherently* intimidating, the defense of non-harm may not be made to refute this presumption, as it could in a tort action,[14] nor could the defense of "truth" be made, for we saw in the last chapter that the harm exists independently of any truth that may accompany the act of expressive intimidation. The only valid defenses (which may be difficult to prove) would be ignorance of the nature of the target and the likely effect of the speech or (perhaps) miscalculation of the likelihood of hitting a relevant target with the message.[15] This latter defense may involve a careful examination of the facts of the case, as the jury would have to make a prudential judgment based on the "totality of the circumstances."[16]

Whether the rebuttable presumption approach is used or the other approach (in which the burden of proof remains entirely with the prosecution), adjudication in this area would entail a method of evidentiary consideration similar to that of English courts in the adjudication of the Race Relations Act. In the most important prosecution in England brought under the act's Incitement to Racial Hatred law, the court instructed the jury to investigate the "real intent" behind the public demonstrations of Colin Jordan of the National Socialist Movement. This investigation included consideration of Jordan's party platform, his public statements, statements reported in the press or other media, and other relevant material.[17] Had such a consideration been made at Skokie, the NSPA's status would have been much more precarious from a constitutional standpoint (I refer the reader to the discussion above about the leaflets, the press statements, the NSPA platforms, and their previous demonstrations).

This type of jury consideration may be alleged to pose First Amendment problems because it requires delicate judgments which defy perfectly predictable outcomes. Yet, as Hadley Arkes states in his article on the prosecution of racial slurs:

> The premise itself is misconceived. The meaning of words cannot be so arbitrary and subjective. There may, of course, be borderline cases that are difficult to judge. But there are borderline judgments to be made in all kinds of cases, including murder, assault, and rape. Even though the injuries are unambiguous in these cases, they cannot be enough in themselves to determine the verdict. Whether a killing is a murder or a "justifiable homicide" will depend, by definition, on the case that could be made in justification. It will become necessary then to consider matters of intention and provocation, and these things can be judged only by reading the circumstances of the case. But the facts of the case, as we know, are not always so unequivocal . . . a decision, when it is finally made, may have to rest on an educated hunch—an estimate of character or an exercise of conjecture, which may be quite as slippery and "subjective" as anything one is likely to encounter in cases of speech or verbal assault. [18]

Given the harms perpetrated by targeted racial or ethnic vilification, it is hardly irresponsible to endorse Arkes' position on the validity of the jury's consideration of intent in this area of law. Nonetheless, context could make a difference in the area of intent. Collin's intimidations at Skokie were unprovoked. Yet racial insults often arise in response to an immediate stimulus, such as a traffic mishap or in response to other expression. What if the NSPA targeted the swastika at the American Jewish Committee headquarters after an anti-Nazi speech by AJC leaders? In these instances the specific intents to harm are precipitated by actions committed by the targets. The criminal law, of course, recognizes degrees of culpability which depend on context and mental state. Homicides committed with premeditation or malice aforethought constitute first degree murder, whereas homicides committed in the "heat of passion" constitute manslaughter or second degree. [19]

The courts could apply these standards to racial vilification. In this case, unprovoked verbal assault would clearly represent intent to harm (e.g., Skokie). This standard would cover the serious cases analyzed in the previous chapter; and this coverage is our main concern. If provocation existed, depending on the context, a lesser degree of culpability would exist, or none at all. Yet only a racialist provocation could justify a response; as we saw in our "Kike Keefe" hypothetical, the reference to Keefe's ethnicity was unjustified even though Keefe had (allegedly) engaged in panic peddling. Thus, the defendant should be allowed to claim provocation or special circumstances, and, for reasons of practicality and simplicity, success in making such a claim should be a total defense. Yet, once again, the provocation must be significant and shown by objective criteria: it should be such a provocation as to cause an average or reasonable person to retaliate with vilification. Finally, the presence of provocation would also be a factor the police and prosecutor would weigh at the stage of arrest or decision to prosecute.

IV. Targeting

The final prong in my definition of punishable racial vilification is the act of targeting. Targeting must be found for the expressive act to be abridgeable because, as seen in the last chapter, it is targeting which makes vilification *intimidating* and therefore substantial enough a harm to justify abridgement of the speech right. The major difference between the impact of Beauharnais' non-directed leafletting and the impacts of the racialist expressions in Arkes' Cicero example and my "Kike Keefe" hypothetical is precisely the act of targeting.

What does targeting look like? As in the determination of the vilifying or assaultive content of expression, there are degrees. The clearest instance of targeting is already provided for by present constitutional doctrine discussed in the last chapter: the captive audience as defined by *Cohen v. California* and other cases (this doctrine includes the structural basis for determining fighting words). As seen, this test involves continued direct, unavoidable exposure to unwanted ideas or expressions. Because the law already protects against speech that unjustifiably holds captive, there is no need here to deal with the situation of captivity.

The second instance of targeting lies outside the narrow test of *Cohen*: when the expression is *pointed at* or *directed toward* a particular target as defined by the targeter, though the speech does not literally hold the target captive. The determination of targeting in this sense would be more difficult to make, as it could come about by a variety of means. As in the determinations of intent and assaultive content, juries or judges would be required to consider all relevant evidence in the speech act rather than simply focusing on a particular act of presentation of views in the public forum. Skokie is a case in point. Though Skokie counsel presented evidence of the NSPA's leafletting, platform statements, and press statements,[20] the courts eventually disregarded these pieces of evidence in their determination of the NSPA's First Amendment right. Had they considered this evidence in framing a picture of the nature of the NSPA's speech act, the picture would have looked more assaultive than the image of "pure speech" which emerged from the courts' focus on the proposed demonstration at village hall. The courts viewed this proposed speech act in isolation from the *acts which targeted Skokie ahead of time* and which appear to have transformed the denotative and connotative meaning of the speech act from "pure speech" into a calculated assault. The present judicial methodology in this area of law, which requires courts to disregard past statements and acts of hate groups and to consider only the speech act at hand,[21] prevents the courts from comprehending the true meaning of assaultive speech.

Courts should be allowed to consider all relevant criteria to determine whether vilifying racialist or ethnic expression actually targets identifiable groups, thereby rendering it assaultive or a form of invasion (such as occurred at Skokie). In some cases, as in our "Kike Keefe" hypothetical, Arkes' Cicero case, and the types of neighborhood intimidations pointed out by the study of racial intimidation in Contra Costa County, the determination of targeting can be derived from the nature of the speech act itself. Though these cases may not entail strictly captive audiences (if we accept the extreme views of the ACLU's Franklyn Haiman mentioned in the last chapter or even *Cohen v. California*), they do indeed involve unacceptable forms of intimidation through the explicit targeting of *homes* or *neighborhoods.*

In rarer cases, such as Skokie, it may be possible to target not only a specific home or neighborhood, but an *entire ethnic community or set of neighborhoods.* Because these targets are larger, expression targeted at them is less clearly associated with the harms of captivity or direct assault than are invasions of neighborhoods or the area of privacy surrounding the home. Yet our investigation of the Skokie case has shown us that vilifying expression may indeed be felt as assaultive invasions of the community. In such cases, however, the courts (jury or judge) should be required to find sufficient evidence to warrant a finding of targeting. Advance notice of the assaultive intent of the demonstration (e.g., NSPA leaflets and press statements at Skokie) would be material evidence in making this determination, especially if the actual demonstration took place in only a single location on the periphery of the ethnic community. An actual "march" into the community could itself constitute targeting, as well as other dramatic, "pointed" acts at the time of the actual demonstration. In both cases, the speaker would determine the act of targeting by his actions prior to and/or during his demonstration in the public forum. As in the above determinations, the test would be objective, based on what a reasonable person would construe to be targeting.

I suggest the following legal standard of targeting (the formulation is amenable to more definite judicial construction or specification, as was the legislative standard of fighting words in *Chaplinsky*):

> When vilifying or assaultive expression is directed at an individual, home, neighborhood, or community in such a way as to single out an individual or specified group as the definite target of the expression, it is abridgeable.

V. The Final Test and the Problem of Unusual Susceptibility

Our analysis leaves us with the following components of abridgeable speech concerning race in the public forum: 1) assaultive, intimidating speech content, either explicit or symbolic-implicit; 2) the targeting of such expression; 3) the unprovoked intent to target such expression in order to harm. In sum, I suggest the following legal formulation as a first step in the direction of reform. Speech in the public forum involving race or ethnicity may be abridged

> 1) when such expression is accompanied by the advocacy of death or violence perpetrated against that group as determined by a reasonable person; *or,* when such expression explicitly demeans or vilifies through reference to race or ethnicity as determined by a reasonable person; *or,* when such expression so vilifies or demeans in a symbolic or implicit manner as determined by a reasonable person; *and*

> 2) such expression and harm are intended by the speaker and are unjustifiable due to the lack of significant provocation; *and*

> 3) such expression is directed at an individual, home, neighborhood, or community in such a way as to single out an individual or specified group as the definite target of the expression.

The Skokie case raised another point which must be addressed: the fact that the survivors were, in the words of the survivor at the Board of Trustees meeting on April 25, 1977, "a special breed of animal." That is, they were more vulnerable to the NSPA provocation than were other Jews because of the wounds caused by their past experiences (their propitious sociological circumstances notwithstanding). Frank Collin knew of this vulnerability and took advantage of it. Yet our analysis has demonstrated that targeted racial or ethnic vilification is *inherently* traumatic; accordingly, special vulnerability of a target group need not be a factor in determining the perpetration of a harm sufficient to justify the abridgement of speech, as harm is presumed in any case. However, any special vulnerability of the target(s), as well as any knowledge of such vulnerability on the part of the speaker may be factors the court may consider in its determination of intent and culpability. These considerations are especially important if the jury exercises discretion in arriving at its decision; as Arkes pointed out above, juries will often consider factors of circumstance and character in their deliberations concerning guilt.[22] The degree of vulnerability would also be a consideration in the decision to prosecute, which is always discretionary.[23] By providing for special vulnerability in this fashion, uncertainty is not eliminated, but is placed in areas of criminal law in which discretion and concomitant uncertainty have always existed. In this respect, my policy is an improvement upon the tort of the intentional infliction of emotional trauma (in which harm must be proved in court, and in which legal provision is made for special vulnerability)[24] because it does not require the actual presence of harm to be determined in court. The sheer existence of the speech act is enough to constitute guilt because harm is presumed.

VI. Questions and Critiques

Before we conclude, three potential problems must be addressed: the problem of chilling effect, the problem of intent, and the issue of the vilification of groups or individuals who do not belong to a racial or ethnic minority.

A. Slippage and the Problem of Chilling Effect

U.S. District Judge Decker predicated his decision in *Collin v. Smith* on the assumption that assaultive racial slurs cannot be separated in practice from controversial yet legitimate speech about racial issues.[25] I have shown that they are analytically distinguishable, and that assaultive expression should be abridgeable despite the fact that it may be "mixed" with worthy or even truthful speech. This position lessens the weight of the "mixed utterance" doctrine Decker endorses.

But critics may still argue that my policy would jeopardize free speech because it introduces a "slippery slope" problem in two respects: 1) courts would misapply the doctrine, thereby in practice abridging speech which my policy does not analytically cover;[26] 2) even if the courts could implement the doctrine without affecting worthy speech, the mere threat of faulty enforcement of the law could "chill" legitimate speech.[27]

My answer to the criticism of misapplication is straightforward. Yes, there may be misapplication. But misapplication is not a sufficient argument against my policy unless it could be shown that misapplication would have *undue* effect on the exercise of free speech. The threat of misapplication has not prevented the Supreme Court from upholding the constitutionality of the death penalty.[28] Is racialist speech more precious than life itself?[29] Nor has the potential problem of misapplication caused the Supreme Court to abandon its normative exclusion of obscenity from First Amendment protection. In *Young v. American Mini Theatres, Inc.,* Justice Stevens acknowledged that "slippage" could occur in the implementation of Detroit's zoning ordinance concerning pornographic shops. Yet Stevens held that this slippage was not a major problem because the affected expression was of only marginal value to society in terms of the social value norm found in *Chaplinsky*:

> The only vagueness in the ordinances relates to the amount of sexually explicit activity that may be portrayed before the material can be said to be "characterized by an emphasis" on such matter. For most films the question will be readily answerable; to the extent that an area of doubt exists, we see no reason why the statute is not "readily subject to a narrowing construction by the state courts." *Since there is surely a less vital interest in the uninhibited exhibition of material that is on the border line between pornography and artistic expression than in the free dissemination of ideas of social and political significance,* and since the limited amount of uncertainty in the statute is easily susceptible of a narrowing construction, we think this is an inappropriate case in which to adjudicate the hypothetical claims of persons not before the court.[30]

Steven's logic is appropriate in the regulation of targeted racial vilification, as well. Even if my proposals were to "slip" and "chill" some racialist expression, this slippage would affect only expression of low value (as low as obscenity). Yet to accept this position, one must take seriously *Chaplinsky's* norm of social value in the adjudication of speech. That is, the *ends* of free speech (their relation to substantive justice) would have to be considered.

B. The Problem of Intent

Libertarian speech theorists assert that free speech interests would be harmed if courts took the intent of speakers into consideration in determining the validity of free speech claims.[31] Yet the courts explicitly consider intent (on the part of government or private citizens, depending on the case) in many vital areas of law, including constitutional law and First Amendment cases. The prosecution must demonstrate a defendant's specific intent to break a law in most serious criminal cases (acts *mala in se*).[32] In constitutional law, the plaintiff must show the intent to discriminate on the part of the government in a suit concerning the equal protection clause,[33] and the Supreme Court even considers intent in such First Amendment areas as commercial speech and libel suits brought by public officials. In-person solicitation by lawyers may be prohibited because its "aim and effect" is often to compel people in distress to use a particular lawyer, making its commercial aspect and intent more important than its "speech" value.[34] Likewise, libel of public officials made with "malice" is constitutionally tortious according to the Court in the *Sullivan* case (a watershed pro–free speech decision).[35] The consideration of intent in the area of targeted racial vilification, therefore, is valid, *a fortiori.*

C. The Vilification of Majority Groups

Finally, readers will ask about the proper policy concerning minority groups' vilification of majority group members. My discussion of the *Gooding*[36] and *Lewis*[37] cases in Chapter One foreshadowed my position on this issue, as I criticized how these decisions in favor of angry black defendants watered down *Chaplinsky*'s fighting words doctrine.

Though it is true that racism directed against minorities is especially vicious because of the history of racial oppression in this country (a factor in making racial classifications "inherently suspect," as pointed out in the last chapter), I recommend that my policy reforms apply across the board to all forms of targeted racial vilification. First, whites who are targeted for vilification because of their race may feel just as intimidated as blacks, Jews, or other minorities. Second, the very act of *targeting* adds to the assaultive nature of the expression, so whites may be expected to feel unjustifiably assaulted in these instances. Third, it seems unfair to treat races differently in this area of law, especially because the basic values at stake concern the *fundamental principle that people should not be unduly abused on account of their race.* Whites who target racial vilification at blacks may be punished for violating this principle. Is it sensible to then turn around and allow blacks to commit the same harm against whites? I think not. Finally, such a double standard seems to constitute a subtle, new form of patronizing racism — it assumes that some minorities must be treated differently because they are less able to control themselves. Such assumptions undermine the constitutional principles of equality and individual responsibility.[38]

For these reasons, I endorse an evenhanded policy of application and enforcement in terms of race (subject, as above, to legitimate police and prosecutorial discretion). Richard Delgado espouses a similar approach in the tort area. His conclusion may be applied to my policy:

> The cause of action outlined is intended primarily to protect members of racial minority groups traditionally victimized. However, in some situations racial insults may cause harm when directed at members of the majority. The best example of such a situation would be the insult "You dumb honkey" directed at a white child by a black teacher in a predominantly black school. The potential for psychological harm in such a situation is obvious. And although the basis for the tort, the legacy of slavery and race discrimination, might seem to limit the class of those who can bring such actions to members of traditionally victimized minorities, it is the use of race to make invidious distinctions that is the ultimate evil the tort is designed to combat.[39]

VII. Substantive Justice and Community

In the Skokie litigation the courts ignored the intent and latent meaning of the NSPA's proposed speech act. Their limited view was a function of both their doctrinal commitment to the content neutrality rule and to their refusal to consider evidence pertaining to the NSPA's actions and statements leading up to Skokie. As a result, the legal decisions appeared out of touch with the facts and, therefore, out of touch with justice.

The Skokie decisions were the result of a free speech jurisprudence which is excessively libertarian. They upheld the NSPA's speech right despite the harms such speech caused (and would cause) the Skokie survivor community. The delicate balance of liberty and social value which the Supreme Court practiced in *Chaplinsky* was absent. My analysis of the Skokie case (both empirical and normative) has demonstrated that it is time the Supreme Court took the *Chaplinsky* social value principle and fighting words doctrine seriously once again. Such reconsideration would reconnect the First Amendment with substantive justice and the civility and protective functions of the just community.

The method of free speech adjudication I have proposed in this chapter would require the courts to consider community values. The present method of adjudication is anti-communitarian for two reasons: (1) It does not allow the courts to consider the *context* of political speech or its concrete application. Yet context and concreteness are important values of community or *gemeinschaft*.[40] (2) By forbidding courts to consider all relevant evidence in order to ascertain the intent and therefore the full meaning of speech, the method resembles the anti-community principle (or principle of "analysis") which Roberto Unger criticizes in *Knowledge and Politics*. Simply stated, the principle of analysis involves the dissection of "wholes" into constituent parts which then stand isolated from their former contextual meaning. This nominalism results in "the proposition that in the acquisition of knowledge the whole is the sum of its parts."[41] The relation between the principle of analysis and the principle of libertarian individualism is apparent: each focuses on individual entities in isolation from the contexts or environments within which they are embedded.[42] Unger contrasts the principle of analysis with the principle of "synthesis," which maintains that we cannot understand facts or individuals outside of their place in larger wholes.[43] In social terms, the principle of synthesis recognizes the individual as a social person.

If Unger is right, it is no accident that First Amendment jurisprudence concerning political speech in the public forum exalts an individualism abstracted from the community at the same time as it practices a method which is analytical in nature: the context, intent, and associated expression that give meaning to any individual speech act are ignored in honor of the individual's particular right at a particular time to exercise uninhibited free speech. It was this type of jurisprudence which prohibited the judicial consideration of wider context in the *Gooding, Lewis, Collin* and *Skokie* cases. Nor is it an accident that the courts downplayed *Chaplinsky*'s deeper "social value" principle in reaching these results.

But man is a political, communal animal in addition to being an individual.[44] Indeed, his development and growth require adequate socialization and learning from his culture. And the acts of individuals have important consequences, as the science of ecology teaches us in a different realm. Accordingly, the most prudent jurisprudence should *balance* individualism and community, the principles of analysis and synthesis. Alexander Meiklejohn achieves this balance in his theory of free speech. Though he is often considered an extreme libertarian,[45] Meiklejohn justifies free speech in terms of its contribution to the political and communal practice of self-government. His theory is incomprehensible outside of this teleological context. Significantly, Meiklejohn asserts that the citizens who practice self-government must possess "self-control" and virtue, and that selfishness and inconsideration (incivility) are inimical to freedom, properly understood.[46] Meiklejohn's theory is consistent with both *Chaplinsky*'s civility principle and its definitional (two-level) approach to free speech adjudication that emphasizes social value.[47] By these means, a propitious balance is struck between individualism and communitarianism. Frank Collin's abuse of free speech at Skokie and similar precedents have upset this delicate balance. It is time courts set the balance aright.

Notes

Chapter One

1. Tape of Skokie Board of Trustees meeting, April 25, 1977.
2. Ibid.
3. David Hamlin, *The Nazi/Skokie Conflict: A Civil Liberties Struggle* (Beacon Press, 1980), p. 172.
4. See *Brandenburg v. Ohio,* 395 U.S. 444 (1969).
5. On the aspects of the content neutrality rule, see Laurence Tribe, *American Constitutional Law* (Foundation Press, 1978), ch. 12, secs. 1–5.
6. See Hannah Arendt, *The Crises of the Republic* (Harcourt Brace Jovanovich, 1972), pp. 88–96. See also David Garrow, *Protest at Selma: Martin Luther King, Jr., and the Voting Rights Act* (Yale University Press, 1979); Jack Greenberg's fine text, *Judicial Process and Social Change: Constitutional Litigation* (West, 1975), particularly ch. II: Hugo Adam Bedau, ed., *Civil Disobedience: Theory and Practice* (Pegasus, 1969). For an explicit connection between the content neutrality doctrine and the expression and protest in favor of blacks' rights, see Harry Kalven, *The Negro and the First Amendment* (University of Chicago Press, 1965), esp. ch. 1.
7. Kenneth Karst, "Equality as a Central Principle in the First Amendment," 43 *U. Chi. L. Rev.* 20, 28 (1975). See also Tribe, op. cit., pp. 672–74. A key case is *Chicago Police Department v. Mosley,* 408 U.S. 92 (1972).
8. See Martin Shapiro, *Freedom of Speech: The Supreme Court and Judicial Review* (Prentice Hall, 1966), in which Shapiro champions the Court as a political body representing the claims of groups denied access to other political institutions. See also *U.S. v. Carolene Products Co.,* 304 U.S. 144, 152, n. 4; and John Hart Ely, *Democracy and Distrust* (Harvard University Press, 1980). On how administrative law reflects group theory, see Shapiro, "On Predicting the Future of Administrative Law," *Regulation,* May/June 1982, pp. 20–21.
9. See Karen Orren, "Standing to Sue: Interest Group Conflict in the Federal Courts," 70 *Amer Pol Sci Rev* 723 (1976).
10. See Richard Stewart, "The Reformation of American Administrative Law," 88 *Harvard L. Rev.* 1669 (1975); Richard Stewart and Stephen Breyer, *Administrative Law and Regulatory Policy* (Little, Brown, 1979), ch. 10, "Public Interest" Ad-

ministrative Law: Representation and Disclosure." On politics as group behavior and public interest as the outcome of this struggle, see David Truman, *The Governmental Process* (Knopf, 1971); Glendon Schubert, *The Public Interest* (Free Press, 1960). See also Orren, op. cit.

11. See Philippe Nonet and Philip Selznick, *Law and Society in Transition: Toward Responsive Law* (Harper Torchbook, 1978), ch. IV.

12. See Archibald Cox, *The Warren Court: Constitutional Decision as an Instrument of Reform* (Harvard University Press, 1968), ch. 1. On constitutional "ethos" as a mode of interpretation, see Philip Bobbitt, *Constitutional Fate: Theory of the Constitution* (Oxford University Press, 1982), chs. 7-12.

13. *Collin v. Smith,* 447 F. Supp. 676 (1978), 687. There is a difference between procedural, or civil, "commutative" justice and "distributive" or "social" justice. The liberal regime is more comfortable with the former than the latter. See Geoffrey Hazard, "Social Justice Through Civil Justice," 36 *U. Chi. L. Rev.* 699 (1969). On justice as open participation, see also Robert Paul Wolff, *The Poverty of Liberalism* (Beacon Press).

14. Alexander Meiklejohn, *Political Freedom* (Oxford University Press, 1965), p. 75. On free speech as also necessary to the fundamental liberal value of autonomy, see Thomas Scanlon, "On Freedom of Expression," 1 *Philos. and Pub. Affs.,* 1972; Harry Wellington, "On Freedom of Expression," 88 *Yale L. J.* 1105 (1979); Thomas Emerson, *The System of Freedom of Expression* (Vintage, 1970), ch. 1. Shapiro portrays administrative legal theory in terms similar to Meiklejohn in "The Future of Administrative Law," p. 21. On how too much group participation in administrative decision-making *weakens* the state, see Stewart, op. cit. See also Theodore Lowi: *The End of Liberalism* (Norton, 1969).

15. The "concept" (or basic definition) of a right is not the same thing as its "conception" (i.e., application in a particular case or instance). Thus, the *exercise* of a right may contradict the basic principle inherent in the right. See Ronald Dworkin, *Taking Rights Seriously* (Harvard University Press, 1978), pp. 134–36. Hanna Pitkin, *Wittgenstein and Justice* (University of California Press, 1973), pp. 186–92, and Jack Donnelley, "Human Rights and Human Dignity: An Analytical Critique of Non-Western Conceptions of Human Rights," 76 *Amer Pol Sci Rev* 303 (1982), pp. 303–4.

16. Stephen interview.

17. See *Freedom, Virtue, and the First Amendment* (Gateway, 1965). Berns' position relies strongly on the political theory of Leo Strauss. See *Natural Right and History* (University of Chicago Press, 1953), in which Strauss criticizes the modern conception of right or "rights" in favor of the natural "right" orientations of the ancients, particularly those of Plato and Aristotle. See also Berns, *The First Amendment and the Future of American Democracy* (Basic Books, 1976).

18. See Stewart, op. cit.; Shapiro, "Future of Administrative Law"; and Richard Neeley, *Why Courts Don't Work* (McGraw-Hill, 1983), Preface and ch. 1.

19. Berns, *Freedom,* ch. IX. Berns' position is similar to the "bad tendency" test developed by the Supreme Court in World War I cases. See *Schenck v. U.S.,*

249 U.S. 47 (1919); *Debs v. U.S.,* 249 U.S. 211 (1919). On the weaknesses of Berns' and Strauss' natural law approach, see Judith Shklar, *Legalism* (Harvard University Press, 1964). On bad tendency, speculative harm, and the McCarthy era Communist Party cases, see Tribe, op. cit., pp. 608–17. On the type of balance entailed in this logic, see Craig E. Ducat, *Modes of Constitutional Interpretation* (West Publ., 1978), pp. 130–35.

20. See Southern Poverty Law Center Report; *Klan Watch Intelligence Report*; the special Southern Poverty Law Center Report, *The Ku Klux Klan: A History of Racism & Violence,* 1982; and California Fair Employment and Housing Commission Report and Recommendations on Public Hearings on Racial, Ethnic, & Religious Conflict & Violence in Contra Costa County, issued April 8, 1982. Also see California Assembly Report on Bill 267, Against Inciting Racial Hatred, 1981.

21. *Schenck v. U.S.,* 249 U.S. 47, 52 (1919). See Robert Bork, "Neutral Principles and Some First Amendment Problems," 47 *Ind. L. J.* (1971); Meiklejohn, op. cit.

22. See Bork, op. cit.; Meiklejohn, op. cit.; Laurent Frantz, "The First Amendment in the Balance," 71 *Yale L. J.* 1424 (1962) and Melville B. Nimmer "The Right to Speak from *Times* to *Time*: First Amendment Theory Applied to Libel and Misapplied to Privacy," 56 *Cal. La. Rev.* 935 (1968), esp. 942–48.

23. 315 U.S. 568, 571–2 (1942).

24. See Tribe, op. cit., p. 606, on *Chaplinsky,* as concerned with the *manner* of expression. Some theorists criticize definitional balancing as mere ad hoc balancing in disguise. See Shapiro, *Freedom of Speech,* ch. 3.

25. On the "civility" value in *Chaplinsky,* see Hadley Arkes, "Civility and the Restriction of Speech: Rediscovering the Defamation of Groups," in Kurland, ed., *Free Speech and Association: The Supreme Court and the First Amendment* (University of Chicago Press, 1975); and Arkes, *The Philosopher in the City* (Princeton University Press, 1981), part one.

26. *New York Times v. Sullivan,* 376 U.S. 255 (1964). On *Sullivan* and definitional balancing, see Nimmer, op. cit., 942–48.

27. Harry Kalven states that the most important litmus paper test of a democracy is its position on seditious libel. A society's stance on obscenity, he says, is of secondary importance compared to its position on free political speech. See "The New York Times Case: A Note on the 'Central Meaning' of the First Amendment," in Kurland, op. cit., p. 98. It is ironic that Kalven, whose position here seems to vindicate *Chaplinsky*'s two-level approach, elsewhere disparaged it in the name of libertarianism. See "The Metaphysics of the Law of Obscenity," 1960 *Sup. Ct. Rev.* 1.

28. Some contemporary social critics maintain that there is a disturbing undercurrent in a society of *excessive* libertarianism, for such a society undermines the intermediate institutions and the psychological bases that promote psychological sublimation and maturation. See Christopher Lasch, *Haven in a Heartless World: The Family Besieged* (Basic Books, 1977), and *The Culture of Narcissism* (Norton, 1978); Philip Rieff, *The Triumph of the Therapeutic* (Harper, 1966). A classical example of this logic is Tocqueville's *Democracy in America* (Schocken, 1961 trans.), which located freedom between solipsism and absolutism.

29. Kalven, *The Negro and the First Amendment* (University of Chicago Press, 1965), pp. 140–45. The Warren Court's treatment of speech in these respects may have been part and parcel of its approach to criminal sanctions in general. Cox, *The Warren Court*, p. 11, states that the Court was influenced in its criminal law jurisprudence by sociologists and psychologists who "have cast doubt upon the efficacy of punishment and deterrence in the face of the social, economic, and psychological causes of criminal conduct." Interestingly, Herbert Packer maintains that a similar suspicion of criminal sanctions and the exercise of legal authority characterizes the "Due Process Model" of criminal procedure (the model sanctioned by the Warren Court, and opposed to the "Crime Control Model"). Advocates of the Due Process Model are suspicious of the authoritative discernment and articulation of facts and motives in human (and criminal) action. See Packer, *The Limits of the Criminal Sanction* (Stanford University Press, 1968), ch. 8, esp. pp. 163–71. It will be seen, however, that the Burger Court (allegedly a "crime control" court) accelerated *Chaplinsky*'s demise.

30. *Edwards,* 372 U.S. 229 (1963); *Cox,* 379 U.S. 536 (1965); *Gregory,* 349 U.S. 111 (1969); and *Cohen,* 403 U.S. 15 (1971). For a good discussion of these cases in terms of our present discussion, see Tribe, op. cit., pp. 600–601, 617–23.

31. See *Cohen v. California,* 403 U.S. 15 (1971); *Public Utilities Comm'n v. Pollak,* 343 U.S. 451 (1952); *Rowan v. Post Office,* 397 U.S. 728 (1970); *Lehman v. Shaker Heights,* 418 U.S. 298 (1974); *Erznoznik v. Jacksonville,* 422 U.S. 205 (1975).

32. 315 U.S. 568, 571–72.

33. 403 U.S. 15, 25. Harlan's opinion constitutes a judicial acceptance of the epistemological premises of liberal psychology as depicted (critically) by Roberto Unger in *Knowledge and Politics.* These premises, according to Unger, include: 1) the separation of reason and desire, with the latter being the primary part of the self; 2) the arbitrariness of desire from the perspective of the understanding; 3) the principle of analysis: the sum is not greater than its parts, i.e., there is no real community of shared value beyond atomized individuals. The results of these principles are "absolute moral skepticism" and extreme individualism: "Given the postulate of arbitrary desire, there is no basis on which to prefer some ends to others." See *Knowledge and Politics* (Free Press, 1973), pp. 31–53. Unger's theory of liberal psychology parallels the "group theory" of politics and law discussed earlier: both downplay end values in favor of values that arise due to experience or participation. It also parallels the discussion of the Warren Court's suspicion of the criminal sanction above. For another superb critique of arbitrary desire, or "emotivism," as a basis for moral evaluation see Alasdair MacIntyre, *After Virtue* (University of Notre Dame Press, 1981).

34. See Hadley Arkes, op. cit., for excellent discussions of *Cohen*'s impact on *Chaplinsky* to which I am indebted.

35. In this respect we see the similarity between the political and speech theories of Meiklejohn and Hannah Arendt. Both posit speech as an essential attribute of political life, the very substance of a public order. Each also envisions politics as a preeminently creative enterprise which brings a distinctly human meaning into

the world which is different from the laws of nature and the necessities of survival. Free politics, while involving awesome burdens of responsibility, nonetheless represents a relative freedom from necessity. In this sense, political freedom parallels the psychological freedom of the mature individual depicted by psychologists, as the mature ego gives the self *some* freedom from the demands of the instincts ("inner necessity," to Freud). See Meiklejohn, *Political Freedom,* particularly ch. 1, on freedom vs. behaviorism and totalitarianism; Arendt, *The Human Condition* (University of Chicago Press, 1958). See also Joseph Tussman, *Obligation and the Body Politic* (Oxford University Press, 1962), ch. 1. For a philosophical position that expresses many of the values underlying the theory of the First Amendment as an "experiment," see William James, *Pragmatism* (New American Library, 1974). James dedicated his *Pragmatism* lectures to Mill. See also Unger's elaboration of modernism in *Passion: An Essay on Personality* (Free Press, 1984).

36. On the priority of security as a value, see Ernest van den Haag, *Punishing Criminals: Concerning a Very Old and Painful Question* (Basic Books, 1975), p. 36. See also Charles Silberman, *Criminal Violence, Criminal Justice* (Vintage, 1980), ch. 1; and Hobbes, *Leviathan* (Pelican, 1968).

37. *Gooding, Warden v. Wilson,* 405 U.S. 518 (1972).

38. Ibid., pp. 528-29. Burger's critique essentially accuses the majority of engaging in what Unger calls the *principle of analysis,* in which the contextual, communitarian meaning of speech and action is lost in the exclusive focus on individual terms or persons. In grammatical terms, there is no syntactic meaning, only words. In sociological terms, there is no community, only the individual. In proverbial terms, there is no forest, only the trees. This modernistic tendency is also depicted in Ferdinand Tönnies' distinction between society and community in *Community and Society (Gemeinschaft und Gesellschaft),* trans. Loomis (Michigan State University Press, 1957), Pts. I and II, in which the meaning of "community" is defined in terms of empathy and context, "society" as individualistic "rational will" divorced from context. Justice Blackmun's dissent in *Lewis* II, quoted below, should be read in terms of Tönnies. See also Arendt's analysis of the concomitant declines of public community and "common sense" in *The Human Condition,* pp. 208-9, 274-75, 283-84. See also Blackmun's dissent in *Gooding*: The majority's reading of the statute defies "common sense," 405 U.S. 518, at 535.

39. See Franklyn Haiman's recent treatise, *Speech and Law in a Free Society* (University of Chicago Press, 1981), for many prominent examples of this practice. Haiman is national secretary of the ACLU, a post he held during the Skokie controversy. He was an interviewee. In *The Philosopher in the City,* Arkes attributes this tendency to an undue reliance on the outmoded philosophy of logical positivism, which bans prescriptive meaning from discourse. See pp. 69-72.

40. 408 U.S. 901, 913, 914, and 415 U.S. 130, respectively.

41. 415 U.S. 130, 136-7. See also Arendt on "common sense," *The Human Condition.*

42. See John Noonan's critique of legalism's "masking" of empirical reality in *Persons and Masks of the Law: Cardozo, Holmes, Jefferson, and Wythe as Makers*

of the Masks, (Farrar, Straus, and Giroux, 1976). Noonan's critique of legalism is reminiscent of Tönnies' critique of rational will and abstractionism in *Community and Society.* See also Jackson's dissent in *Terminiello v. Chicago,* 337 U.S. 1 (1949), at 24-37. Jackson wrote the dissent after presiding over the Nuremburg trials. Terminiello's conviction for inciting racial violence had been overturned by the Court (per Douglas) because of an "improper" instruction to the jury. Not once did Douglas acknowledge the exceptional violence that characterized the case. The Skokie decisions relied on Douglas' *Terminiello* decision.

43. Herbert Packer, "The Courts, the Police, and the Rest of Us," 57 *Crim. L. C. and P. S.* 238-39 (1966). See also Henry J. Friendly, "The Bill of Rights as a Code of Criminal Procedure," 53 *Calif. L. Rev.* 929 (1965). For a favorable view of this approach, see Ely, *Democracy and Distrust,* pp. 124-25.

44. Erna Gans interview.

45. *NSPA v. Skokie,* 373 N.E. 2d. 21 (1978).

46. Ibid., at 23; and "Brief & Argument of Village of Skokie, A Municipal Corp, Plaintiff Appellee," pp. 5-6.

47. *NSPA v. Skokie,* at 23-25.

48. *Collin v. Smith,* 447 F. Supp. 676 (1978).

49. Ibid., at 686.

50. Ibid.

51. Ibid.

52. Ibid., at 688-89; see also Skokie brief.

53. *Collin v. Smith,* at 692-93.

54. See *The Prince* and *The Discourses* (Modern Library, Random House, 1950). See also J. G. A. Pocock, *The Machiavellian Moment: Florentine Political Thought and the Atlantic Republican Traditions* (Princeton University Press, 1975); and also Hanna Pitkin's *Wittgenstein and Justice* on Machiavelli's notion of "virtu" as manly energy, pp. 308-12. The notion of accepting painful reality and dealing with it is also akin to Freud's model of mature ego-formation, in which the psyche accepts the reality principle despite the pleas of the pleasure principle to ignore it. See Freud, *General Psychological Theory* (Collier, 1963), ch. I; *New Introductory Lectures on Psychoanalysis* (Norton, 1965). This notion of republican virtue ignores the more classical notion that pertains to goodness. In the American context, see Gordon Wood, *The Creation of the American Republic* (Norton, 1972).

55. See Glenn Tinder, *Community: Reflections on a Tragic Ideal* (Louisiana State University Press, 1980); Meiklejohn, op. cit., p. 75; and Holmes' notions of the democratic "experiment" in *Abrams v. U.S.* See also Karl Popper, *The Open Society and Its Enemies* (Harper, 1962).

56. *Whitney v. California,* 274 U.S., 357 (1927), 375-77.

57. Other theorists have stressed similar ends of free speech. See, for example, Emerson, *The System of Freedom of Expression* (Vintage, 1970), ch. 1; Karst, op. cit., pp. 23ff; Bork, "Neutral Principles," p. 20. One recent work makes a powerful argument against the "truth" justification of free speech, maintaining that no one has satisfactorily demonstrated that free speech engenders truth in a systematic sense.

See Frederick Schauer, *Free Speech: A Philosophical Enquiry* (Cambridge University Press, 1982). Schauer's point does not weaken the utility of this model for our ensuing analysis, however.

58. See, for example, Fred Berger, *Freedom of Expression* (Wadsworth, 1980), ch. 1.

59. Mill, *On Liberty* (Henry Holt, 1898), pp. 95-96. See also the excellent treatment of the relation between factual truth and its psychological acceptance in Walter Laqueur's book on the Jewish and non-Jewish refusal to accept the truth of the Holocaust in *The Terrible Secret: Suppression of the Truth about Hitler's "Final Solution"* (Little, Brown, 1980). Laqueur concludes that the refusal to accept the "terrible secret" must be based on the mysterious but real operation of a psychological process involving *recognition* and *willingness* to *grasp* and *accept* painful facts. Bruno Bettelheim addresses the same matter in his controversial critique of Anne Frank; Bettelheim accuses her family of denying reality in favor of wishful and "magical" fantasy, which, in psychoanalytic terms, represents a primitive, infantile form of thinking. See "The Hidden Lessons of Anne Frank," in Bettelheim, *Surviving and Other Essays* (Vintage, Random House, 1980). The relevance of these works to our depiction of Machiavelli and republican virtue is obvious. See also Arendt, *Eichmann in Jerusalem* (Penguin, 1963), and Raul Hilberg, *The Destruction of European Jews* (Penguin, 1963) for critiques of Jews' refusal to face the harsh facts of Nazi intentions.

60. Judith interview.

61. See Meiklejohn's discussion of political freedom as primarily the responsibility of the citizenry in their roles as "We, the rulers." *Political Freedom,* ch. 2.

62. See Hadley Arkes, "Civility and the Restriction of Speech," op. cit., pp. 418-20. In speaking about crowds' intimidations of innocent citizens on account of their race (e.g., *Kristallnacht* 1938 in Germany; white racists outside a black family's home), Arkes states: "No government may hold back in these instances and properly claim the allegiance of its citizens, for if we may use an older phrase, it would have shown itself at that moment to be destructive of those ends for which governments are instituted. It would have defaulted then on the first obligation of government as it was understood by the men who framed the Declaration of Independence." See also Van den Haag, op. cit., Hobbes, op. cit. Freud provides a parallel psychological analysis: a mature ego (the agent of autonomy and freedom) arises only out of the resolution of the Oedipus complex, which entails the internalization of authority and order. See *The Ego and the Id* (Norton, 1962).

63. See James Q. Wilson, "The Urban Unease: Community vs. City," 12 *Public Interest,* 25 (1968), cited in Hadley Arkes, "Civility and the Restriction of Speech," op. cit., pp. 390-91. See also Van den Haag and Silberman, op. cit.

64. Aristotle, *The Politics,* Barker, trans. (Oxford University Press, 1962), p. 6. Hobbes also viewed civil society as constituted by the common (public) agreement about the basic terms of justice. A strong sovereign is needed to enforce this commonality. See *Leviathan,* Part I, on the state of war as due to the passions and the disagreement over the terms of right, and Part II, ch. 17, on the commonwealth

as the cure. Locke held a similar view in *The Second Treatise of Government* (Mentor, 1963), esp. chs. II and III. On Hobbes in this regard, see Eric Voegelin, *The New Science of Politics* (University of Chicago Press, 1952), pp. 152–62. See also Walter Berns, "Judicial Review and the Rights and Laws of Nature," 1982 *Sup. Ct. Rev.* 49, 58–75. On the distinction between conflict over basic or fundamental values and over secondary values (the former is destructive, the latter may be beneficial), see Lewis Coser, *The Functions of Social Conflict* (Free Press, 1956), pp. 73–75; and Ortega, *Concord and Liberty,* quoted at front of this book.

Chapter Two

1. The following references to dates, actions, and characteristics of the relevant parties are based on many sources, including David Hamlin, *The Nazi/Skokie Conflict: A Civil Liberties Battle* (The Beacon Press, 1980); Hamlin, "Swastikas and Survivors: Inside the Skokie Case," *Civ. Lib. Rev.,* May–June, 1978; Aryeh Neier, *Defending my Enemy: American Nazis, The Skokie Case, and Risks of Freedom* (Dutton, 1979); "Skokie Chronology," a report of the Midwest Office of the Anti-Defamation League, Chicago; and press reports.

2. See Ellerin Report on American Nazis, American Jewish Committee, Chicago, "American Nazis – Myth or Menace?" Domestic Affs. Dept., Nov, 1977, #77-970-13; and ADL report, "The U.S. Neo-Nazi Movement: 1978," in *Facts,* 24(2), March 1978.

3. John Boguta in the *Chicago Journal,* July 19, 1978, p. 6. Boguta once made a film on Marquette Park for PBS.

4. See Jerome Skolnick, Director, *The Politics of Protest: A Task Force Report Submitted to Skolnick, Director, the National Commission on the Causes and Prevention of Violence* (Simon and Schuster, 1969), pp. 225–26. On the issue of white working class backlash and conflict, see also Robert O'Neil, *Classrooms in the Crossfire* (Indiana University Press, 1981), ch. 1; J. Harvie Wilkinson, III, *From Brown to Bakke: The Supreme Court and School Integration: 1954–1978* (Oxford University Press, 1979), ch. 8; John Gaventa, *Power and Powerlessness: Quiescence and Rebellion in an Appalachian Valley* (University of Illinois Press, 1980).

5. See *Chicago Tribune,* June 27, 1978.

6. See *Chicago Sun-Times,* July 9, 1978.

7. See the California Fair Housing and Employment Commission *Report on the Incitement of Racial Hatred in Contra Costa County.* Young men and teen-aged boys are targets of hate group recruitment and incitement because they are vulnerable to excitement, adventure, and the ideological appeal offered by such groups. Many are angry and in need of "commitment" in a period of "drift" in their lives. See Charles Silberman, *Criminal Violence, Criminal Justice,* ch. 3; Erik Erikson, *Insight and Responsibility* (Norton, 1964), ch. III; Kenneth Keniston, *The Uncommitted: Alienated Youth in American Society* (Dell, 1965).

8. Hamlin, "Swastikas and Survivors."

9. Ibid.

10. See *Collin v. Chicago Park District,* 460 F.2d 746 (1972). The Federal District Court ruled in Collin's favor by holding that the right of free speech naturally includes the right to present it in a forum that is effective, that is, in which sympathetic or interested audiences are likely to be present. "Hyde Park" forums are insufficient.

11. See testimony in *Collin v. Smith,* in U.S. District Court, N. D. Illinois, Eastern Division, 78-1381, Collin testimony, p. 4.

12. DKT. No. 76 C 2024 (N. D. Illinois, 1976); see Hamlin, *The Nazi/Skokie Conflict,* pp. 15–19.

13. Skokie corporate counsel Harvey Schwartz said that years of watching Collin had taught him that Collin will obey the law for two reasons: 1) he wants police to *protect* him in demonstrations and in general; 2) he is afraid of being sent to Cook County Jail, where the "enemy" waits behind bars to seriously mistreat him. On racial violence and mistreatment in prisons (particularly black against white) see Silberman, op. cit., ch. 10. It is ironic that after the Skokie affair Collin was sentenced to prison for sexually molesting young boys.

14. See Hamlin, *The Nazi/Skokie Conflict,* p. 17.

15. Ab Rosen interview.

16. The Federal courts ruled against him in the late summer of 1976 and spring of 1977. See discussion in *Collin v. O'Malley,* 452 F. Supp. 577(1978), and the *Chicago Tribune,* April 19, 1977. It was not until the pressures of Skokie arose that the O'Malley litigation was reviewed and decided in favor of Collin. See infra.

17. Hamlin, *The Nazi/Skokie Conflict,* pp. 18, 23. Compare Hamlin's portrayal of Collin's need for public confirmation of his inner needs with Erich Fromm's depiction of Hitler's narcissistic needs in *The Anatomy of Human Destructiveness* (Fawcett, 1973), ch. 13; see also Jürgen Syberberg's film, *Our Hitler.*

18. See *Demographic Characteristics: Village of Skokie; U.S. Department of Housing and Urban Development Community Development and Housing Plan Summary: Community Profile, Village of Skokie,* June 13, 1979; *"Skokie," A Report on Skokie;* and *The Comprehensive Plan: Skokie Illinois,* a report prepared for the Village Planning Commission and the Village Board of Trustees, September, 1969.

19. See Hamlin, *The Skokie/Nazi Conflict,* p. 26 and Hamlin interview.

20. The German *Bund* movement in America was fairly substantial across the land and supported by many Germans. Their leader was the redoubtable *Bundesleiter* Fritz Julius Kuhn. See Sander A. Diamond, *The Nazi Movement in the United States, 1924–1941* (Cornell University Press, 1974).

21. See *"Skokie," A Report on Skokie,* p. 8.

22. There are no exact figures available for Skokie's Jewish population, but reliable expert sources estimate the number is 30,000, not the 40,000 figure that appears in law casebooks and also appeared in the press during the Skokie controversy. See Marvin Bailey interview (Bailey is the Skokie director of housing development).

23. This is the figure given to me by survivor leaders.

24. See ADL chronology, op. cit.

25. Hamlin interview.

26. Hamlin, *The Nazi/Skokie Conflict,* p. 32.

27. Ibid., p. 32.

28. See Mayor Smith's deposition in *Collin v. Smith,* U.S. District Court, N. D. Illinois, Eastern Division, 77c 2982, pp. 15–16.

29. Hamlin, *The Nazi/Skokie Conflict,* p. 132. Beauharnais also cloaked his intent this way in *Beauharnais v. Illinois.* Justic Black accepted the masquerade in his dissent. See Kalven, *The Negro and the First Amendment,* ch. 1.

30. See ADL and American Jewish Committee reports on Skokie and the quarantine policy. ADL Memorandum, National Law Committee, September 20, 1979; *NJCRAC Annual Report;* Rice interview; DuBow interview; Ab Rosen interview; and Hal Rosen interview.

31. See Walter Berns' concept of "moral anger" in *For Capital Punishment* (Basic Books, 1979); and Margaret MacDonald, "Natural Rights," in A. I. Melden, ed., *Human Rights* (Wadsworth, 1970), pp. 40–60.

32. Gordon Allport, *The Nature of Prejudice* (Addison-Wesley, 1979), p. 430. See also Seymour Lipset and Earl Raab, *The Politics of Unreason* (Harper, 1970), chs. 1 and 12; Arendt, *The Human Condition;* and Meiklejohn, *Political Freedom.* They define political freedom as freedom from necessity. In terms of extremism as we define it, extremists are not free from their own inner passions. See also Sartre's "Portrait of an Antisemite," in Kaufmann, ed., *Existentialism from Dostoevsky to Sartre* (New American Library, 1975).

33. Allport, op. cit., pp. 380–89, 404.

34. See Richard Sennett, *The Fall of Public Man,* chs. 5, 10, and 11, for accounts of the way in which extremist political behavior represents projection of psychological matter rather than objective clarification.

35. Daniel Boorstin, *The Image* (Atheneum, 1977), p. 11.

36. Ibid., p. 47.

37. See Lipset and Raab, chs. 3 and 4; John Higham, *Strangers in the Land: Patterns of American Nativism 1860–1925* (Atheneum, 1969), ch. 10; Nathan C. Belth, *A Promise to Keep: A Narrative of the American Encounter with Anti-Semitism* (Times Books, 1979), ch. 3; and *The Ku Klux Klan: A History of Racism and Violence* (Southern Poverty Center, 1982).

38. Herbert Gans, *Deciding What's News* (Vintage, Random House, 1980).

39. Ibid., pp. 52–57.

40. Epstein, *News From Nowhere: Television and the News* (Random House, 1973), pp. 173, 241, 262–63.

41. The image of irrationality actually serves as a strategic advantage in bargaining and extortionate relationships because it shows that the extortioner is capable of cruelty. See William Ker Muir, *Police: Streetcorner Politicians* (University of Chicago Press, 1977), pp. 43–44 and ch. 8; and Thomas Schelling, *The Strategy of Conflict* (Oxford University Press, 1963), pp. 16–18.

42. *New Order* (NSPA newsletter), March, 1979, p. 8.

43. Allport, op. cit., pp. 37, 151-53 on self-hate and concomitant hate of ingroups. See also Fromm, *Anatomy of Human Destructiveness,* on Hitler's self-hate.

44. Allport, op. cit., p. 152.

45. See Mike Royko, "'Ol' Daddy o' Mine' isn't a Nazi favorite," *Chicago Daily News,* June 23, 1977; Jack Mabley, "This Nazi's Got a Real Problem," *Chicago Tribune,* June 26, 1977; Hamlin, *The Nazi/Skokie Conflict,* pp. 5-8; and "Curse of Dachau Survivor: Son is Jewish-hating Nazi," *Detroit News,* July 28, 1977.

46. See Henry Krystal, ed., *Massive Psychic Trauma* (hereafter, *MPT*) (International University Press, 1968), pp. 29, 65, 85, 333, 343-44 on "identification with the aggressor" and self-hate in survivors of torturous treatment. These problems also afflict some children of such survivors. See Helen Epstein, *Children of the Holocaust* (Putnam, 1979), especially pp. 136-37 where she identifies Frank Collin as an example of self-hate and identification with the aggressor. On the general phenomenon of Jewish self-hate, see Raphael Patai, *The Jewish Mind* (Scribner's, 1977), ch. 17.

47. Tedor quoted in "The Nazi," *Chicago Magazine,* June, 1978.

48. "Lying has always been a highly approved Nazi technique. Hitler, in *Mein Kampf,* advocated mendacity as a policy," said Justice Jackson in his closing address at the Nuremburg Trial; see London, II, *The World of Law* (Simon and Schuster, 1960), pp. 467 and 505. See also Syberberg's masterful and extraordinary film *Our Hitler,* in which he utilizes the leit motif of projection onto film to illuminate the inner meaning of Hitler and the Third Reich.

49. Ab Rosen, Midwest director of the ADL, stressed this point to me more assiduously than anyone. Every single interviewee criticized the press for "sensationalizing" the issue — even Collin! See also *Evanston Review,* June 22, 1978, "Northwestern University Study: Skokie Residents Say Too Much Media Play."

50. *Midweek Magazine,* May 4, 1977, p. 5.

51. See Frances Fox Piven and Richard A. Cloward, *Poor People's Movements: Why They Succeed, How They Fail* (Vintage, Random House, 1974), pp. 18-22; Michael Lipsky, *Protest in City Politics* (Rand McNally, 1970); Arendt, "On Violence" in *Crises of the Republic*; Schelling, *The Strategy of Conflict,* pp. 12, 16-18; Muir, *Streetcorner Politicians,* pp. 43-44; and James Q. Wilson, "The Strategy of Protest," *Journal of Conflict Resolution,* 5 (1961), pp. 292-93.

52. See Harvey Schwartz interview; Hamlin, *The Nazi/Skokie Conflict*; and Hamlin interview.

53. See Schelling, op. cit., pp. 20, 121, 135, 239; Muir, op. cit., pp. 38-40.

54. Greene column, "Chicago's Nazis switch — main target now is the Jews," *Chicago Sun-Times,* September 29, 1976.

55. See *Chicago Tribune,* April 19, 1977, "Judge's refusal of Nazi plea upheld." The appeals court upheld Leighton's decision in April.

56. See *Village of Skokie v. NSPA,* 51 Ill. App. 3d. 279; 366 N.E. 2d. 347, (1977).

57. Ibid.

58. Village Ordinance 77-5-N-994.

59. Village Ordinance 77-5-N-996.

60. Village Ordinance 77-5-N-995.

61. See *Collin v. Smith,* 447 F. Supp. 676 (1978) 578 F. 2d. 1197 7th Cir. (1978).

62. On the expense and burdens of litigation, which favors the wealthy and powerful, see Marc Gallanter, "Why the 'Haves' Come Out Ahead: Speculation on the Limits of Legal Change," 9 *Law and Society Rev.,* 1 (1974), p. 95; and Stuart Scheingold, *The Politics of Rights: Lawyers, Public Policy, and Political Change* (Yale University Press, 1974).

63. See *Chicago v. Lambert,* 47 Ill. App. 2d 151, 154.

64. See *Jewish War Veterans v. American Nazi Party,* 260 F. Supp. 452 (1966). Interviewee Herman Moses, national chairman of the JWV, argued this case for the JWV in court.

65. See Neier, *Defending My Enemy,* ch. 5; Charles Lam Markman, *The Noblest Cry: A History of the ACLU* (St. Martin's Press, 1965); and Hamlin, *The Nazi/Skokie Conflict.*

66. Topol, "Village decries ACLU doggedness on Nazis," *Skokie Life,* July 11, 1977.

67. Hamlin interview.

68. Hamlin, *The Nazi/Skokie Conflict,* pp. 81-2.

69. Ibid., pp. 65-66.

70. Ibid., pp. 64-66; Hamlin interview.

71. Hamlin, *The Nazi/Skokie Conflict,* p. 132.

72. Ibid., p. 119.

73. Four thousand letters specified Skokie as the reason for resignation—way more than the withdrawal specifications which followed in the wake of the ACLU's defense of Rockwell in the 1960s. See Neier, op. cit., pp. 78-9; and, generally, ch. 6, on past ACLU policy and the nature of the membership.

74. Ibid., p. 78.

75. On the struggles between these factions, which are membership based, and also struggles between state divisions (whose decisions are not subject to veto by the national ACLU, though the national division has discretion to support or not support state division causes), see Neier, op. cit., ch. 6; and Jim Mann, "How the ACLU Created Its Skokie Problem," *The New Republic,* June, 1978; J. Anthony Lukas, "The ACLU Against Itself," *New York Times Magazine,* July 9, 1978; editorial comment, *The Los Angeles Times,* May 8, 1978. I also conducted an interview with a leader of the "progressive" revolt against the ACLU, Ann Fagan Ginger, in Berkeley. Her views support Neier's depiction.

76. Neier, op. cit., p. 80; Hamlin, *The Nazi/Skokie Conflict,* pp. 81-84.

77. *Chicago Tribune,* June 16, 1977; see Edward J. Epstein, op. cit.; and Gans, op. cit. on press coverage of legal struggles.

78. See Schattschneider, *The Semi-Sovereign People* (Holt, Rinehart, Winston, 1960), pp. 3-7. A similar process, which relies on federal governmental power to equalize or overcome local power disadvantages, is espoused and analyzed by Grant McConnell in *Private Power and American Democracy* (Vintage, Random House,

1965), esp. chs. 4 and 10. The Federalist constitutional scheme was adopted, in part, to foment this process. See James Madison, *The Federalist Papers,* Federalist No. 10; judicial review in support of minority rights may also be construed in terms of Schattschneider's socialization process, as it provides national institutional support of minority rights which may not be provided for by local and state political institutions, or by Congress. See McConnell, *Private Power and American Democracy*; Shapiro, *Freedom of Speech,* ch. 1; and *United States v. Carolene Products Co.,* 304 U.S. 144, 152, n. 4. See also Garrow, *Protest at Selma.*

79. See McConnell, op. cit. Examples are *Brown v. Board of Education,* 347 U.S. 483 (1954) *Cooper v. Aaron,* 358 U.S. 1(1958); *Green v. County School Board,* 391 U.S. 430(1968).

80. See *Williams v. Wallace,* 240 F. Supp. 100 (1965); and Garrow, *Protest at Selma.* Garrow depicts King's strategy at Selma in terms of Schattschneider's notion of socialization.

81. Schattschneider, op. cit.

82. Ibid., pp. 3-4; Garrow, op. cit., p. 214.

83. See Shapiro, *Freedom of Speech,* ch. 1. See also Truman, *The Governmental Process,* pp. 472-89.

84. See Donald J. Black, "The Mobilization of Law," II *Journal of Legal Studies,* no. 1 (1973), 125; Scheingold, *The Politics of Rights,* ch. 6 "Rights as Resources," ch. 9 "Legal Rights, and Political Mobilization," and ch. 1 "Legal Rights and Political Action."

85. For an analysis of the problems this type of logic (leave constitutional considerations to the courts) poses for the political system, see Jesse H. Choper *Judicial Review and the National Political Process* (University of Chicago Press, 1980), esp. pp. 224-229.

86. See "Court revises ban on Skokie march," *Chicago Tribune,* July 13, 1977. See also Arendt's notion of power in *The Human Condition,* pp. 200-201. Power is created by the fusion of word and deed in the public realm; it is a force promoted by common purpose, sometimes embodying institutions. Courts are traditional public loci of power.

87. See Schattschneider, op. cit., pp. 3-79.

88. See James Q. Wilson, "The Strategy of Protest," p. 293; Schattschneider, op. cit.; Garrow, op. cit.

89. See Schelling, op. cit., p. 34.

90. See William Benditt, "Compromising Interest and Principles," in XXI *Nomos: Compromise in Law, Ethics, and Politics* (New York University Press, 1979), pp. 30-32. On the distinction between conflict over primary and conflict over secondary, less deep, principles, see Coser, *The Functions of Social Conflict,* pp. 73-75. The former type of conflict is usually destructive, whereas conflict over the latter is often salubrious in interesting and often subtle ways. For a similar view, see Machiavelli, *The Discourses.*

91. Neier in U.P.I. press release of April 18, 1978.

92. "Village decries ACLU doggedness on Nazis," op cit.

93. Hamlin, *The Nazi/Skokie Conflict,* pp. 79–80. Hamlin expressed sincere regrets about this incident in his interview.

94. *Skokie v. NSPA,* Illinois Circ. Ct., Transcript of the Proceedings, No. 77 CH 2702, pp. 79–80.

95. Ibid., pp. 56–7; see generally pp. 54–73.

96. The concept "ethic of responsibility," of course, forms the centerpiece of Weber's notion of responsible political action. See "Politics as a Vocation," in *Max Weber: Essays in Sociology,* Gerth and Mills, ed. (Oxford University Press, 1946).

97. Haiman interview. See also Berns, *Freedom, Virtue, and the First Amendment,* ch. 10, for a critique of this view.

98. Hamlin, "Swastikas and Survivors."

99. *Skokie v. NSPA,* Transcript, Ill. Circ. Ct., pp. 116, 120.

100. On this tumultuous history, see Neier, op. cit., ch. 6, "The Constant Battle." See also Markmann, op. cit. The Court has wavered in the past. In the 1930s, the Court protected more speech than in the 20s. Then it abandoned the First Amendment in the McCarthy era. Compare *Fiske v. Kansas,* 274 U.S. 380 (1927) and *DeJonge v. Oregon,* 299 U.S. 353 (1937), to *Dennis v. U.S.,* 341 U.S. 494 (1951). *Dennis* made even the organized advocacy of communist doctrine a crime under the Smith Act. After *Dennis,* the Court began to construct more "objective" (or positivistic) tests to ensure more protection of speech. Two cases epitomize this movement toward positivism, and they make one wary to attack positivism. In *Yates v. U.S.,* 254 U.S. 298 (1957), the Court modified *Dennis* by allowing the advocacy of abstract communist doctrine. In *Brandenburg v. Ohio,* 395 U.S. 444 (1969), the Court all but overruled *Dennis* by constructing a positivistic incitement test: the direct incitement test. On how more "objective" tests in similar areas of criminal law (such as the law of attempts) are more consistent with liberty and the principle of "legality" (i.e., fair notice, consistent application, etc.), see George Fletcher, *Rethinking Criminal Law* (Little, Brown, 1978), ch. 3.

Chapter Three

1. See *Massive Psychic Trauma. MPT* is my major source on the psychology of survivors of Hitler's persecution. It is a compilation of a conference on this issue at Wayne State University in 1968. The conference was attended by most of the world's leading psychiatrists in this area. The pioneering work on the phenomenon of *surviving* is Robert Lifton's *Death in Life, Survivors of Hiroshima* (Random House, 1968).

2. Erna Gans interview; Richter interview.

3. Erna herself related the story of a survivor friend who was too timid to light candles at a Holocaust ceremony. See also Rabbi Montrose interview.

4. R. D. Laing depicts a similar process at the heart of schizophrenia and other mental illnesses. See *The Divided Self* (Penguin, 1965).

5. See Elie Wiesel, trans. by Stella Rodway, *Night* (Hill and Wang, 1960). See also *One Generation After* (Simon and Schuster, 1970).

6. See Alexander Szatmari, *MPT,* p. 132. Psychiatrists of survivors use the following terms in describing survivors' fantasies and images: fire and smoke (the symbols of the Holocaust), cannibalism, hunted and hunting animals, vermin, night vs. day, dogs, and burning flesh. See *MPT,* pp. 16, 17, 11, 21, 95, 213, 225, respectively. These are the images of the regressive ego. In the survivors' case, regressive fantasy corresponded with reality. On the "beastliness" of the "primitive," pre Oedipal imagination in general, and its resurrection in psychological regression, see Melanie Klein, *The Psycho-Analysis of Children* (Dell, 1975). Freud, of course, addressed this matter in many works.

7. Arendt, *The Origins of Totalitarianism,* p. 445.

8. For other powerful portraits of Holocaust ordeals, see Wiesel, *Night* and *One Generation After*; Victor Frankl, *Man's Search for Meaning* (Beacon Press, 1963); David Rousset, *The Other Kingdom* (Reynal and Hitchcock, 1947).

9. See Bettelheim, "Trauma and Reintegration," in *Surviving.*

10. Survivor guilt seems to be universal after major disasters or afflictions. See *MPT*; and Robert Lifton, op. cit.; and Chapter VII, *MPT,* "The Survivors of the Hiroshima Disaster and the Survivors of Nazi Persecution"; and Kai Erikson, *Everything in its Path* (Simon and Schuster, 1976).

11. All of the foregoing analysis is from Bettelheim, "Trauma and Reintegration," in *Surviving.*

12. See Helen Epstein, *Children of the Holocaust*; *MPT*; Eileen interview.

13. See Harold Laswell, *Power and Personality* (Viking, 1962); and James David Barber, *The Presidential Character* (Prentice Hall, 1972).

14. Bettelheim, "Individual and Mass Behavior in Extreme Situations," in *Surviving,* pp. 56–57. Bettelheim's point is also related to the "self-development" function of free speech and political participation discussed in ch. 1. Free speech and political theorists maintain that politics should enlighten one and make one more responsible. Theorists such as Arendt, Meiklejohn, Mill and Tocqueville stress this role of politics and speech.

15. DuBow interview. See also Ab Rosen interview.

16. See American Jewish Committee report on Skokie chronology. See also Goldstein's testimony in *Collin v. Smith* no. 77C2982, 78-1381, U.S. Dist. Ct., N.D. Ill., pp. 88–101.

17. This tendency signifies prejudice. See Allport, *The Nature of Prejudice,* ch. 25, esp. 397–400. See also Freud, *General Psychological Theory,* for several essays that touch on this issue.

18. See Ab Rosen interview; Hamlin, *The Nazi/Skokie Conflict*; ADL and American Jewish Committee policy papers on quarantine policy. For an example of the quarantine policy in regard to George Lincoln Rockwell, see American Jewish Committee Inst. of Human Relations, Memorandum, "George L. Rockwell and Quarantine," July, 1963, by Dr. S. Andhil Fineburg.

19. ADL and AJC reports, op. cit.; Hamlin, *The Nazi/Skokie Conflict*; Ab

Rosen interview; Harvey Schwartz interview. See Rev. Koenline interview. At an early meeting of local leaders, only one rabbi even questioned the quarantine policy — and his concern was with its feasibility, not with the need to morally support the survivors.

20. Every non-survivor Jewish leader I interviewed originally supported the ADL position. See rabbi interviews: Charney, Montrose, Weiner, Stern; and non-rabbi Jewish interviews: Richter, Ab Rosen, Hal Rosen, Rice, Wishner, DuBow, Schwartz, Topol, Grosberg, Lerner, Torshen, Jacobvitz.

21. See Helen Epstein, op. cit.; *MPT.*

22. "Communality" is the term used by Kai Erikson in his analysis of Buffalo Creek. It pertains to the psychological *sense* of community and order.

23. See John interview; Eileen interview; Helen Epstein, *Children of the Holocaust.*

24. Sennett, *The Fall of Public Man,* ch. 13; see also Sennett, *The Uses of Disorder: Personal Identity and City Life* (Vintage, 1970), esp. Part One.

25. See also Eileen, Erna Gans, and Judith interviews; Jerome Torshen interview. For another empirical account of the survivors' different perspective on civil liberties and the "conversion" of Skokie "elites" to the survivors' position, see David G. Barnum, "Decision Making in a Constitutional Democracy: Policy Formation in the Skokie Free Speech Controversy," *Journal of Politics* 44 (1982), pp. 480-98. On Jewish ethnic politics, see also Daniel Patrick Moynihan and Nathan Glazer, *Beyond the Melting Pot: The Negroes, Puerto Ricans, Jews, Italian, and Irish of New York City* (M.I.T., 1963), p. 139, which stresses the separation of German Jews (higher class and more assimilated) from other Jews which developed in New York City by the 1920s. Yet the authors also point out that outbreaks of anti-Semitism *unify* the different classes of Jews, a phenomenon that clearly occurred at Skokie (see pp. 139-40, 292-3). See also *Moving Up: Ethnic Succession in America,* by Daniel Elazar and Murray Friedman (Institute for Pluralism and Group Identity, 1976).

26. See Dr. Bychowski, "Permanent Character Changes as an Aftereffect of Persecution," *MPT,* p. 78.

27. Guttman Deposition to *Collin v. Smith,* U.S. Dist. Ct. N.D. Ill. No. 77 c2982, p. 47.

28. Kai Erikson, *Everything in its Path,* p. 234.

29. Judith interview. See also the third Skokie law suit (described, infra), *Goldstein v. Collin.* The suit's brief spoke of "the destruction of their enjoyment of Skokie as a sanctuary from Nazi horror and its psychological aftermath." See Plaintiff's Memorandum, Circ. Ct. Cook County, Ill. County Dept., Chancery Div., No. 77 C H 4367, Aug. 16, 1977.

30. See Henry Krystal, *MPT,* p. 4. "Another variety of personality change is that of a compensation for an 'unfinished problem' . . . they have a perpetual need to atone for cowardice or other 'failures.' There is either real personal shame or assumption of collective shame for the failure of the Jews to fight the Nazis." See also the sometimes virulent debate over the findings of Hannah Arendt and Raul

Hilberg in the early 1960s that the Jews were partly responsible for their fates. Hannah Arendt, in *Eichmann in Jerusalem* and Raul Hilberg in *The Destruction of the European Jews* demonstrate the ways in which the Final Solution was assisted by a combination of general Jewish submissiveness (what Bruno Bettelheim calls "denial" in his critique of the Anne Frank method of coping in "The Hidden Lessons of Anne Frank" in *Surviving*) and the assistance rendered the Nazi killing bureaucracy by the *Judenräte* and other Jewish leadership. "The reaction pattern of the Jews was characterized by almost complete lack of resistance," Hilberg asserts. In a review of Hilberg's book, Oscar Handlin epitomizes the moral outrage engendered by the Hilberg-Arendt thesis. "Such accusations are 'defaming the dead and their culture'." See "Jewish Resistance to the Nazis," *Commentary,* Nov. 1962. Gershom Scholen directed similar recrimination against Arendt a year later in "Eichmann in Jerusalem," *Commentary,* 1963. Yet despite the "objective" validity of the conclusions of the respective sides, the fact remains that the shame of cowardice and/or not having done enough exists as a psychological fact independent of the more objective validity of the feelings of shame and guilt. The phenomenon of *collective* shame exists, as Krystal suggests. As we proceed, we will see that survivor interviewees at Skokie were quite concerned about not reacting submissively again. In general, on the issue of resistance and Jewish complicity in the Final Solution, see Lucy Dawidowicz, *The War Against the Jews* (Bantam, 1975).

31. See also Bettelheim, *Surviving,* p. 27.

32. Nietzsche points out that debt ("Schulden") and guilt ("Schuld") in German are etymologically connected. See *The Genealogy of Morals,* Kaufman, trans. (Vintage, 1967), Second Essay, sec. 4.

33. See Rem Blanchard Edwards, *Freedom, Responsibility, and Obligation* (Martinus Nischoff, 1969), p. 114. "A fifth and final condition of my being able to do my duty in the face of temptation is that I must be an agent who in some sense exercises some control over his desire." For a contrary view, see W. D. Ross, *The Nature of Moral Responsibility,* (Wayne State University Press, 1973).

34. See Joseph Tussman, *Obligation and the Body Politic,* chs. 1 and 2. "To be a member is thus to subordinate oneself . . . to acknowledge that one's own interests are only a part of a broader system of interests . . ." (pp. 26–28) See also Meiklejohn, *Political Freedom,* chapters 1 and 4; and Michael Walzer, *Obligations: Essays on Disobedience, War, and Citizenship* (Simon and Schuster, 1970), chapter 1. Walzer states that "One does not acquire any real obligations, however, simply by being born or by submitting to socialization within a particular group. These come only when to the fact of membership there is added the fact of willful membership commitments to principles that usually are also commitments to other men." (p. 5) Walzer's view should be read in relation to the discussion above about the survivors' priority of commitment to their own community over their commitment to the First Amendment.

35. In this respect, Stephen's view supports Arendt's thesis that "doing the unthinkable," a Nietzschean ethic, constituted one of the inner drives of Nazi totali-

tarianism. See *The Origins of Totalitarianism,* pp. 436–37. See also David Rousset, *The Other Kingdom.*

36. *Chaplinsky v. New Hampshire,* 315 U.S. 568 (1942).

37. In "direct" civil disobedience, the law that is broken is the alleged unjust law itself. In "indirect" disobedience, the law is not considered to be *itself* unjust, but it is broken in order to facilitate the act of disobedience. See Carl Cohen, *Civil Disobedience, Conscience, Tactics, and the Law* (Columbia University Press, 1971), ch. III. Indirect civil disobedience is more difficult to justify than direct disobedience.

38. See, for example, Martin Luther King's appeal to the basic principles underlying the Constitution in his "Letter From a Birmingham Jail," written during the civil rights struggle in the early 1960s, in Bedau, ed., *Civil Disobedience.* King was no revolutionary, except, perhaps, *qua* the South. For treatments of the inevitable conflicts between individual laws and the principles of the legal order, see Locke's *Second Treatise on Government* (Mentor, 1963) on revolution, civil law, and natural law; and Margaret MacDonald, "Natural Rights," in Melden, ed., *Human Rights,* p. 43. On the differences between outright civil disobedience, which is punishable by law, and forms of disobedience which are "legitimated" by law, see Mortimer and Sanford Kadish, *Discretion to Disobey: A Study of Lawful Departure from Legal Rules* (Stanford University Press, 1973), esp. ch. 3.

39. On cognitive or attitudinal dissonance, see Harry C. Triandis, *Attitude and Attitude Change* (Wiley, 1971), ch. 3; see also Roger Brown, *Social Psychology* (Free Press, 1964).

40. King also appeals to the "higher law" in his Birmingham letter. Yet King also points out that the justice he sought was *constitutional,* as well.

41. See Berns, *For Capital Punishment,* introduction and pp. 153–56, on the role of "moral anger" in supporting and promoting the legitimate sense of moral community. Berns uses Martin Luther King as an example. For a different sympathetic treatment of the relation between emotion and morality, see, for example, Stuart Hampshire's excellent analysis of morality, emotion, and what he calls "rational computational morality" in "Morality and Pessimism," in Stuart Hampshire, ed., *Public and Private Morality* (Oxford University Press, 1978).

42. Schelling, *The Strategy of Conflict,* p. 13.

43. See Scheingold, *The Politics of Rights,* and Black, "The Mobilization of Law," for accounts of the use of law as a mobilizing tool.

44. Muir, *Police: Streetcorner Politicians,* pp. 37, 47–48. See also Schelling, op. cit. For *six* modes of conflict that are further refinements of the categories Muir forms, see Raven and Kruglanski, "Conflict and Power," in Swingle, ed., *The Structure of Conflict* (Academic Press, 1970).

45. *Village of Skokie v. NSPA,* 51 Ill. App. 3d 279 366 N.E. 2d 347.

46. Ibid.

47. See Hamlin, *The Nazi/Skokie Conflict,* pp. 71–74, and *Midweek Magazine,* May 4, 1977.

48. *Village of Skokie v. NSPA,* op. cit. Exparte injunctions are considered highly suspect by the U.S. Supreme Court. See *Carroll v. President and Commissioners,*

393 U.S. 175 (1968). Skokie's return to court on Monday for a full adversary hearing on the injunction may represent a requirement after *exparte* injunctions have been granted, as such injunctions must be justified by a normal hearing. *Exparte* injunctions must be allowed under emergency conditions, of course; yet they must be justified after the emergency by a normal hearing.

49. See *Carroll v. President and Commissioners*; *Freedman and Maryland*, 380 U.S. 51 (1965); and *Shuttlesworth v. Birmingham*, 394 U.S. 147 (1969).

50. Hamlin interview.

51. *NSPA v. Skokie*, 432 U.S. 43, 44, (1977). The Supreme Court did not rule on the substance of the case in deference to the Illinois courts.

52. *Skokie Life,* June 26, 1977; *Chicago Tribune,* June 24, 1977; June 30, 1977; *American Jewish Committee Skokie Chronology (AJC Chronology)*. For an example of Kahane's Jewish "fundamentalism" and extreme commitment to Jewish causes, see Kahane, *Why Be Jewish? Intermarriage, Assimilation, and Alienation* (Stein and Day, 1977).

53. *Chicago Tribune,* June 29, 1977; *AJC Chronology*.

54. See Hamlin's depiction of the coverage in "Swastikas and Survivors."

55. *Skokie v. NSPA,* 51 Ill. App. 3d. 279, 295.

56. *Skokie Life,* July 14, 1977; *Chicago Tribune,* July 13, 1977.

57. *Goldstein v. Collin,* No. 77 CH 4367 (Chancellery Court, Sept. 1, 1977).

58. *Goldstein v. Collin,* No. 50176 (Ill. Jan. 27, 1978).

59. See *AJC Chronology,* p. 14.

60. See Coser's distinction between "consensual" and "nonconsensual" conflict in Coser, op. cit., pp. 73-4. See also Swingle, op. cit., and Schelling, op. cit., pp. 4-5, 83-96, on the difference between "zero-sum" conflicts and those that are "variable sum." See also Kenneth Terhume, "The Effects of Personality in Cooperation and Conflict," in Swingle, op. cit., pp. 208-12, on how *distrust* exacerbates conflict.

61. Muir points out that one of the "paradoxes of coercive power" is the "paradox of irrationality": "the more delirious the threatener, the more serious the threat; the more delirious the victim, the less serious the threat." Muir, op. cit., pp. 42-44; see also Schelling, op. cit., pp. 16-17. By acting irrationally in reaction to the NSPA threat, the survivors lower the power of the initial threat, and create one of their own.

62. Hamlin interview.

63. *Village of Skokie v. NSPA,* Transcript of Proceedings April 28, 1977. Circ. Court Cook County, 77 Ch 2702, p. 67.

64. See Schelling. op. cit., pp. 2-8.

65. Making promises constitutes "the force" that keeps people "together" and which sustains the "public space in existence," according to Arendt. See *The Human Condition,* pp. 244-45. On self-subordination as the basis of membership in a political community, see Tussman, *Obligation and the Body Politic,* ch. 2, and Meiklejohn, op. cit. ch. I. On the uses of promises and binding oneself in bargaining, see Schelling, op. cit., pp. 22, 43.

66. The willingness to die in the name of the cause is a sign of true membership in a community, as it signifies the mastery of the baser passions of self interest

and survival by the self formed in relation to the community. Walter Lippman's depiction of Socrates' decision to die rather than to leave Athens illustrates the point: "If Athens was to be governed it must be by citizens who by their second nature preferred the laws to the satisfaction of their own impulses, even their own will to live . . . This is the image of a man who has become fit to rule. He is ruled within by his second and civilized nature. This true self exercises the power of life and death over his natural self." *The Public Philosophy,* (New American Library, Signet, 1955), p. 106. See also Meiklejohn, *Political Freedom*; chs. 1 and 2; and George F. Will, *Statecraft as Soulcraft* (Simon and Schuster, 1983), ch. 4.

67. *Skokie Life,* June 26, 1977.

68. See *Chicago Tribune,* March 8, 1978. "Skokie Countermarch Studied."

69. Strategic advantage is gained by tying oneself to an immovable ally. See Schelling, op. cit., pp. 21, 27, 40.

70. Muir, op. cit., p. 44.

71. See Lipsky, *Protest in City Politics,* p. 167. Relatively powerless groups must cross a "threshold" to engage in politics. Many groups fail to emerge because they fail to "surface."

72. DuBow interview.

73. This quotation and the following remarks quoted from the April 25 meeting were taken from the tape recordings of the Board of Trustees' weekly meetings.

74. On how elites and others with responsibility often are more moderate than claimants in roles of narrower responsibility, see James Q. Wilson, *Political Organizations* (Basic Books, 1973) and "The Strategy of Protest," pp. 291–93; Jack Walker, "Protest and Negotiation: A Case Study of Negro Leadership in Atlanta, Georgia," VII *Midwest Journal of Political Science,* no. 2 (1963), 99, 104–08, 121; Lipsky, op. cit. Elites (especially governmental elites) also value civil liberties such as free speech more broadly and consistently than do non-elites. See S. Stouffer, *Communism, Conformity, and Civil Liberties* (Doubleday, 1955), and literature discussed in Chapter Seven.

75. See Richter, Montrose, Charney interviews.

76. See Arendt, "On Violence," in *The Crises of the Republic*; Piven and Cloward, *Poor People's Movements,* ch. 1; Lipsky, op. cit.

77. See Schelling, op. cit., p. 117: "talk is not a substitute for moves. Moves can in some way alter the game . . . they nevertheless have an evidential quality that mere speech has not."

78. One journalistic account after the controversy called April 30, 1977 the most important social event in the controversy, though it was not played up too much by the press. See Max Wiley, "The Law, the Press, and the Nazis," *Chicago Journal,* July 19, 1978, p. 6.

79. See footnote 74.

80. Weiner stressed the relationship between Mayor Smith and Goldstein.

81. See also Weiner interview: Goldstein and Smith had arranged the pattern of the meeting in advance. On the need for established Jewish leadership to fill the space of leadership filled by the JDL, see the June 28, 1977 letter of the well-

known Rabbi Herbert Bronstein, Head of the North Shore Congregation Israel, to Jewish leaders in the Chicago area. On Bronstein's basic posture of resistance in the controversy, and how he tied it to the eruption of anti-Semitism around the world and in historical terms, see Bronstein, "Again, the Nazis—What is to be Done?" Message delivered to North Shore Congregation Israel, Glencoe, Ill., February 17, 1978.

82. Lipsky stresses this role of public opinion. See also Schelling. op. cit.; Garrow, op. cit.

83. See Bettelheim, *Surviving,* p. 30; and Helen Epstein, op. cit.

84. Bettelheim argues that the sense of abandonment in the persecution camps precipitated the triumph of the death instinct over the life instinct. See *Surviving,* p. 101, "The Holocaust—One Generation Later." See also *MPT,* pp. 65–67. On the phenomenon of European and American denial of the Final Solution and their refusals to help the Jews, see Arthur D. Morse, *While Six Million Died; A Chronicle of American Apathy* (Random House, 1967); and Laqueur, *The Terrible Secret,* chs. 2, 3. See also Montrose interview. Montrose stressed this point concerning Skokie.

85. See Raven and Kruglanski, op. cit., on how "reference" and identification are aspects of exhortation and moral persuasion.

86. One major interpretation of the eruption of conflict at Skokie is that the long latency period of survivor silence had ended, and it was now appropriate from a psychological standpoint to communicate and act out the past. That is, survivors had waited a generation in silence, and were now psychologically ready to openly, publicly deal with the past as soon as the proper stimulus presented itself. For similar viewpoints about Skokie and other incidents of survivor behavior, see Eileen int.; Reeve Brenner, *The Faith and Doubt of Holocaust Survivors* (Free Press, 1980), ch. 1; Helen Epstein, op. cit., ch 1.

87. Rousset, quoted in Arendt, *The Origins of Totalitarianism,* p. 436; see also Timerman, *Cell Without a Number, Prisoner Without a Name.* On Nazi moral metaphysics, see Hitler, *Mein Kampf* (Houghton Mifflin, 1971), Vol. II, ch. 1.

88. See Laqueur, op. cit.

89. This quotation is Montrose's own version of Stephen's speech, which Montrose maintains is virtually verbatim. Emphases in the quotation were based on Montrose's own inflections.

Chapter Four

1. *Village of Skokie v. NSPA,* Circuit Court of Cook County, Illinois County Department, Chancery Division. No. 77 CH 2702; 51 Ill. App. 3d. 279.

2. *Skokie v. NSPA,* 366 N.E. 2d. 347 (1977), 352–3.

3. Ibid., at 353.

4. Ibid., at 352–3.

5. Ibid., at 354.

6. Ibid., at 356.

7. 403 U.S. 15 (1971).

8. 315 U.S. 568 (1942).

9. *Skokie v. NSPA,* 366 N.E. 2d. 347 (1977) 356.

10. See Sol Goldstein testimony in *Skokie v. NSPA,* Circ. Ct. Cook County, No. 77 CH 2702, April 28, 1977, pp. 66-70; and in *Collin v. Smith,* U.S. Dist. Ct. N.D. Ill. no. 1381, Dec. 2, 1977, pp. 86-101. The appellate court wrongly held that this transcript supported the distinction it drew. Nor did my interviewees only stress the swastika.

11. *Skokie v. NSPA,* 373 N.E. 2d. 21 (1978).

12. Ibid., at 23.

13. Ibid., at 23-4.

14. Ibid.

15. Hamlin interview.

16. Hamlin, *The Nazi/Skokie Conflict,* p. 140.

17. *Skokie v. NSPA,* 373 N.E. 2d. 21 (1978), 26.

18. *Goldstein v. Collin,* Ill. Sup. Ct., No. 50176.

19. The Illinois Supreme Court dismissed on the following grounds: 1) that the *Goldstein* suit was a mere duplication of *Skokie v. NSPA;* 2) that Goldstein and the survivors therefore lacked standing; 3) that the enjoinment would violate the First and Fourteenth Amendments; 4) the plaintiff's complaint stated no cause of action; 5) the normal civil remedies at law should bar injunctive relief in the case at hand. See *Goldstein v. Collin,* Plaintiff's Petition for Rehearing of Ill. Sup. Cts. Summary Order of January 27, 1978, Dismissing the Plaintiff's Complaint. No. 50176. See also ACLU (Respondent) Brief in Opposition to Petition for Writ of Certiorari to the Supreme Court of Illinois, *Goldstein v. Collin,* U.S. Supreme Court, Oct. Term, No. 77-1788, p. 5.

20. See ACLU Brief, p. 5.

21. See Petition for Writ of Certiorari to the Supreme Court of Illinois, *Goldstein v. Collin,* U.S. Supreme Court, Spring Term, 1978. June 16, 1978.

22. See Hamlin, *The Nazi/Skokie Conflict,* pp. 105-17; and Hamlin interview. David Hamlin considered the suit a fraud because of Sol Goldstein's personal willingness to confront Collin head on.

23. See *Chicago Tribune,* March 18, 1978; *Skokie Life,* March 19, 1978; *Chicago Tribune,* April 1, 1978.

24. *Collin v. Smith,* 447 F. Supp. 676 (1978), 686-7.

25. Ibid., at 684-6.

26. Ibid., at 686.

27. Ibid., at 700.

28. Ibid., at 686-700.

29. Ibid., at 687-8; *Whitney v. California,* 274 U.S. 357, 375-76 (1927); and p. 21, *Brandenburg v. Ohio,* 395 U.S. 444 (1969); the danger test was first formulated by Justice Holmes in *Schenck v. U.S.,* 249 U.S. 47 (1919).

30. *Collin v. Smith,* ibid., at 688; *Brandenburg v. Ohio,* ibid.

31. Defendant's Brief in Response to Plaintiff's Memorandum of Law, *Collin v. Smith,* No. 77 C 2982, U.S. Dist. Ct., Northern Dist. Ill., Eastern Div., p. 2. *Collin v. Smith,* ibid., at 688.

32. Skokie Brief, pp. 3-9.

33. 343 U.S. 250 (1952); Skokie Brief, ibid., p. 2.

34. Hadley Arkes makes such an association in his excellent article on *Beauharnais and Chaplinsky,* written in 1974, four years before *Collin v. Smith.* See "Civility and the Restriction of Speech," p. 390; see also Arkes, *The Philosopher in the City,* part 1.

35. Skokie Brief, pp. 2-6.

36. *Collin v. Smith,* at 692; see 690-2.

37. Ibid., at 692.

38. Ibid., at 692. On the role of the "chilling effect" (or deterrent effect) doctrine in free speech adjudication, see Note, "The First Amendment Overbreadth Doctrine," 83 *Harv. L. Rev.,* 844, 875 (1970); Tribe, *American Constitutional Law,* pp. 711-12; Lillian Bevier, "The First Amendment and Political Speech: An Inquiry into the Substance & Limits of Principle," 30 *Stan. L. Rev.* 299 (1978). See also *N.Y.T. v. Sullivan,* 376 U.S. 254, 270 (1964). *Sullivan* proclaimed the crime of seditious libel inconsistent with the First Amendment. See Harry Kalven, "The New York Times Case: A Note on the 'Central Meaning of the First Amendment,'" in Kurland, ed., op. cit., p. 84.

39. See, for example, *Garrison v. Louisiana,* 379 U.S. 64 (1964); *Gertz v. Robert Welch,* 418 U.S. 323, 349 (1974).

40. *Collin v. Smith,* at 694. Examples of critical commentary include Emerson, *The System of Freedom of Expression,* p. 396, cited by Decker; and Tribe, op. cit., pp. 632, 670.

41. *Collin v. Smith,* at 695.

42. 379 U.S. 64 (1964).

43. 418 U.S. 323 (1974).

44. *Collin v. Smith,* at 695-6.

45. Ibid., at 696; *Beauharnais v. Ill.,* 343 U.S. 250, at 265-66.

46. *Collin v. Smith,* ibid., at 697.

47. See *U.S. v. Darby,* 312 U.S. 100 (1941); *Williamson v. Lee Optical,* 348 U.S. 483 (1955); *Railway Express Agency v. N.Y.,* 336 U.S. 106 (1949); and *New Orleans v. Dukes,* 427 U.S. 297 (1976).

48. *Collin v. Smith,* at 698. Emphasis added.

49. See Tribe, op. cit., pp. 602-05 (on content-based abridgements of speech), 684-87 (on non-content-based abridgements), 1000-60 (on equal protection). See also the different approaches taken in *Regents of Univ. of Calif. v. Bakke,* 438 U.S. 265 (1978). On strict review of "fundamental rights," see DuCat, *Modes of Constitutional Interpretation,* op. cit., ch. 4.

50. Eugene DuBow interview; see PAC Subcommittee on Individual Liberty & Jewish Security, Summary Report of Meeting held at Mayer Kaplan JCC in Skokie, Feb. 27, 1978. At this meeting the Northwest Suburban Synagogue Council and the

Committee members asserted their dedication to "a counterdemonstration by the total American community." This position was more strongly asserted than before.

51. *Chicago Tribune,* March 8, 1978; March 9, 1978.
52. *Collin v. Smith,* at 702. Emphasis added.
53. *Chicago Tribune,* April 7, 1978; *Skokie Life,* April 9, 1978.
54. Brief for Plaintiffs-Appellees, *Collin v. Smith,* U.S. Court of Appeals, 7th Circ., No. 78-1385, p. 5; *Smith v. Collin,* U.S. Crt. of Appeals, 7th Circ., Nos. 78-1381 and 78-1385, May 22, 1978, p. 4.
55. *Chicago Tribune,* April 16, 1978; AJC Chronology.
56. *Smith v. Collin,* 578 F. 2d. 1197 (7th Cir. 1978).
57. *Skokie Life,* June 8, 1978.
58. Respondent's Brief in Opposition to Petition for Writ of Certiorari to the U.S. Crt. of Appeals for the 7th Circ., *Smith v. Collin,* U.S. Sup. Crt., No. 77-1736 (A-1037), p. 4.
59. *Chicago Tribune,* October 17, 1978; *Skokie Life,* October 19, 1978.
60. See *Chicago Tribune,* May 3, 1978; May 11, 1978; June 7, 1978, ("2 Nazi March bills lose"); June 14, 1978.
61. Hamlin, *The Nazi/Skokie Conflict,* p. 172.
62. *Chicago Tribune,* editorial, May 25, 1978.
63. Hamlin, *The Nazi/Skokie Conflict,* p. 139.
64. Ibid., pp. 139-40.
65. See *Collin v. O'Malley,* 452 F. Supp. 577 (1978), 579.
66. See Richard Salem interview (Salem is Midwest director of CRS); *Chicago Tribune* editorial, May 25, 1978; *Chicago Tribune,* May 25, 1978; *Skokie Life,* June 15, 1978. CRS's function is to mediate local disputes to avoid violence and undue conflict.
67. Hamlin, *The Nazi/Skokie Conflict,* pp. 164-72.
68. Ibid.; Salem interview.
69. Salem interview; DuBow interview.
70. Hamlin, *The Nazi/Skokie Conflict,* p. 171.
71. Ibid., p. 172.
72. Salem interview. On the "split" in the NSPA, see *The Daily Herald,* Buffalo Grove, Ill., June 16, 1978, "Nazi leadership split."
73. Ibid.
74. Hamlin, *The Nazi/Skokie Conflict,* p. 139. See also *Chicago Tribune,* June 17, 1978.
75. *Chicago Tribune,* June 22, 1978; *Sun Times,* June 22, 1978.
76. See *Chicago Tribune,* June 25, 1978; Erna Gans interview; and Alex interview.
77. *Chicago Tribune,* July 10, 1978; Richter interview.
78. DuBow interview; Hamlin interview; Skokie Police Chief Chamberlain, testimony in *Collin v. Smith,* (U.S. Dist. Ct.), pp. 49-65.
79. Charney interview. Charney was head rabbi of the NWSSC. See also Federation meeting notes. And DuBow interview; Rice interview; Hal Rosen interview; Richter interview. See Kevin Philips' plan submitted to PAC: "The Skokie March —

A Battle Plan; 'Proposal for Dealing with Nazi Demonstration,'" Mayer Kaplan Center, Skokie, Feb. 20, 1978; DuBow's and Richter's personal notes on counter-demonstration plans.

80. The Skokie Public Library has thousands of reports from newspapers from all over America, from which I obtained this information.

81. *L.A. Times,* June 24, 1978, and June 26, 1978.

82. David Lerner interview; James Rice interview; Hal Rosen interview. See NJCRAC report on Executive Committee's policy recommendation for inclusion in Joint Program Plan: "Jewish Security and Individual Freedom." This is a report of the Tucson meeting and its politics; and see the finished product in NJCRAC, *Joint Program Plan, 1979-80: Fed. Jewish Comm. Relations, Guide to Program Planning of the Constituent Orgs.,* pp. 31-32, "Individual Freedom & Jewish Security," "Combatting Nazi Groups."

83. Ab Rosen interview; DuBow interview; and Lerner interview.

84. See James Rice interview; Hal Rosen interview; and DuBow interview.

85. See Richter interview. Richter said violence was certain, and that it would have scarred the entire controversy. See also Rice interview, Rosen interview, and DuBow interview.

86. I attempted to interview police department leaders in the controversy, but was rebuffed. I then sought the aid of Trustee Conrad and the new city manager (Matzer resigned after the controversy after sixteen years on the job — another sign of the tensions created) in eliciting an interview. Their efforts on my behalf failed, too.

87. Several interviewees mentioned this matter.

88. See *Skokie Life,* May 11, 1978, "Skokie Spirit planning begins"; May 14, 1978, "Skokie unveils 'image' marketing plans"; May 25, 1978, "PR firm kicks off Skokie positive image campaign"; 2-1-79, "PR firm contract ended" (after much cynical commentary). See also report on the project by the public relations firm: "1978 Progress Report and 1979 Goals," Aaron D. Cushman, & Assocs., Chicago. Skokie also developed an office of "Public Information Officer" — see "Confidential" report from Al Bernstein to Village Board. And, Skokie developed a monthly newsletter about civic affairs called "Skokie Spirit" (replete with a logo that was used on buttons and other objects). The first issue came out, interestingly, in June 1978. The head of the Skokie Spirit Campaign was Rev. Thomas O'Connor of St. Peter's Church, an interviewee. O'Connor was an ally of Rabbi Weiner, and deeply concerned about Christian-Jewish unity and the *image* of Skokie.

Chapter Five

1. See Dworkin, *Taking Rights Seriously,* pp. 134-36; and Donnelley, "Human Rights and Human Dignity," pp. 303-4, for discussions of the difference between a "concept" of a right and its "conception." The latter has to do with a right's *application.*

2. See Weber, "Politics as a Vocation," in *Essays in Sociology.*

3. *Chaplinsky v. New Hampshire.* On consequentialist versus non-consequentialist theories of free speech, see Fred Berger, *Freedom of Expression,* (Wadsworth, 1980), introduction.

4. Mill, *On Liberty*; Mill's utilitarian approach to speech has been criticized on the grounds that it provides a basis for limiting speech if speech's non-utility can be empirically established. See H. J. McClosky, "Liberty of Expression: Its Grounds and Limits," 13 *Inquiry* 219 (1970).

5. Bychowski, "Permanent Character Changes as an Aftereffect of Persecution," *MPT,* p. 78.

6. See Montrose, Richter, Matzer, Schwartz, Conrad, etc.

7. See Alex and Erna Gans interviews, and *Midweek Magazine* report, "Fighting for the Freedom to Hate," May 4, 1977, p. 4.

8. See Conrad, O'Connor, Richter, Matzer, etc. Matzer, for example, said: "On that Saturday, my observations are the same as Schwartz's. They had lost control of themselves. There would have been violence. There was no question that for the survivors it was a reliving of the whole thing. This is what changed my attitude about the issue." Rabbi Montrose portrayed their fears in terms similar to my divided-self hypothesis: "He [Collin] released the suppression valve that was keeping all this down and could only come out in the form of nightmares. This valve was opened and now the nightmare was in the daytime reconfirming these old experiences." Psychological literature on the survivors emphasizes the role of bad dreams in the survivor syndrome. Also, there is sometimes a difference between cognition and feelings associated with the day and those associated with the night. Some survivors become anxious, withdrawn, and generally regressive as the night approaches, as if the "valve" that separates the world of consciousness from the world of the unconscious (of sleep) is disintegrating. See *MPT,* p. 95.

Many Skokie survivors received vicious phone calls in the early hours of the morning, at the mental period of greatest vulnerability. There is no concrete evidence linking these calls to the NSPA, however. See testimony in *Collin v. Smith,* U.S. Dist. Ct., N.D. Ill., no. 78-1381, pp. 50–65 (Police Chief Chamberlain testimony).

9. See also Hamlin, *The Nazi/Skokie Conflict,* p. 152.

10. See also Stephen and John interviews.

11. On this matter of passivity and fear, see the discussion in the next chapter on "mastery" and what Erik Erikson calls "agens."

12. See Richard Rubenstein, *Rebels in Eden: Mass Political Violence in the United States* (Little, Brown, 1970); and Charles Silberman, *Criminal Violence, Criminal Justice,* ch. 1. On the Appalachian miners' reactions to new textbooks in their school which they viewed as invasions, see Robert O'Neil, *Classrooms in the Crossfire.* On South Boston's resistance to busing due to the same feeling, see Wilkinson III, *From Brown to Bakke,* ch. 8.

13. See Michael Novak, *The Experience of Nothingness* (Harper and Row, 1970).

14. See Plaintiff's Memorandum, *Goldstein v. Collin,* p. 24.

15. See Guttman deposition in *Collin v. Smith,* quoted in Chapter Three.

16. These are the terms of Rabbi Montrose.

17. See *MPT,* esp. pp. 335ff.

18. See, for example, Robert Lifton's portrayal of the Hiroshima survivors in *Death in Life*; and Kai Erikson, *Everything in Its Path.* In *Massive Psychic Trauma,* conferees at the Wayne State conference on survivor psychology establish several psychological similarities between the consequences of the Hitler persecution and the dropping of the atom bomb. Both of these consequences, in turn, are similar to Buffalo Creek in terms of psychological regression, trauma, and the breakdown of community. Yet the conferees also drew important distinctions.

19. According to George Mosse in *The Crisis of German Ideology: The Intellectual Origins of the Third Reich* (Schocken, 1981), anti-Semitism was one of the most important ingredients in the cosmology of the German *Volk,* which was an intellectual, moral, and cosmological precursor of Hitler. In the metaphysics of the *Volk,* rooted in a racial theory of blood purity and instinct, the Jew's very being constituted a violation of the laws of nature. Hitler posits a similar view in *Mein Kampf,* pp. 232, 287, 300–308, 312–13, 447. See also Syberberg's cosmological treatment of anti-Semitism in *Our Hitler*; and Max Frisch, *Andora* (Hill and Wang, 1966).

20. See Hitler in *Mein Kampf.* Hitler and Germans *are* what the Jew *is not.* Purification of the putative moral community can be achieved only by purging or exorcising the disease which is the victim. See also Mosse, op. cit. On the psychology and anthropology of "purification," see Mary Douglas, *Purity and Danger: An Analysis of Concepts of Pollution and Taboo* (Penguin, 1966); Ernest Becker, *Escape from Evil* (Free Press, 1972); and Sennett, *The Uses of Disorder.*

21. Niederland, *MPT,* pp. 14, 20–21. Terror is "ineffable." This point refers to point made in Chapter Three, about the incommunicability of the survivors' experiences.

22. See Bettelheim, in *Surviving,* pp. 26–27.

23. See Roberto Unger, *Law in Modern Society* (Free Press, 1975), ch. 3.

24. See also Arkes, in Chapter One, on the obligation of the government to protect citizens from unjustified intimidation.

25. See Arkes, "Civility and the Restriction of Speech."

26. See Sennett, *The Fall of Public Man,* pp. 264–65. On distancing and individuation as signs of maturity, see the various works of Ortega y Gasset, e.g., *What Is Philosophy?* pp. 106–13; and *Revolt of the Masses,* ch. 8.

27. Wilson, "The Urban Unease," p. 25.

28. See Alexander Bickel, *The Morality of Consent* (Yale University Press, 1975), p. 74.

29. Tussman, *Government and the Mind.* See also Hampshire, "Morality and Pessimism," in Hampshire, ed., *Public and Private Morality*; and Wilson, "The Urban Unease."

30. See *Cohen v. California,* 403 U.S. 15, 21, (1971).

31. For a good analysis of how Skokie's features, such as those mentioned, rendered it not subject to constitutional doctrines providing for the restriction of speech,

see Carl Cohen, "Skokie: the Right to be Offensive. The Extreme Test of our Faith in Free Speech," *The Nation,* April 15, 1978.

32. Bickel, op. cit., p. 73. See also Stuart Hampshire, "Morality and Pessimism," in Hampshire, ed., *Public and Private Morality.*

33. See Gordon Allport, *The Nature of Prejudice,* p. 470. A legal norm "creates a public conscience and a standard for expected behavior that check overt signs of prejudice." On law as a teacher, see also Richard Delgado, "Words That Wound: A Tort Action for Racial Insults, Epithets, and Name-Calling," 17 *Harv. Civ. Rts.-Civ. Libs. Law Rev.,* 133, 148–49 (1982); and Berns, *For Capital Punishment,* ch. 4, esp. pp. 138–47, and *Freedom, Virtue, and the First Amendment.*

34. Some theorists maintain that the higher stages of moral development entail both tolerance and recognition of the distinction between legality and morality. See June Louin Tapp, "The Psychological Limits of Legality," and John W. Patterson, "Moral Developments and Political Thinking: The Case of Freedom of Speech," *Western Political Science Quarterly,* 1979. Tapp and Patterson employ the moral stages of Piaget and Kohlberg. In the process, they forget Chesterton's warning that open-mindedness may become "open-mindlessness" under extreme conditions.

35. See, for example, *Gregory v. Chicago,* 394 U.S. 111 (1969); *Cohen v. California,* op. cit.

36. See Arkes, "Civility and the Restriction of Speech," p. 432, and *The Philosopher in the City,* p. 77.

Chapter Six

1. See Machiavelli, *The Discourses*; Coser, *The Functions of Social Conflict,* pp. 73–75.

2. See Emerson, *Freedom of Expression,* pp. 6–7; Mill, *On Liberty*; Meiklejohn, *Political Freedom*; and Bork, "Neutral Principles and Some First Amendment Problems." For a strong critique of the justification of speech based on truth, see Frederick Schauer, *Free Speech: A Philosophical Inquiry,* ch. 2. Schauer is convincing, but consideration of his views is beyond our present task.

3. Emerson, *Freedom of Expression,* p. 6; Mill, op. cit.; Bork, op. cit.; Brandeis, *Whitney v. California,* 274 U.S. 374, 377.

4. Erik Erikson, *Insight and Responsibility,* p. 89.

5. Ibid., p. 87.

6. See Kai Erikson, *Everything in Its Path,* for a portrayal of the devastating consequences of being overwhelmed by "fate." See also Pocock, *The Machiavellian Moment,* for an excellent analysis of the ways in which sixteenth-century theorists viewed a strong republican community and *agens* as a means of tempering the ravages of *Fortuna* or fate. Communality is a protector against fate and *patiens.* See also Lifton, *Death in Life.*

7. See also Frankl's portrayal of the roulette wheel-like nature of the "selection" process at the death camps in *Man's Search for Meaning.*

8. See Rousset, *The Other Kingdom*; Bettelheim, *Surviving*; Frankl, op. cit.; and Wiesel, *Night*.

9. Krystal, "Patterns of Psychological Damage," *MPT*, p. 4. Jewish hostility to the Arendt and Hilberg thesis about Jewish responsibility may signify this passion.

10. In general, those survivors who were most devastated by their experiences in the camps (controlling for the different intensities and brutalities of the experiences) were those who had not yet developed mature egos which would protect them against regression and the unleashing of primitive inner emotions which attacked the ego from within, parallel to the external attack perpetrated by the Nazis. See *MPT*, pp. 13, 248, 256.

11. See *Insight and Responsibility*, p. 92; see also Sennett's critique of Frantz Fanon and other revolutionary anti-colonialists in the introduction to *The Uses of Disorder*, and Camus' criticism of the Algerian revolutionists' use of terrorism in *Resistance, Rebellion, and Death* (Vintage, Random House, 1974), pp. 111-53.

12. See the notion of "Gestalt" in Erik Erikson, *Insight and Responsibility*, p. 92. Gestalt entails a mature, ordered openness.

13. Hegel, *The Phenomenology of Mind* (Harper, 1967), p. 229.

14. Ibid., pp. 232-33. For a similar view on the noble self-consciousness, as distinguished from the "mass," see Ortega's *The Revolt of the Masses,* esp. ch. 7.

15. See Ivan Soll, *An Introduction to Hegel's Metaphysics* (University of Chicago Press, 1969), pp. 73-75.

16. In a sense, this project entails the development or molding of a "second nature" based on true inner freedom and control out of the "first nature" of the passions. For an interesting discussion of this project, see George F. Will, *Statecraft as Soulcraft*, ch. 4.

17. See Arendt, *The Origins of Totalitarianism,* pp. 301-2; A. I. Melden, *Rights and Persons,* (University of California Press, 1977), pp. 23-24.

18. Melden, op. cit., pp. 23-24. Melden's position (and Arendt's) is also relevant to the debate over the nature of rights; the "entitlements" school defines rights as *a priori* entitlements, whereas the "claims" school emphasizes the *act* of *making* the claim. While the entitlements position makes sense philosophically, the claims position makes more sense *politically,* as it is more informed in practical terms. It also entails the notion of *agens* and the psychology of autonomy presently under discussion. For a "claim" view, see Joel Feinberg, "Duties, Rights, and Claims," *Amer. Philos. Quarterly,* no. 2 (1966), p. 137. For the entitlement view, see H. J. McClosky, "Rights," 15 *Philos. Quarterly,* p. 115 (1965); Donnelley, "Human Rights and Human Dignity"; and Dworkin, *Taking Rights Seriously.*

19. See the discussion of the Nazi's view of Jews as inherent "cowards" in the chapter on terror above, in which Mosse's *The Crisis of German Ideology* is discussed. *Mein Kampf,* of course, is full of this logic.

20. See Bettelheim, "Individual and Mass Behavior in Extreme Situations," in *Surviving,* pp. 56-83. The concentration camps, however, were less debilitating than the death camps. Compare, for example, Rousset's discussion of death camp politics in *The Other Kingdom* with Bettelheim's portrayal. Rousset's camp was fraught

with the sheer, perverted will to power, even on the part of the inmates. See also Weisel, *Night*; Frankl, op. cit.; and Arendt, *The Origins of Totalitarianism.*

21. Albert Memmi, *The Colonizer and the Colonized* (Beacon Press, 1965), pp. 86-87.

22. Frantz Fanon, *The Wretched of the Earth* (Grove Press, 1968), pp. 293-94.

23. Krystal, op. cit., pp. 4-5.

24. See Wiesel's portrayal of the liberation in *Night*; and Bettelheim, *Surviving.*

25. See Arendt, *The Human Condition,* pp. 35-36, 186.

26. Brenner, *The Faith and Doubt of Holocaust Survivors,* p. 8. On the psychology of survivors in Israel, see Samai Davidson, in "Psychiatric Disturbances of Holocaust Survivors." Symposium of the Israel Psychoanalytic Society, *Israel Annals of Psychiatry & Related Disciplines* 5:1 (1967).

27. Brenner, op. cit., p. 7.

28. Rosenberg, "The Trial of Eichmann," *Commentary,* Nov. 1961.

29. See also Stephen interview, "Only over our dead bodies will they come to our city." Stephen's emphasis made this remark more than a mere cliche.

30. Weiner interview.

31. Smith interview; Richter interview.

32. See, for example, *Chicago Tribune* report of Wiesenthal's visit to Skokie in May, 1977, "Wiesenthal speaks out on Nazis," May 22, 1977.

33. Emphasis added. On children of survivors and their need to prove themselves, see Heleñ Epstein, *Children of the Holocaust.*

34. See Mill, *On Liberty*; Brandeis, *Whitney v. California,* 274 U.S. 357, 377 (1927), concurring opinion; Arendt, *The Human Condition*; and Meiklejohn, *Political Freedom.*

35. Bettelheim, "Individual and Mass Behavior in Extreme Situations," in *Surviving,* p. 83.

36. See Gordon Allport, *The Nature of Prejudice,* pp. 380, 382, 387f; Erikson, *Insight and Responsibility*; Sennett, *The Fall of Public Man,* ch. 10.

37. See Sennett, *The Fall of Public Man,* esp. ch. 13.

38. Tussman, *Obligation and the Body Politic,* p. 25, and generally, ch. 2. See also Meiklejohn, *Political Freedom,* p. 73, on the inadequacies of Holmes' notion of the "marketplace of ideas" in this regard. Tussman was Meiklejohn's respectful student.

39. See Charles Schultze, "The Public Use of Private Interest," *Harper's,* May, 1977, p. 43; Theodore Lowi, *Private Life and Public Order* (Norton, 1968).

40. Tocqueville, *Democracy in America,* vol. II, pp. 124-25.

41. Muir, *Police: Streetcorner Politicians,* pp. 50-51. On Weber's important effort to teach prudence and reality-testing in the face of the rigid politics of ideological commitment (as well as Weber's failures in this regard), see Voegelin, *The New Science of Politics.* Also see Sennett, *The Fall of Public Man,* ch. 13, for an analysis of "compromise" as an indicator of political virtue; and Mario Cuomo, *Forrest Hills Diary* (Vintage, 1974).

42. See the polls presented in the next chapter on public support for Nazi speech rights.

43. See Klaus Hoppe, "Psychotherapy with Concentration-Camp Survivors," in *MPT,* p. 215.

44. Neier, *Defending My Enemy,* ch. 8; Hamlin, *The Nazi/Skokie Conflict.*

45. On the First Amendment rights as fundamental due to their provision of input into the system, see Ely, *Democracy and Distrust,* ch. 5. See also my analysis of free speech as a vehicle of dissent in Chapter One, and the discussion of "socialization" in Chapter Two.

46. Stephen interview.

47. Judith's view is similar to the psychologists' notion of "projection." See Allport, op. cit., pp. 380, 382, 387f.

48. See also DuBow, Rice, Hal Rosen interviews. These other leaders of established groups expressed similar views as Ab Rosen.

49. Elites characteristically support civil liberties more consistently and universally than do non-elites. See Samuel Stouffer, *Communism, Conformity, and Civil Liberties*; Herbert McClosky, "Consensus and Ideology in American Politics," 58 *Amer. Pol. Sci. Rev.* (1964) 361. On how established groups generally have more competing commitments than less established groups, see Wilson, *Political Organizations.*

50. "Village Decries ACLU Doggedness on Nazis," *Skokie Life,* July 11, 1977.

51. Torshen interview; Hamlin, *The Nazi/Skokie Conflict,* pp. 113–15. Ab Rosen said this view of Torshen was correct.

52. Haiman interview.

53. Montrose interview.

54. See, for example, Rabbi David Polish's column, "Minority Report," in the Jewish publication, *Sentinel,* on how some Jews who publicly supported the ACLU at Skokie were traitors to the cause. "Hiding Jewish identity for years, now they support ACLU as Jews." Rabbi Polish is a prominent national Jewish leader.

55. Hamlin, *The Nazi/Skokie Conflict,* and Hamlin interview.

Chapter Seven

1. Neier, *Defending My Enemy,* p. 145.

2. See also Koenline interview.

3. Coser, *The Functions of Social Conflict.* Coser's propositions are distilled from George Simmel's *The Web of Social Conflict.*

4. See *New York Times v. Sullivan,* 376 U.S. 255 (1964); *Cohen v. California,* 403 U.S. 15 (1971).

5. See NJCRAC annual report, 1979; NJCRAC Executive Comm. approval of new position, May 1, 1978; and ADL Memoranda to National Law Committee from New York Office during the controversy.

6. Lerner interview; Grosberg interview; DuBow interview; Charney interview; Ab Rosen interview; Hal Rosen interview; and James Rice interview.

7. Jacobvitz interview. See also NJCRAC, Background Paper for Joint Program Planning Session, For Consideration by Member Agencies Prior to Plenum, "Individual Freedom and Jewish Security: A Local Perspective," by Norman A. Stack, Jan. 23, 1979; NJCRAC Memo, "Response to Nazi Provocation – Philadelphia," April 5, 1979; Jewish Community Relations Council of Greater East Bay, Memo, Aug. 13, 1979, "Tentative Neo-Nazi Rally," from Madeline Weinstein; Walnut Creek, Mayor's Office, News Release, Aug. 27, 1979.

8. In some respects the Jewish establishment appears to have been characterized by what Michels calls the "iron law of oligarchy," a process whereby elites come to commit themselves to their own institutional needs which may be independent of the needs of the larger membership the elites represent. It then takes an unusual set of elements (a revolt or crisis, for example) to reunite the interests of the elites and the membership. See Robert Michels, *Political Parties* (Free Press, 1962). See also Wilson, *Political Organizations.*

9. *Swastika 1960,* David Caplovitz and Candace Rogers (Anti Defamation League, 1961), p. 53. See also Kurt and Gladys Lang, *Collective Dynamics* (Crowell, 1961), ch. 4. Columnist William Safire made a similar point in a column on Skokie: "America has no vivid reminder of that horror [Holocaust] . . . Let them march through Skokie and through the media, into every American living room . . . Let the networks then reach into film files of Dachau and Buchenwald, to which young Americans have never been exposed. We need that reminder . . . to teach a new generation of Americans the extreme to which anti-Semitism can lead." "Let us be Grateful for Skokie," in *Milwaukee Journal,* April 5, 1978, p. 27.

10. See *Protest in City Politics,* p. 2. Lipsky says that "reference groups" are important as allies, and that many actions in politics are symbolic devices to make appropriate messages to these allies. See also Murray Edelman, *The Symbolic Uses of Politics* (University of Illinois Press, 1964), and Doris A. Graber, *Verbal Behavior and Politics* (University of Illinois Press, 1976), esp. ch. 8.

11. My emphasis.

12. Neier, op. cit., p. 145.

13. Hamlin, *The Nazi/Skokie Conflict,* pp. 66–67, and Hamlin interview. See also Goldberger interview in *L.A. Times,* June 7, 1978. "The Press doesn't understand what the real issues are," Goldberger asserted.

14. See *Chicago Tribune* June 10, 1978; June 23, 1978, p. 1: "Nazis cancel their march in Skokie," read the headline.

15. See Barnum, "Decision Making in a Constitutional Democracy," 44 *Journal of Politics* (1982), p. 480. Barnum labels the anti-ACLU view at Skokie the "anti-democratic consensus." Below and in Chapter Eight I will criticize this view, which is consistent with the major behavioral and survey research into attitudes about civil liberties.

16. One poll was commissioned by Gannett News Service May 6–7 and carried out by the National Center for Telephone Research. The Center surveyed 1003 reg-

istered Illinois voters. See Barnum, ibid., p. 492. The other was commissioned by the *Chicago Sun-Times* and conducted by Mid-America Research of Chicago. They telephoned 304 Skokie residents. See *Chicago Sun-Times,* March 12, 1978; and Barnum, op. cit., p. 492.

17. This poll·was done by telephone between May 8 and May 21, 1978 by Communication Research Center of Northwestern University. See *The National Jewish Monthly,* July–August 1978, pp. 32–34. The question asked, however, seems to be subject to differing interpretations: "Do you think that the Nazis have a constitutionally guaranteed right to march in Skokie?" Though the question appears to pertain to the *factual* status of the Nazis' right, it *could* be interpreted to ask the interviewee what he thinks the constitutional right *should* be. Similar polls were taken in Minnesota and Wisconsin, with quite similar results. All these polls support the findings of other researchers that the public tends to wane in its support of controversial speech rights in concrete cases. See Herbert McClosky, "Consensus and Ideology in American Politics," p. 361; Stouffer, *Communism, Conformity, and Civil Liberties*; and Barnum, op. cit.

18. My own reading of editorials (especially the *Chicago Tribune*) makes me agree with Goldberger. The distinction between reportage and editorials in terms of style, content, and quality appears to be the norm.

19. See Leo Strauss, *Natural Right and History,* p. 125: "All understanding presupposes a fundamental awareness of the whole . . ."

20. John J. Camper, "Jews confront American nazism and the First Amendment," *The National Jewish Monthly,* July–August 1978, p. 33.

21. Ibid., p. 34.

22. The very title of Camper's article suggests this fact.

23. Dworkin has held that "rights" or "principles" cannot be canceled by considerations of utility, preference, or "policy." See *Taking Rights Seriously,* pp. 22–28, 71–80. The heckler's veto essentially says that the preference of audiences cannot overcome the principle of free speech. But Dworkin maintains that rights or principles must be balanced or compromised when they conflict with other rights or principles.

24. See the distinction between the "concept" and the "conception" of a right discussed in Chapter One. Dworkin also makes this distinction; ibid., pp. 134-6, 226.

25. *The Structure of Scientific Revolutions* (University of Chicago Press, 1970).

26. See Machiavelli, *The Discourses*; and Coser, *The Functions of Social Conflict.* Though it should be recalled that Coser also says that conflict over primary values may engender too much conflict to handle. Yet at Skokie the courts ultimately decided the legal issue, so the conflict was tempered, at least in this regard. See Barnum, op. cit., pp. 501-7 on the courts' role in elevating and defusing conflict at Skokie and in general. It should also be recalled that Mill's theory of free speech is predicated upon the notion that speech conflict engenders necessary change and the renewal of commitment. Recall also Ortega's depiction of the relation between social conflict and stability in *Concord and Liberty,* cited at the front of this book.

27. See *Gooding v. Wilson,* 405 U.S. 518 (1972); Tribe, *American Constitutional Law,* pp. 711-12. In *Palko v. Connecticut,* 302 U.S. 319 (1937), Justice Cardozo stated that "freedom of thought and speech" is "the matrix, the indispensable condition, of nearly every other form of freedom."

Chapter Eight

1. *Collin v. Smith,* 447 F. Supp. 676 (1978), 692.

2. See, for example, Erna Gans, Stephen, Alex, Montrose, and Richter interviews. Neier of the ACLU maintained that the most prevalent anti-ACLU position concerned Skokie's uniqueness. See *Defending My Enemy,* pp. 126-7. See also Hamlin, *The Nazi/Skokie Conflict.*

3. *Skokie v. NSPA,* 69 Ill. 2d.605; *Goldstein v. Collin,* Plaintiff's Memorandum, Circ. Ct. Cook County, No. 77 C.H. 4367.

4. See Roscoe Pound, *An Introduction to the Philosophy of Law* (Yale University Press, 1922), pp. 62-64; Aristotle, *Nichomachean Ethics,* World Classics (Oxford University Press, 1969), pp. 132-34.

5. See Richard Wasserstrom, *The Judicial Decision* (Stanford University Press, 1961), esp. ch. 7.

6. On the need for clear, general rules which constitute a "system" of free speech rules, see Emerson, *The System of Freedom of Expression* and BeVier, "The First Amendment and Political Speech." On the limits of equity, see Wasserstrom, op. cit., ch. 5; Unger, *Law in Modern Society,* ch. 3. On chilling effect and vagueness and overbreadth, see *Papachriston v. Jacksonville,* 405 U.S. 156 (1972).

7. 10 *Poverty Law Report,* no. 3; *Klanwatch,* p. 12. May/June 1982.

8. California Fair Housing and Employment Commission, *Report on the Incitement of Racial Hatred in Contra Costa County. Public Hearings on Racial, Ethnic, and Religious Conflict in Contra Costa County.* Issued April 8, 1982, p. 51.

9. Kant, *Groundwork of the Metaphysic of Morals* (Harper, 1964), pp. 95-96.

10. Rawls explicitly predicates his theory of civil liberty and rights in *A Theory of Justice* on Kantian principle. On Kant and constitutional core values, see Arkes, *The Philosopher in the City*; Richards, *The Moral Criticism of Law*; Nomos, *Constitutionalism,* op. cit.

11. Arkes, *The Philosopher in the City,* p. 7. See also pp. 47-48.

12. See Schauer, *Free Speech: A Philosophical Inquiry,* Part I, esp. ch. 1. See also Emerson, *The System of Freedom of Expression,* for a similar yet less theoretical position; and Meiklejohn, *Political Freedom.* It could also be said that *political prudence* unavoidably operates in the world of "contingency," for politics must deal with a complex empirical world of changing facts. See, for example, Aristotle's distinction between theoretical truth and practical wisdom in *The Nicomachean Ethics,* Book VI, ch. 5: "Plainly, then, practical wisdom is a virtue and not an art. There being two parts of the soul that can follow a course of reasoning, it must be a virtue of one of the two, i.e., of that part which forms opinions; for

opinion is about the variable and so is practical wisdom." And Book VI, ch. 7: "It is evident also that philosophic wisdom and the art of politics cannot be the same . . . Nor is practical wisdom concerned with universals only—it must also recognize the particulars; for it is practical, and practice is concerned with particulars."

13. On the compelling interest test of strict judicial review in the free speech area, see Tribe, *American Constitutional Law,* chs. 11, 16; and Ducat, *Modes of Constitutional Interpretation,* ch. 4.

14. See Aristotle on practical political prudence, op. cit. This balancing is *principled,* because it seeks to accommodate competing principles of equal merit (free speech and ultimate ends). See Dworkin's distinction between "principle" and "policies" in *Taking Rights Seriously,* pp. 22–28; 90–100.

15. In this regard Kant's maxim involves the element of mental state, or specific intent, which is necessary to constitute criminal liability. On the mental element in criminal law, see Jay A. Sigler, *Understanding Criminal Law* (Little, Brown, 1982), pp. 31, 56–59; and Inbau, Thompson, and Zagel, *Criminal Law and Its Administration* (Foundation Press, 1980). See also Hyman Gross, *A Theory of Criminal Justice* (Oxford University Press, 1979), ch. 1, on degrees of culpability. On the moral development in the individual's accounting of mental state, see Jean Piaget, *The Moral Judgment of the Child* (Free Press, 1964).

16. Charles Fried, *Right and Wrong* (Harvard University Press, 1978), pp. 32–33.

17. *Terminiello v. Chicago,* 337 U.S. 1 (1948).

18. See Coser, *The Social Function of Conflict;* Machiavelli, *The Discourses.*

19. 436 U.S. 447 (1978). It should be noted that success is not required for a person to be guilty of solicitation. Yet the free speech principle requires showing of successful harm in the area of racialist expression in order to secure speech values. Solicitation is *not* "speech," yet some racialist expression *is.*

20. *New York Times v. Sullivan,* 346 U.S. 255 (1964).

21. *Collin v. Smith,* op. cit. On how the Court legitimately employed institutional and implementational concerns in fashioning the *Sullivan* standards (and how principles must be modified by pragmatic concerns in application), see BeVier, "The First Amendment and Political Speech," op. cit., p. 299. See also Wellington, "On Freedom of Expression," op. cit., p. 1115.

22. *New York Times v. Sullivan,* op. cit.

23. *Gertz v. Robert Welch,* 418 U.S. 323 (1972).

24. Bob Greene column, "Chicago's Nazis switch—main target now is the Jews," *Chicago Sun-Times,* September 29, 1976.

25. 379 U.S. 536 (1965).

26. 372 U.S. 229 (1963).

27. 240 F. Supp. 100 (1965).

28. See Garrow, *Protest at Selma,* pp. 221–23, 322. A strict Kantian position would not allow for King's acts of coercion, either. See also Reinhold Niebuhr, *Moral Man and Immoral Society* (Scribner's, 1932).

29. King's letter is found in Bedau's anthology, *Civil Disobedience.* See also

Erik Erikson, *Gandhi's Truth* (Norton, 1969), on Gandhi's theory of the *humanity* of the opposition.

30. On the public, moral character of many civil disobeyers, see Bedau, op. cit.; and Cohen, *Civil Disobedience,* chs. I and II.

31. See Berns, *For Capital Punishment,* discussed in Chapter Three.

32. 240 F. Supp. 100 (1965). Emphasis added. See also Johnson, "Civil Disobedience and the Law," 44 *Tulane Law Rev.,* 4, for Johnson's articulation of the "commensurity theorem." The Supreme Court expressed a similar logic based on the substance of the First Amendment claim in its cases dealing with legislative investigations in the early 1960s. The Court honored the claims of the NAACP much more faithfully than the claims of the Communist party because the Communist party was held to be subversive in its nature, organization, and goals. That is, the Court compared the *ends,* of the organizations, and ruled accordingly. Compare *Barenblatt v. U.S.,* 360 U.S. 109 (1959) (upheld contempt of Congress conviction of Communist party members) to *Gibson v. Florida Legislative Investig. Comm.,* 372 U.S. 539 (1963) (overturning a similar conviction against an NAACP leader).

33. See "Protest, Politics, and the First Amendment," 44 *Tulane Law Rev.,* 443, 445; and Garrow, op. cit., p. 279.

34. See Johnson, op. cit.

35. The distinction between *general advocacy* and *targeted, direct harm* is a refinement which Rawls fails to draw in his discussion of "toleration of the intolerant" in *A Theory of Justice.* Rawls states that strong libertarian institutions are not threatened by the rights of the intolerant to express and practice their beliefs (p. 219). He would limit suppression to situations in which the security of society or its institutions were threatened (p. 220). This position is similar to *Brandenburg v. Ohio*'s incitement test (the most liberal clear and present danger test). Yet Rawls addressed only this *macro* issue, ignoring the case of suppression in instances of direct harm to discrete individuals (*micro*), which fall within the terms of *Chaplinsky v. New Hampshire* (fighting or assaultive words). His analysis supports the same *general* (macro) right for hate groups which our position supports; yet it fails to consider the *limits* of this general right in concrete instances of application. Thus, his position concerning toleration of the intolerant does not contradict ours — it simply does not deal with the application of the general principle and the principle of direct harm. Nonetheless, it seems that individuals in Rawls' "original position" might rationally agree to limit the speech right in the fashion I will suggest.

36. See Meiklejohn, *Political Freedom,* especially p. 27. Meiklejohn, of course, has been criticized for restricting the First Amendment to *political* speech. On one hand, libertarian critics say such freedom should extend to *all* forms of expression, not just the political. See Richards, *The Moral Criticism of Law,* ch. 3. On the other hand, critics point out that it is virtually judicially impossible to define "what is "political" with any regularity. See Chafee, "Book Review," p. 891. Chafee's view, however, would undermine the entire scheme of definitional balancing upon which modern free speech adjudication rests. For a defense of this type of balancing against claims such as Chafee directs against Meiklejohn, see Frantz, "The First Amend-

ment in the Balance;" and Nimmer, "The Right to Speak From *Times* to *Time*," op. cit.

37. Scanlon, "A Theory of Freedom of Expression," p. 213. See also Wellington, "On Freedom of Expression," p. 1105.

38. Scanlon, op. cit.

39. *Whitney v. California,* 274 U.S. 357. On Brandeis' notion of mental time and space for deliberation, see Tribe, op. cit., p. 611.

40. *Organization for a Better Austin v. Keefe,* 402 U.S. 415 (1971).

41. My approach, as stressed in the Introduction, is minimalist. Compare Berns, *Freedom, Virtue, and the First Amendment.*

42. *Org. for a Better v. Keefe,* at 419. Burger's position is at odds with a strict Kantian categorical imperative concerning ultimate ends. My support of Burger is another example of my prudential deviation from Kant.

43. Some social and psychological theorists depict society and culture as, at least in part, a conservative defense mechanism against anxiety. If so, advocacy of change or the pointing out of unpleasant truths can engender the desire to repress the speech. A small sampling of such theorists whose views could be utilized in this fashion includes Geza Roheim, *The Origin and Function of Culture* (Anchor Doubleday, 1971); Emile Durkheim, *Suicide* (Free Press, 1951); and Sebastian De Grazia, *The Political Community: A Study of Anomie* (University of Chicago Press, 1948).

44. See the discussion of Schattschneider's theory of socialization in Chapter Two.

45. See Meiklejohn, op. cit., pp. 18, 34–35, on how Article I, section 6 of the Constitution grants immunity to the speech of Congressmen on the floor of either house; citizens must also have strong speech rights if they are "rulers."

46. See Arkes, *The Philosopher in the City,* on how racial vilification violates the principle of autonomy in this respect. See also the discussion on rights and autonomy, Rawls, Dworkin, and Arkes, supra.

47. See Allport, *The Nature of Prejudice;* G. Simpson and J. Yinger, *Racial and Cultural Minorities: An Analysis of Prejudice and Discrimination* (Harper & Row, 1972), pp. 70–75; "Group Vilification Reconsidered," Note 89, *Yale L.J.* 308, (1980) 311–14. These works stress how racism is the product of internal, subconscious stresses and conflicts. For a more general and powerful treatment of racism in America, see Gunnar Myrdal, *An American Dilemma: The Negro Problem and Modern Democracy* (Pantheon, 1972), esp. ch. 4.

48. See *Yale L.J.* Note, pp. 312–13.

49. See *Korematsu v. U.S.,* 323 U.S. 214; *Regents of University of California v. Bakke,* 438 U.S. 265. See also Ely, *Democracy and Distrust;* Lockhart, Kamisar, and Choper, eds., *Constitutional Rights and Liberties* (West Publishing Co., 1981), pp. 1002–7, 881–902.

50. See Locke, *A Letter Concerning Toleration* (Martinus Nijhoff, 1963), esp. pp. 17–19; Hume, *A Treatise of Human Nature,* ed. Hendel (Scribner's, 1955). Leonard Levy argues that this belief in the lack of free will in the choice of values

is a major justification for speech libertarianism: we cannot punish people for be-lieving that which they cannot help believing. See *Legacy of Suppression,* epilogue. See also Stuart Hampshire, *Thought and Action* (Viking Press, 1960), for a thought-ful, balanced discussion of this issue. Although Hampshire is characteristically cognizant of the complexity in this area of value determination, he rejects sheer determinism.

51. See Berns, *For Capital Punishment,* Introduction; Van den Haag, *The Pun-ishment of Criminals* (Basic Books, 1975), ch. 10; Gross, op. cit., ch. 3; *Mullaney v. Wilbur* 421 U.S. 684 (1975); Sigler, op. cit.; Inbau, Thompson, and Zagel, op. cit., ch. 7.

52. On realistic conflict theory, see S. Cummings, "White Ethnics, Racial Preju-dice, and Labor Market Segmentation," *Amer. Jour. Sociology* (1980); Ra. A. Le-vine and D. T. Campbell, *Ethnocentricism* (Wiley, 1972); M. Rothbart, "Achieving Racial Equality: An Analysis of Resistance to Social Reform," in P. A. Katz, ed., *Towards the Elimination of Racism* (Pergamon, 1976); and D. Kinder and L. Rhode-beck, "Continuities in Support for Racial Equality" (paper prepared for *Public Opinion*). For more theoretical and sociological treatments of the difference be-tween rational and irrational conflict, see Sennett, *The Fall of Public Man*; Coser, op. cit.

53. See Kant, *Groundwork of the Metaphysic of Morals,* pp. 80–81, and, gen-erally, ch. II. On the role of agency in moral responsibility and accountability, see Rem Blanchard Edwards, *Freedom, Responsibility, and Obligation,* ch. VI, and p. 114.

54. See the discussion in ch. 6 of Memmi, *The Colonizer and the Colonized*; Fanon, *The Wretched of the Earth*; and Arendt, *The Origins of Totalitarianism,* esp. chs. 6 and 7. On German racist metaphysics, see Mosse, *The Crisis of German Ideology.*

55. Yale Note, op. cit., p. 313. See also Allport, op. cit. On uncertainty and rac-ism, see Sartre, "Portrait of an Anti-Semite" in Walter Kaufmann, ed. *Existential-ism from Dostoevsky to Sartre* (New American Library, 1975), which is consistent with *Being and Nothingness* (Washington Square Press, 1969) in its depiction of the weakness of consciousness. The anti-Semite's hatred of Jews is a manifestation of a fundamental weakness of character—the anti-Semite escapes this weakness in his hatred.

56. See *Herbert v. Lando,* 441 U.S. 153 (1978).

57. Arkes, "Civility," p. 418.

58. *Cohen v. California,* 403 U.S. 15 (1971).

59. See *Garrison v. Louisiana,* 379 U.S. 65 (1964). *Sullivan* "absolutely pro-hibits punishment of truthful criticism" of public officials, even if made with malice.

60. 310 U.S. 88 (1940).

61. 312 U.S. 287, 294 (1941).

62. See *Bakery & Pastry Drivers v. Wohl,* 315 U.S. 769, 776 (1942).

63. *Brandenburg v. Ohio,* 395 U.S. 444 (1969).

64. *Int'l Brotherhood v. Vog't, Inc.,* 354 U.S. 284, (1957); and see *Giboney v. Empire Storage and Ice Co.,* 336 U.S. 490 (1949).

65. On picketing as inducement, see Archibald Cox, "Strikes, Picketing, & the Constitution," *Vand. L. Rev.* 4 (1951): 574, 591-602. See also Emerson, *The System of Freedom of Expression,* pp. 592-602, on picketing as "signal" and "publicity."

66. The same point applies to other justifications of free speech such as the "marketplace of ideas." Paul G. Chevigny adds another justification based on the philosophy of language. Using Wittgenstein, Barthes, Habermas and others, he argues that the meanings and truths of a political community are articulated through an ongoing process of communication and speech—through *discourse.* Consequently, the right to speak must be honored, as well as the right to listen. Yet he fails to recognize that while this *discourse* justification is significant, it is superceded by the principle of harm in certain instances for the same reason other essentially utilitarian justifications are superceded. See Chevigny, "Philosophy of Language and Free Expression," 55 *N.Y.U Law Rev.* 157 (1980). For a critique of the grounding of free speech theory on such premises, see Schauer, *Free Speech,* ch. 4.

67. On how *moral laws* have a different epistemological status from *scientific* truth values, see Tussman, *Obligation and the Body Politic,* p. 130. To say something is *unjust* is different from saying something about the laws of physics. On the weaknesses of the "truth" justification of free speech, see Schauer, op. cit., ch. 2.

68. On obscenity and patent offensiveness, see Harry Clor, *Obscenity and Public Morality* (University of Chicago Press, 1968), pp. 62-65, 69-73; Bickel, *The Morality of Consent,* pp. 73-74. On the evidence linking obscenity to sexual behavior, see Clor, op. cit., ch. 4.

69. *Brent v. Morgan,* 221 Ky. 765, 766 (1927), quoted in Arkes, "Civility," p. 411.

70. See Kalven, "Privacy in Tort Law—Were Warren and Brandeis Wrong?" *Law and Contemporary Problems* 31 (1966), 326; cf. Warren and Brandeis, "The Right to Privacy," *Harv. L. Rev.* 4 (1890), 193.

71. Arkes, "Civility," p. 411.

72. See, for example, *Schneider v. State,* 308 U.S. 147, 162 (1939); *Martin v. City of Struthers,* 319 U.S. 141, 148 (1943); *Rowan v. Post Office,* 397 U.S. 728, 736-37 (1970); *Kovacs v. Cooper,* 336 U.S. 77 (1949); *PUC v. Pollak,* 343 U.S. 451 (1952); *Org. for a Better Austin v. Keefe,* op. cit.

73. *Cohen v. California,* 403 U.S. 15, 21 (1971).

74. Stone, "Fora Americana: Speech in Public Places," in Kurland, ed., op. cit., pp. 372-73.

75. Ibid., p. 376.

76. See *Carey v. Brown,* 100 S. Ct. 2286 (1980): "the state's interest in protecting the well-being, tranquility, and privacy of the home is certainly of the highest order."; *Moore v. East Cleveland,* 431 U.S. 494 (1977).

77. Haiman, *Speech and Law in a Free Society,* pp. 144, 146. Emphasis added.

78. Bickel, *The Morality of Consent,* pp. 73-74. See also Tussman, *Government and the Mind,* ch. 1: "A community is constituted by—its very existence de-

pends upon — a condition or state of mind. It is not a mere collection of physical entities or a herd of biological organisms." See also George F. Will, *Statecraft as Soulcraft,* for arguments in favor of laws affecting *the mind.* Haiman sees only the physical aspect of captivity, thereby treating man as a biological entity rather than a rational and spiritual entity. In this respect, Haiman's view represents the reduction to the physical and animalistic nature of man so characteristic of modern libertarianism. For insight into this reductionism, see Berns, *The First Amendment and the Future of American Democracy,* ch. 5. This reduction is also related to Unger's notion of the primacy of emotion over reason in *Knowledge and Politics.* See also Philip Rieff, *The Triumph of the Therapeutic;* and Alasdair MacIntyre, *After Virtue.*

79. *Beauharnais v. Illinois,* 343 U.S. 250; Ill. Crim. Code, Sec. 224a, Ill. Rev. Stat., 138, Div. 1, Sec. 471 (1949). See Arkes, "Civility," pp. 396-97; and Kalven, *The Negro and the First Amendment,* ch. 1.

80. In its stead, the Illinois constitution now says that such expression "should be condemned," thus making the moral condemnation (not the *legal prohibition*) of such speech a constitutional exhortation. See Illinois constitution, Art., Sec. 20 (1970); *Goldstein v. Collin,* Plaintiff's Memorandum, Circ. Ct. Cook County, No. 77 CH 4367, Aug. 16, 1977, p. 18.

81. See Emerson, *Freedom of Expression,* pp. 389-401; Hamlin, *The Nazi/Skokie Conflict,* pp. 77-78; Neier, *Defending My Enemy,* pp. 140, 165; Joseph Tannenhaus, "Group Libel," *Cornell L. Q.* (1950).

82. *Beauharnais v. Ill.,* 343 U.S. 250-252; Arkes, "Civility," p. 397.

83. Frankfurter favored "balancing" as opposed to giving a "preferred position" to speech (strict scrutiny). See Frankfurter's opinions in *Dennis v. U.S.,* 341 U.S. 494, 525, and *West Virginia State Board of Education v. Barnette,* 319 U.S. 624, 662. On this logic of balancing, see Ducat, *Modes of Constitutional Interpretation,* pp. 132-33, and generally, ch. 3; Berns, *Freedom, Virtue, and the First Amendment,* ch. 7; Shapiro, *Freedom of Speech,* ch. 3.

84. See Frantz, "The First Amendment in the Balance," for a critique of *ad hoc* balancing in favor of definitional balancing.

85. On how free speech requires the strict judicial review of facts and danger *in each case independent* of legislative judgement about classes of speech contained in statutes, see Tribe, *American Constitutional Law,* pp. 608-17. Tribe refers to the *Dennis* case and other cases dealing with the advocacy of subversion.

86. See, for example, Wellington's general analysis, in "On Freedom of Expression," esp. pp. 1132-1142, which deals with autonomy, self-government, and laws against racially disruptive speech.

87. See Tribe, op. cit., pp. 711-12.

88. *Cohen v. California,* 403 U.S. 15, 20.

89. See the Ellerin report on Nazi and hate group activities for the American Jewish Committee, "American Nazis — Myth or Menace?" Nov. 22, 1977; and *Facts,* March, 1978, vol. 24, no. 2., ADL, "The U.S. Neo-Nazi Movement: 1978."

90. *Chicago v. Lambert,* 47 Ill. App. 2d. 151, 154. See Arkes, "Civility," pp. 430-32.

91. Arkes, op. cit.

92. Tanenhaus, "Group Libel"; on Hitler's *Putsch* trial, see John Toland, *Adolf Hitler* (Ballantine, 1976), pp. 252-61.

93. See Patricia M. Leopold, "Incitement to Hatred—the History of a Controversial Offense," *Public Law* (1977): 397, for an account of how the *Southern News* in England won a publicity coup by *winning* in court.

94. Tanenhaus, op. cit., p. 301. See also Neier, op. cit.; and Alexander Greenfeld talk at American Jewish Congress meeting in Berkeley, 1979.

95. On the problem in England, see Leopold, op. cit.; and Anthony Dickey, "English Law and Race Defamation," 14 *N. Y. L. Forum,* 1968. For a favorable view of the Race Relations Act, see Anthony Lester and Geoffry Bindman, *Race and Law in Great Britain* (Harvard University Press, 1972). For an excellent defense of group libel laws written before *Beauharnais,* see David Riesman's classic essay, "Democracy and Defamation: Control of Group Libel," XLII *Colum. L. Rev.* 727 (1942). For negative appraisals of group libel laws in America, see Tanenhaus, op. cit.; Neier, op. cit.; Hamlin, *The Nazi/Skokie Conflict*; Geoffrey Stone, "Group Defamation," "Occasional Paper, Univ. Chicago Law School," 15, Aug. 10, 1978; Pemberton, "Can the Law Provide a Remedy for Race Defamation in the United States?" *N.Y.L Forum* (1968); Franklyn Haiman, *Speech and Law in a Free Society,* p. 90; Loren P. Beth, "Group Libel and Free Speech," *Minn. L. Rev.* (1955); Emerson, *Freedom of Expression,* ch. 10. For a favorable view, see Arkes, "Civility"; Berns, *Freedom, Virtue, and the First Amendment,* pp. 148-155. On the institutional and implemental weakness of courts, especially in the area of free speech concerning "mixed utterances" and coexisting good and bad speech, see BeVier, "The First Amendment and Political Speech." On the general institutional incapacities of courts, see Donald Horowitz, *The Courts and Social Policy* (Brooking, 1977); and Alexander Bickel, *The Least Dangerous Branch: The Supreme Court at the Bar of Politics* (Bobbs-Merrill, 1962).

96. See Arkes, "Civility," for a recommendation of a *total* return to *Chaplinsky* that represents a *strong* Kantian position.

97. See Arkes, *The Philosopher in the City,* esp. pp. 7-8, 48, 387-91.

98. See Hugo Adam Bedau, "Egalitarianism and the Idea of Equality," in IX *Nomos: Equality* (Atherton, 1967), on this issue. Equality *must* mean equality *in essence,* but might not entail the right to equal wealth or resources. The heated debate over the scope of equality is important, but beyond our purview. For a recent account of the ways to think about equality, see Douglas Rae, et al., *Equalities* (Harvard University Press, 1981).

99. This distinction is employed by Dworkin, *Taking Rights Seriously,* ch. 12; and Hazard, "Social Justice through Civil Justice."

100. Compare Dworkin, op. cit., who limits his doctrine of "treatment as an equal" to state action, to Arkes, "Civility," who does not.

101. Berns, "Religion and the Founding Principle," in Robert H. Horwitz, ed., *The Moral Foundations of the American Republic,* (University of Virginia, 1979), p. 171. See also Berns, *The First Amendment and the Future of American Democracy,* ch. 1.

102. Tussman and ten Broek, "The Equal Protection of the Laws," 37 *Calif. L. Rev.* 3 (1949) 341, at. 353.

103. See Douglas Rae, "The Egalitarian State: Notes on a System of Contradictory Ideals," 20 *Daedulus* (1980), p. 37.

104. In the names of liberty and constitutional interpretation, the Supreme Court has limited the scope of the equal protection clause to "state action." See Civil Rights Cases, 109 U.S. 3 (1883). The Court has never abandoned the basic concept of state action created in these cases, though the "conception" of state action has varied over time.

105. See Hazard's distinction between "commutative" and "distributive" justice in "Social Justice through Civil Justice."

106. "The Equal Protection of the Laws," p. 354.

107. In this respect, those survey-researchers and democratic theorists who automatically label the anti-Nazi free speech position "non-democratic" or "anti-democratic" are too simplistic. Even if one disagrees with the conclusion of this chapter, it should at least be clear that an anti-free speech position on this issue deserves more than an "anti-democratic" rap. For representative works of this position, see Barnum, "Decision Making in a Constitutional Democracy," pp. 480, 487ff; Stouffer, *Communism, Conformity, and Civil Liberties*; James W. Prothro and Charles M. Grigg, "Fundamental Principles of Democracy: Bases of Agreement and Disagreement," *J. Politics* 22 (1960), 276; and Herbert McClosky, "Consensus and Ideology in American Politics," p. 361. On how the Federal Republic of Germany's Federal Constitutional Court enforces, in the name of individual dignity, substantive constitutional provisions against racial vilification, see my colleague, Donald P. Kommers, "The Jurisprudence of Free Speech in the United States and the Federal Republic of Germany," 53 *S. Cal. L. Rev.* 657 (1980). Is West Germany really "anti-democratic" in this regard?

Chapter Nine

1. Hadley Arkes does not specify context in his treatment of *Chaplinsky*. This is one reason that he is able to treat *Chaplinsky* and *Beauharnais* as comparable (whereas I distinguished them in the last chapter). See Arkes, "Civility and the Restriction of Speech: Rediscovering the Defamation of Groups", in Kurland, ed., *Free Speech and Association,* p. 390. Of course, Arkes' strong Kantian position precludes the consideration of context because context is an empirical "contingency."

2. The advocacy of death violates (in speech) the most fundamental taboos of civilized society. On the importance of honoring taboos by maintaining *fear* of

breaking them, see Hampshire, "Morality and Pessimism," in Hampshire, ed., *Public and Private Morality.* On how the "speakable" may eventually become the "doable," see Bickel, *The Morality of Consent,* p. 73. On the *"special"* harm of the advocacy of death, see also Maynard Wishner interview: "It is a question of categories to define when speech is permissible. The question here is, is it not equally "obscene" to applaud the extermination of 6,000,000 people in what everyone calls mankind's most obscene act? It is okay to come to people and say this? The question is, is there anything the advocacy of which is beyond the pale of the First Amendment?" Wishner became Chairman of the American Jewish Committee a year after the Skokie conflict.

3. Wellington addresses the issue of the advocacy of death or genocide and the application of the autonomy principle in "On Freedom of Expression," pp. 1141-42. Wellington states: "It is the privilege of each individual in a democracy to make up his own mind, on the basis of all the evidence, on every political-moral issue that arises . . . It remains unfortunately imaginable that genocide could be implemented in a secular democracy: the state — including the courts — could be captured by a coalition of sick and evil minorities. But I do not believe that more restrictive control of expression would prevent such a catastrophe: unlike his cruelty, man's laws do have effective limits." Of course, our survivor interviewees disagree with this assessment because of their own experience in Europe. We should also remember what Bickel and a host of other commentators have maintained: that law is a teacher.

4. See *Goldstein v. Collin,* Plaintiffs' Memorandum in Support of Complaint for Injunction, Circ. Ct. Cook County, No. 77 CH 4367, pp. 13-20; see also Second Restatement of Torts, Sec. 46(1), (1965); and *Knierim v. Izzo,* 174 N.E. 2d 157 (1961), a case the Goldstein Memorandum relied on a great deal.

5. On this racial slur tort, see Richard Delgado, "Words That Wound: A Tort Action for Racial Insults, Epithets, and Name Calling," 17 *Harv. Civ. Rts.—Civ. Libs. L.R.* 133 (1982).

6. See Delgado, op. cit., p. 133; and *Contreras v. Crown Zellerbach, Inc.* 88 Wash. 2d 735, 565 P. 2d. 1173.

7. Delgado, op. cit., pp. 150-51; and *Fisher v. Carrousel Motor Hotel, Inc.,* 424 S.W. 2d 627 (Tex. 1967), 630.

8. Delgado, op. cit., pp. 151-7; *Contreras; Alcorn v. Aubro Engineering, Inc.,* 468 P. 2d. 216 (1970); *Agarawal v. Johnson,* 603 P. 2d. 58 (1979); *Wiggs v. Courshon,* 355 F. Supp. 206 (1973). "Extreme and outrageous" conduct must be shown. Verdicts against the plaintiffs in similar cases were returned in *Irving v. J.L. March Inc.,* 360 N.E. 2d. 983 (1977); and *Bradshaw v. Swagerty,* 563 P. 2d. 511 (1977). See Delgado, pp. 155-7.

9. Delgado, op. cit., pp. 157-59; *Irving*; and *Bradshaw.*

10. Delgado, op. cit., pp. 159-65.

11. Delgado, ibid., p. 172, states that, surprisingly, "the question whether racial insults are protected by the First Amendment has not arisen in any case involving a racial insult" since *Collin v. Smith.* Accordingly, the effect of the Skokie

decisions on tort law has yet to be determined. Had the Illinois courts chosen to decide the *Goldstein* suit, this hiatus would have been filled.

12. Ibid., p. 174.

13. Ibid., p. 179.

14. On the need to show harm in the tort of racial insult, see ibid., pp. 150–59, 179–80.

15. These defenses would be successful if they were proved, say, by a "preponderance of the evidence," which is the level of proof courts sometimes require the state to meet. See, for example, *Lego. v. Twomey*, 404 U.S. 477 (1972) (burden on prosecution to show voluntariness of a confession by a "preponderance of the evidence"). The *presumption* of intent in this area is based on the fact that when vilifying expression is targeted, it is "more likely than not" that it is intended. On the "more likely than not" test for the validity of presumptions, see *Leary v. U.S.*, 395 U.S. 6 (1969). On the theory of "mistakes" and "excuses" in criminal law (based on the issue of "mental state"), see George Fletcher, *Rethinking Criminal Law*, chs. 9 and 10.

16. This test is used by the courts in determining whether a party has voluntarily consented to a search of his premises by authorities without a search warrant. See *Schneckloth v. Bustamonte*, 412 U.S. 218 (1973); and Charles H. Whitebread, *Criminal Procedure, An Analysis of Constitutional Cases and Concepts* (Foundation Press, 1980), p. 197. It is also the old test used by courts to determine the voluntariness of custodial confessions, though it was abandoned (or redirected) by *Miranda*. See *Fikes v. Alabama*, 352 U.S. 191 (1957); *U.S. v. Blocker*, 354 F. Supp. 1195 (D.C. 1973); and Whitebread, op. cit., pp. 283, 301.

17. See Leopold, "Incitement to Hatred – The History of a Controversial Criminal Offense," pp. 395–97; and Dickey, "English Law and Race Defamation," pp. 17–20. See also Lester and Bindman, *Race and Law in Great Britain*, pp. 361–74.

18. Arkes, "Civility," p. 433. The issue of "subjectivity" which Arkes raises is similar to Roberto Unger's portrayal of the epistemological basis of liberal moral theory. See Unger, *Knowledge and Politics*, ch. 1. Arkes, however, counters the position that values are subjective in liberalism by predicating his argument against the First Amendment protection of racial vilification on the normative ends of the liberal state: "No government may hold back in these instances and properly claim the allegiance of its citizens, for if we may use an older phrase, it would have shown itself at that moment to be destructive of those ends for which governments are instituted. It would have defaulted then on the first obligation of government as it was understood by the men who framed the Declaration of Independence: to protect its subjects from lawlessness in the taking of their lives, the abridgement of their liberty, or the destruction of their property." Arkes, op. cit., p. 420.

19. On the degrees of culpability in homicide cases, see *Mullaney v. Wilbur*, 421 U.S. 684 (1975); *State v. Flory*, 276 P. 458 (1929) (on voluntary manslaughter); *People v. Decina*, 138 N.E. 2d 799 (1956) (involuntary manslaughter). On provocations in general, see Inbau, Thompson, and Zagel, op. cit., pp. 313–16 (see p. 315: "We understand, too, that provocation, whether by assault or by words, would be

regarded in most countries of Western Europe as a mitigating circumstance which might justify reduction of the maximum penalty for homicide." From *1953 Report of Royal Comm. on Capital Punishment*). On how juries often take provocation into consideration in deciding cases of assault and homocide, see Harry Kalven and Hans Zeisel, *The American Jury* (Little, Brown, & Co., 1966), pp. 222n, 227-236.

20. See, for example *Collin v. Smith,* Hearing on Dec. 2, 1977, U.S. Dist. Ct. N.D. Ill., No. 78-1381, testimony of Frank Collin, cross examination, pp. 13-19; and *Skokie v. NSPA,* Hearing on April 28, 1977, Cook County Circ. Ct., no. 77 CH 2702, pp. 51-70.

21. See *Kunz v. New York,* 340 U.S. 290 (1951): past conduct of speaker not a grounds for denying a permit; *Healy v. James,* 408 U.S. 169 (1972). The methodology used here employs essentially what Unger calls the "principle of analysis," which will be discussed in the conclusion of this chapter.

22. For a classic study of the factors juries use in their discretionary determination of guilt, see Kalven and Zeisel, *The American Jury.*

23. On the decision to prosecute and the exercise of discretion in that decision see Kenneth Culp Davis, *Discretionary Justice: A Preliminary Inquiry* (University of Illinois Press, 1979), chs. VI and VII: Dworkin, *Taking Rights Seriously,* ch. 8; Kadish and Kadish, *Discretion to Disobey,* pp. 80-85, 137-38.

24. See the tort test in *Knierim v. Izzo,* 174 N.E. 2d. 157 (1961), 164: "whether the aggressive invasion of mental equanimity was unwarranted or unprovoked, whether it is calculated to cause severe emotional disturbance in the person of ordinary sensibilities, and whether there was special knowledge or notice of [atypical sensibilities]." See also Second Restatement of Torts, Sec. 46(1), (1965).

25. Lilian BeVier calls this the "mixed utterance" problem. "The First Amendment and Political Speech," pp. 299, 326.

26. On the institutional problem of implementation of principle, see ibid., pp. 322-45. BeVier argues that the implementation of principle will always involve such "slippage" in the real world. Therefore, since the right of free speech is so important (even "transcendent"), standards and policies of law (the application of principle) must err in the direction of safety — they must provide "breathing space," as the Supreme Court provided for political speech in *New York Times v. Sullivan,* 376 U.S. 254 (1964). Another good example of the recognition of the difference between principle and implementation is Justice Brennan's switch from support of the exclusion of obscenity from First Amendment protection in *Roth v. U.S.,* 354 U.S. 476 (1957), (based on the two-level approach discussed in Chapter One) to his abandonment of this position due to the alleged chaos of adjudication in this area in *Paris Adult Theatre v. Slaton,* 413 U.S. 49 (1973). See also Schauer, *Free Speech,* ch. 9, for a good treatment of institutional competence and the free speech principle.

27. BeVier also deals with this issue, demonstrating its central role in *Sullivan.* See BeVier, op. cit., p. 326.

28. See *Gregg v. Georgia,* 428 U.S. 153 (1976). It has been observed that misapplication of the death penalty is unavoidable. See Charles Black, *Capital Punish-*

ment (Norton, 1974) and "Death Sentences and our Criminal Justice System," in Bedau, ed., *The Death Penalty in America* (Oxford University Press, 1982), p. 359.

29. Meiklejohn holds the value of political speech over the value of life itself, maintaining that Socrates held a similar view in his acceptance of death in the *Crito* as opposed to his refusal to stop talking about political philosophy in the *Apology*. See Meiklejohn, *Political Freedom,* pp. 21–24. But targeted racialist expression is not what Meiklejohn had in mind.

30. 427 U.S. 50 (1976), 62. Emphasis added.

31. See, for example, Haiman, *Speech and Law in a Free Society.*

32. Sigler, *Understanding Criminal Law,* p. 31; on *mens rea* (guilty mind) and specific intent, ibid., pp. 56–59. For a case that discusses both of these concepts, see *People v. Hernandez,* 61 Cal. 2d. 529 (1964). See also Fletcher, op. cit., ch. 10.

33. See *Washington v. Davis,* 426 U.S. 229 (1976) *Arlington Heights v. Metropolitan Housing Dev. Corp.* 429 U.S. 252 (1977).

34. See *Ohralik v. Ohio State Bar,* 436 U.S. 449 (1978).

35. *New York Times Co. v. Sullivan,* 376 U.S. 255 (1964).

36. *Gooding v. Wilson,* 405 U.S. 518 (1972).

37. *Lewis v. New Orleans,* II, 415 U.S. 130 (1974).

38. For a good argument against easier standards for minorities because of their debilitating impact on the quest for excellence and responsibility, and, therefore, on these groups themselves, see Lasch, *The Culture of Narcissism,* ch. 6.

39. Delgado, op. cit., p. 180, footnote 275.

40. See Tönnies, *Community and Society,* especially the discussion "Natural Will" v. "Rational Will" in part 2.

41. Unger, p. 46.

42. Ibid., pp. 81–83.

43. Ibid., p. 47. See also Leo Strauss, *Natural Right and History,* pp. 125–26, on how knowledge and understanding presuppose "a fundamental awareness of the whole."

44. Unger's theory does not annihilate the notion of the individual as do totalitarian theories, but rather seeks a propitious balancing of individualism and communalism. Indeed, he maintains that this balance is necessary to achieve individual fulfillment. Tocqueville attains a more convincing yet similar type of balance in *Democracy in America.*

45. See Berns, *Freedom, Virtue, and the First Amendment,* pp. 198–201, 256.

46. See Meiklejohn, *Political Freedom,* chs. 1 and 4. Meiklejohn's theory is consistent with those conservatives who maintain that free citizens must honor their "second natures" over their "first natures" (i.e., natural passion). See George F. Will, *Statecraft as Soulcraft,* ch. 4; and Walter Lippmann, *The Public Philosophy.* See also the discussion of Hegel in Chapter Six, on "mastery."

47. Meiklejohn distinguishes political from non-political speech, or "freedom" (a political and communal good) from "liberty" (an individual, negative freedom). This distinction parallels the "second nature" thesis, as well as Tocqueville's distinction between political freedom and selfishness in *Democracy in America.*

Index

Abolitionist treatment of blacks, 97–98

Administrative law, 3–4

Agens: basic definition, 95; and claims of rights, 97; link with participation in a communal enterprise based on trust, 103; regaining by survivors in Skokie conflict, 101; relation to fear of death, 98; transformation from *patiens*, 96, 99. *See also* Mastery; Survivors

Allport, Gordon, 23–25

Alex (Skokie survivor), 43–44, 47, 48, 86

American Civil Liberties Union (ACLU): assistance to NSPA at Skokie, 2; assistance to NSPA against Chicago Park District, 20; and content neutrality doctrine, 31, 36; criticism of its Skokie stand by participants, 31; doctrinaire and absolutist position on free speech, 119; factional splits exacerbated by Skokie, 33; hostile public and membership reaction to Skokie stand, 32; Illinois division and board accept Skokie case, 30–32; litigation and experience since World War I, 37, 184 n.100; moves to expedite injunction case in courts, 56; national board takes the Skokie case, 33; past defenses of hate groups, 31; position on the consequences of speech, 84; principle and polarization at Skokie, 35; role in final bargaining game with Collin over Skokie, 79–81; socializes the dispute, 33. *See also* Gelder, Michael; Goldberger, David; Haiman, Franklyn; Hamlin, David; Neier, Aryeh

American Jewish Committee, 23, 83, 114

American Jewish Congress, 114

American Nazi Party, 31, 148

Anti-Defamation League (ADL): and *Goldstein v. Collin* suit, 57; Midwest division's revision of quarantine policy, 114; quarantine policy, advocacy at Skokie, 45; quarantine policy, national branch's consideration of reform, 83; quarantine policy, traditional posture, 23

Anti-Semitism: acts in New York City area in 1960, 115; deterrence of Anti-Semitic groups, 116

Anti-Vietnam War Movement, 9

Arendt, Hannah: bifurcation thesis of survivor personality, 61; on extraordinary knowledge of survivors, 65; on incommunicability of survivor experience and bifurcated self, 39–40; on Nietzschean ethic of "doing the unthinkable" and Nazi Final Solution, 187–88 n.35; on political freedom as "freedom from necessity," 180 n.32; on "common sense," 175 nn.38,41; on relation of free speech to political protest and civil rights movement, 171 n.6; on significance of making promises to political obligation and public realm, 189 n.65; similarities to free speech theories of Alexander Meiklejohn, 174–75 n.35; thesis in *Eichmann in Jerusalem* on Jewish role in Final Solution, 186–87 n.30

Aristotle, 18, 204 n.12

217